D0085499

ARMED FOR LIFE

ARMED FOR LIFE

The Army of God and Anti-Abortion Terror in the United States

Jennifer Jefferis

PSI Guides to Terrorists, Insurgents, and Armed Groups
James J. F. Forest, Series Editor

 PRAEGER

AN IMPRINT OF ABC-CLIO, LLC
Santa Barbara, California • Denver, Colorado • Oxford, England

363.44
J452a

Library of Congress Cataloging-in-Publication Data

Jefferis, Jennifer L.
    Armed for life : the Army of God and anti-abortion terror in the United States / Jennifer Jefferis.
        p. cm. — (PSI guides to terrorists, insurgents, and armed groups)
    Includes bibliographical references (p.   ) and index.
    ISBN 978-0-313-38753-1 (alk. paper) — ISBN 978-0-313-38754-8 (ebook)
    1. Pro-life movement—United States—Case studies.   2. Abortion—United States—Case studies.   3. Religion and politics—United States—Case studies.   I. Title.
    HQ767.5.U5J44   2011
    363.460973—dc22   2011014742

ISBN: 978-0-313-38753-1
EISBN: 978-0-313-38754-8

15   14   13   12   11   1   2   3   4   5

This book is also available on the World Wide Web as an eBook.
Visit www.abc-clio.com for details.

Praeger
An Imprint of ABC-CLIO, LLC

ABC-CLIO, LLC
130 Cremona Drive, P.O. Box 1911
Santa Barbara, California 93116-1911

This book is printed on acid-free paper (∞)

Manufactured in the United States of America

To my parents,
For getting me through childhood . . . and for paying for college.

Contents

Acknowledgments

I am indebted to many people for the writing of this book. For an organization that is hard to catch, the Army of God is easy to reach. Many "members," supporters, and affiliates of the Army of God have made themselves readily available to me and my endless questions, and for that I am grateful. I am also grateful to James Forest at West Point for his willingness to read and edit the roughest version of the book and to the editors at Praeger for their willingness to walk me through this process. I owe Jessica Medhurst endless thanks and probably a new computer. If Synthia Suarez develops gray hair before her time, I take full responsibility for a year of urgent e-mails and sudden deadlines. Her patience and attention to detail have made this process much easier. And of course, Adam, for whom, and to whom, I am endlessly thankful.

Introduction

In the classic film *The Sound of Music,* there is a famous scene in which a group of nuns fret (in melodious rhythm and perfect pitch) about how to solve a problem involving a fellow nun. In the song, they equate their conundrum to trying to capture a cloud for the purpose of tying it down and catching an ocean wave to keep it on the beach. They go on to lament the impossibility of defining their troublesome sister and then summarize the issue by harmonizing "How do you hold a moon beam in your hand?" Notwithstanding the rather important difference in issues (the nuns were concerned about getting Sister Maria to come to meals on time instead of spending hours singing in the hills), and denomination (the nuns were—obviously—Catholic), the song could be nearly as appropriate in explaining the challenges of studying the Army of God: an organization that is not at all organized; a pro-life group justifying the use of fatal force; a shadowy movement composed of individuals ready and willing to talk to anyone who will listen about why they do what they do; a group of only a few dozen able to paralyze an industry. How do you find a word that describes this? How do you hold a moonbeam in your hand?

For the most part, the answer has been "you don't." Most books on the antiabortion movement in the United States to date have devoted a few pages to this perplexing group, content to leave the lines between the Army of God and the rest of the pro-life movement blurred. These books provide invaluable knowledge about the antiabortion movement as a whole and the many groups that form its different parts. There are outstanding resources available that identify leaders in the movement and provide excellent historical context.[1] There are others that trace the long path from nonviolent to aggressive forms of protest and offer insightful explanations for the shift.[2] There are others still that provide chilling case studies of specific instances of near-fatal violence and use social movements theory to offer some explanation.[3] But all of these stop short of providing a comprehensive understanding of the Army of God. Perhaps owing to the ambiguous character of this organization, most accounts stop short of detailing where this organization ends and the rest of the pro-life movement begins. Few look closely at the words of these individuals and provide an overview of the ideology that holds the organization together.

As a result there are important questions left unanswered about the antiabortion movement specifically, and the evolution of terrorism more generally. The Army of God forces a reconsideration of what it means to be an organization in the 21st century, and it challenges previous conceptions about the significance of ideas in the influence of action. As a result, studying the Army of God offers critical insight to the future of terrorism. This book endeavors to contribute to that effort.

WHAT IS AN ORGANIZATION AND WHY DOES IT MATTER?

In 1994, President Clinton ordered an investigation of the Army of God, in an effort to understand the relationships between members. A grand jury was convened and numerous members were subpoenaed for questioning. The grand jury disbanded two years later, after concluding that there was no discernible organizational structure connecting the individuals.

Sixteen years later, law enforcement's understanding of terrorism has evolved dramatically. Terrorism studies of the early 1990s were only just beginning to recognize the evolution of structure taking place in terrorist organizations. Terrorist organizations of the 1950s, 1960s, and 1970s were generally structured along hierarchal lines[4] consistent with studies that established clear links between hierarchy and the use of violence.[5] Because information was tightly controlled by those at the top of the hierarchy and only distributed as necessary to those lower in it, there were consistent lines connecting the upper and lower levels of organizations. The advantage (for law enforcement) to this type of structure was the identifiable leadership structure. Law enforcement officials could identify one individual in an organization and often trace that individual up or down the chain of command to locate and detain others.

Ideas mattered—but only to the extent that the organization permitted them to. Because information was largely controlled and thereby distributed by top levels of individuals, ties were built on interaction rather than on compatibility of worldviews. In fact, organizational structure was recognized to have enormous implications for action. Following World War II, Hannah Arendt explained the heinous acts of the Nazis as a gradual descent.

The tightly controlled nature of the Germany Army and the Nazi regime meant that opportunities for cognitive dissonance were carefully limited.[6] Philip Zimbardo confirmed Arendt's findings in his notorious Stanford Prison experiment. In less than three days, Zimbardo's experiment had to be shut down because of how quickly "ordinary" human beings descended into the use of violence when part of a restrictive hierarchy.[7] Milgram went further and proved that when an oppressor is in some way removed from his/her victim, he is far more likely to harm the individual. "Hierarchy provides a system of rules and norms that insulate members from their culpability in committing violence. The structure has the potential to isolate the would-be perpetrators from the would-be victims . . . when the perpetrator has little or no interaction with his victim, he or she is less likely to perceive the individual as a person deserving of empathy and, as a result, the perpetrator is not forced to identify with the victim or feel guilt for the pain he/she has caused."[8]

But as law enforcement capabilities developed and tracking of information became more consistent, hierarchies became far less tenable to sustain. Valdis Krebs points out that terrorist organizations face a "constant dynamic between keeping the network hidden and actively using it to accomplish objectives."[9] In essence, terrorist organizations are constantly assessing the cost of secrecy against the benefit of action.

One might hope that as hierarchies—which had been found to be more conducive toward producing violence—were infiltrated and destroyed by law enforcement officials, terrorism would also decline. Instead, something different happened. Ideas began to matter.

In 1996, John Arquilla and David Ronfeldt published a report about the changing nature of terror organizations.[10] In the report, Arquilla and Ronfeldt noted that terrorist organizations were dealing with this tension between action and secrecy by shifting their structures to cells rather than hierarchies. Arquilla and Ronfeldt focused specifically on the way the Internet could be used to facilitate these more elusive ties between members, and largely as a result of this work, the study of networks became critical to the study of terrorism.

Networks are understood to be "a set of diverse, dispersed 'nodes' who share a set of ideas and interests and who are arrayed to act in a fully internetted 'all channel' manner."[11] The primary difference between the cell structure and the hierarchical structure is found in the way information is shared. In networks, information travels from one node to another but not in a linear direction. The benefit (to the members of the network) is that the capture or discovery of a single individual will usually only result in the destruction of a single cell. Network analysts studying the al Qaeda network after September 11 concluded that even if Mohammed Atta, who was the most centrally connected node in the network, had been identified as a threat prior to the attacks, at most only one cell would have been destroyed.[12]

Network analysis tells us that "the rise of networked arrangements in terrorist organizations is part of a wider move away from formally organized, state-sponsored groups to privately financed, loose networks of individuals or subgroups that may have strategic guidance but enjoy tactical independence. Related to these shifts is the fact that the terrorist groups are taking advantage of information technology to coordinate the activities of dispersed members. Such technology may be employed by terrorists not only to wage information warfare, but also to support their own networked organizations."[13]

From this, we can conclude that organization shifted from personal contact, to technological connections, usually formed through some emphasis on similarities of ideals. But this description only partially fits the Army of God. Indisputably, the Army of God is not a hierarchical organization, and much of the communication between members is conducted over the Internet, but this does not explain the 1994 grand jury's inability to find any evidence of "tactical guidance" that characterizes the definition of the new type of terrorist organization.

To address this missing link, some have turned to the concept of "leaderless resistance" spearheaded by Louis Amoss in 1962. Louis Beam, creator of *The Seditionist*,[14] first wrote about the concept in 1983,[15] and the idea was adopted and implemented by many right-wing white-supremacy militia movements. Leaderless resistance was Beam's answer to the state's encroaching efforts to impose "federal tyranny." He says "This changing situation makes it clear that those who oppose state repression must be prepared to alter, adapt and modify their behavior, strategy and tactics as circumstances warrant. . . . As honest men who have banded together into groups or associations of a political or religious nature are falsely labeled 'domestic terrorists' or 'cultists' and suppressed, it will become necessary to consider other methods of organization—or as the case may very well call for: non organization."[16] The solution Beam proposes is the rejection of the easily penetrated pyramid (or hierarchical) organizational structure in favor of "leaderless resistance." Beam describes leaderless resistance as "based upon the cell organization, but [without] any central control or direction. . . . Utilizing the leaderless resistance concept, all individuals and groups operate independently of each other, and never report to a central headquarters or a single leader for direction or instruction, as would those who belong to a typical pyramid organization."[17]

Beam points out that this model quickly weeds out the less committed—and thus most vulnerable to outside influence—by its very nature. Because individuals cannot rely on the orders of others, only the firmest believers remain involved with the "organization." This, according to Beam, greatly decreases the risk of discovery. Beam explains that the new model of leaderless resistance calls for unity of purpose, rather than unity of organization, and it is this distinction that is most relevant to discussions of the Army of God.

The difference between cell strategy and leaderless resistance is small, and the Army of God is situated on the very thin line that divides the two. Whereas cell strategy still depends on tactical support among cells—though communication is dramatically more limited than in a hierarchical system—leaderless resistance removes even this tenuous link. When Beam speaks of "unity of purpose," he is giving value to the strength of an idea that is partially lost, even in cell strategy analysis. But emphasis on the idea is critical to understanding the Army of God—and as this book will argue—the future of terrorism.

WHAT IS AN IDEA AND WHY DOES IT MATTER?

In the study of politics, there is an ongoing trend to question the importance of belief on action. Many scholars shy away from using religion as an explanatory variable, in part at least because it is so difficult to operationalize. Indeed, how does one measure belief? Shall we count the number of times a person attends church? Returning to the *Sound of Music* analogy, Sister Maria may not have made the grade, given her penchant for lyrical hiking. Or shall we count how much a person donates financially to a religious establishment? The New Testament would counsel against this method, as the woman who gave two copper coins was judged by Jesus to be more faithful than the man who gave many riches.[18] More often than not, religion, and therefore belief, is rejected as a variable entirely, and scholars choose instead to see it as a mask for more quantifiable variables.[19]

But, as this book will show, there are dangers to avoiding the importance of ideas. Indeed as law enforcement increases its ability to track even the most miniscule of organizational ties, ideas are going to become critical to the connection of organizations.

In fact, this has already begun to occur among organizations other than the Army of God. The 2003 attacks in Casablanca, the 2004 attacks in Madrid, and the 2005 London subway attacks were all undertaken by *individuals* with no organizational ties to al Qaeda. And yet, each perpetrator professed to having been exposed to the ideals of the organization via the Internet and then independently planning these attacks toward the furtherance of these ideals.[20] In fact, Shehzad Tanweer and Mohammad Sidique Khan voluntarily traveled to Pakistan, where they received explosives training, based on the ideology they became exposed to a continent away. Kirby explains the significance of this development. "The current global context is one where both the necessity and the ability for small groups to connect to a larger more organized network have been almost simultaneously, radically diminished. Now, in contrast to many jihadist cells of the past, self-starters demonstrate the features of being largely, if not completely, self-radicalizing and more importantly, self-activating."[21]

After the London bombings took place, law enforcement officials gave interviews to the media professing to be hot on the trails of the extensive support structure that would have allowed the perpetrators to undertake such an act. For months, police sought the "direct links with al Qaeda" that they were certain had to exist,[22] only to eventually conclude that no such connections were present.

The search for organizational ties is inherently understandable. Just as academics avoid giving explanatory power to ideas alone, governments must be cautious in finding ideas to be responsible for acts of terror. After all, how does one prosecute an idea without threatening the very ideals a nation is bound to preserve? But however unappealing a focus on ideas may be, in the climate of terrorism that the world faces, it is fundamentally important

WHERE DOES THE ARMY OF GOD FIT?

The Army of God is often overlooked as a terrorist organization for a number of reasons. First, the group is relatively small. There are perhaps two dozen fully committed and well-known "members" and only dozens more supporters.

Second, in the 30 years that it has been known to exist, there has not been consensus that its members are terrorists at all. Certainly they themselves would deny that they are. They do not consider the killing of abortion providers or the bombing of abortion clinics to be "violence" at all, because violence carries with it negative connotations that do not reflect the Godly work they perceive themselves to be doing. But more significantly, there hasn't been agreement within the law-enforcement community about whether or not the bombings and killings count as acts of terrorism. As will be seen in chapter 5 of this book, the FBI director under Ronald Reagan denied that abortion clinic bombings were acts of terrorism, while Janet Reno, Bill Clinton, John Ashcroft, and Barack Obama have adamantly described them as such.

This book will argue that the ambiguity of the nature of the organization makes the Army of God particularly important to study. As the years since September 11 have shown, there are significant gaps in both domestic and international law regarding how to define and prosecute crimes of terrorism. The Army of God is small and accessible, and the government's actions toward this group could set a valuable precedent about how to protect and preserve rights without condoning violence.

Third, the organization is not an organization in the traditional sense. Stinchcombe defines organizations as "a set of stable social relations deliberately created, with the explicit intention of continuously accomplishing some specific goals or purposes. These goals or purposes are generally functions performed for some larger structure,"[23] and the Army of God does not fit this definition. Certainly the "organization" exists with the explicit intention of continuously accomplishing a specific goal, but the structure can hardly be identified as stable. Stinchcombe's definition rests on the idea of deliberate creation, wherein the institution itself becomes a value of the group that sustains it. This is not the case in the Army of God. While the members interact regularly, the idea of the group is far more important to the members than the institution of it.

Louis Beam's leaderless resistance model is the closest description available, but even this is limited in what it explains. According to Beam's model, leaderless resisters will virtually never interact. The Army of God certainly does. In the 1990s, supporters met yearly at the White Rose banquet to honor and raise funds for members in prison for the sake of the cause. The director of the Army of God website told this author that he knows and regularly interacts—via e-mail, phone, and in-person meetings—with almost everyone listed on the site.[24]

Neal Horsley, one of the more colorful antiabortion proponents, explains the organization as he understands it:

> I have been trying to explode the Army of God myth for many years. This article is simply another example proving that I do not pass up an opportunity to tell anyone who will listen that as far as I can tell there is not now, and probably never has been, an organization that could be reasonably be called The Army of God in the USA. I should know if there was such an organization. I personally know most of the bombers and the arsonists and the assassins who have risen up to strike the abortion industry over the last two decades and there is not even a hint of organization in the entire surviving crew. There is only an "evanescent, amorphous, autonomous and spontaneous" group of individuals, all of whom hate legalized abortion like they hate Satan himself. Who am I talking about? I'm talking about the Reverend Paul Hill, Jim Kopp, Mike Bray, Joshua Graff, John Brockoeft, Clay Waagner, Shelly Shannon, Brenda Phillips, the list goes on and on to include every person who has been arrested for an abortion related crime since 1984. Look at that list and you will see a list of individuals, most of whom acted alone in response to their inability to stand in the face of legalized abortion without autonomously and spontaneously picking up something and trying to hurt it bad. And there is not a scintilla of evidence to the contrary.[25]

Whether or not the organization is actually an organization is important for several reasons. As will be seen in chapter 5 of this book, numerous efforts have been made by law enforcement officials to determine what type of communication goes on between and among affiliates of the Army of God. There has yet to be a successful prosecution (or even firm revelation of evidence) of a conspiracy that would point to a formal organizational structure. This book does not dispute those findings (or lack thereof).

Rather, it will be argued that the Army of God is a model of "organizations" to come and that finding ways to address the presently unique nature of the group is critical to future efforts to deal with terrorism. For the remainder of this book, the author will refer to the Army of God as an organization, bearing in mind the limitations of the term in the circumstances.

Finally, to identify "members" of the Army of God is a bit of a misnomer, but no other term adequately explains the relationship. Members are identified as such not based on an induction ceremony, or the claiming of a recruitment incentive. Rather, individuals share a deep commitment to a particular set of ideals, and this commitment forms the basis of relationship between the members and the organization. In this sense, membership is identified by a shared set of ideals rather than an agreement to participate in an organization. This means that an individual could be identified by someone in the group as a "member" without necessarily considering him/ herself to be one at all.

This distinction presents a challenge to those who would study the organization, as there is no clear difference between "members," "supporters," and "affiliates." This book alternately uses all three classifications, usually reserving "member" for individuals with demonstrable ties (of friendship, kinship, or action) to those who have used force to stop abortion. "Supporters" is generally used to designate individuals who have expressed affinity for the use of force but are not widely recognized as having ties with the organization. "Affiliates" is used to designate those who have signed one of the petitions supporting the use of force, or who have been allegedly linked to individuals in the movements.

But for all the challenges present in defining and studying this small quasi-organization, the benefits are significant. Recent events have proven that terrorism of the future is not going to look the same as terrorism of the past.[26] It is critical to deepen both the academic and practical understanding of the way these organizations operate, develop, and sustain themselves. New models must be developed that can account for quasi-organizational structures and ambiguous membership rosters. The Army of God is unique among these types of organizations because the members are so willing to talk about their goals and the justification for their methods. Members spend extensive amounts of time detailing the processes that led them toward the use of force, and they are remarkably open about their right to do so.

While undoubtedly the goals of the Army of God are different from al Qaeda and Islamic Jihad, the lessons we can learn from them are not markedly so. The Army of God can answer critical questions about the role of ideas in the implementation of terror and the substitution of organization. The response to the Army of God in the United States can establish important precedents for how to handle difficult issues like the preservation of rights to speech and religion while still protecting citizens from intimidation. In short, the Army of God is small, but its potential is significant.

The rest of this book will provide a detailed and comprehensive overview of this important organization. The chapters are organized to answer certain fundamental questions about the organization and its place in American politics.

Chapter 1 asks how the Army of God developed in the context of the abortion debate in the United States. This chapter will show that the debate about abortion has been around for centuries, and that it influences not only the actors themselves, but those who would write about them. With this in mind, the chapter traces the historical developments of perspectives on abortion, paying attention to both empirical and theoretical trends. The chapter demonstrates that although most texts place the Army of God as intimately wedded to the rest of the antiabortion movement, in fact the individuals that make up the Army of God have removed themselves—at least ideologically—from lesser forms of protest. In fact, the Army of God condemns members of the pro-life movement who do not see force as a legitimate and fully justifiable method for ending abortion.

Chapter 2 offers a history of acts attributed to the Army of God. Drawing on confessions from members, court records, and historical accounts, this section provides a timeline of the evolution of tactics and methods. This chapter shows that over time the organization has evolved into more fatal acts of violence. Whereas the 1980s were characterized by bombings and acts of arson, the 1990s and the new millennium have seen targeted killings against individuals associated with the abortion industry.

Chapter 3 explores the themes in the ideology of the Army of God. The chapter examines the four primary justifications used by the organization, including biblical, legal, personal, and pragmatic. While most works written by members of the Army of God use each of these justifications in some way or another, the emphasis shifts according to the individual.

Chapter 4 introduces the reader to the individuals that make up this elusive Army. The chapter highlights the ties that do conclusively exist between members and traces the ideas that unite them. This chapter shows the tenuous nature of "membership" and the influence of affinity in ideology.

Chapter 5 traces the response of other actors involved in the abortion debate to the Army of God. The chapter shows how political affiliation, religious interest, and law enforcement definitions influence the way individuals and organizations respond to acts undertaken by the Army of God. This chapter highlights the challenges facing those who try to stop antiabortion violence, given the centrality of ideas and the absence of organizational structure in the group.

At the end of this book, the reader will be left with some serious questions about the Army of God in particular and the future of terrorism more generally. This book should not be the final word on the Army of God; if anything its purpose is to demonstrate the importance of thinking more carefully about this organization and others like it. The Army of God is not unique among terrorist organizations for its affiliation based on an idea. And as law enforcement becomes more and more sophisticated in its ability to trace all physical relationships, structures, and organizations, this type of "organization" will inevitably become more and more common. It is imperative then, that academics, policy makers, and law enforcement agencies think carefully about how to address this emerging threat. The Army of God is exceptional because its members are so willing to share their idea with others. Future groups may not be so accommodating, and it behooves us to learn the lessons now, before it becomes too late.

NOTES

1. Risen, James and Judy Thomas. 1998. *Wrath of Angels: The American Abortion War*. New York: Basic Books.

2. Blanchard, Dallas A. 1994. *The Anti-Abortion Movement and the Rise of the Religious Right*. New York: Twayne Publishers.

3. Blanchard, Dallas A. and Terry J. Prewitt. 1993. *Religious Violence and Abortion*. Edited by the Gideon Project. Gainesville: University Press of Florida.

4. Hoffman, Bruce. 1999. "Terrorism: Trends and Prospects." In *Countering the New Terrorism*, ed. Ian O. Lesser, Bruce Hoffman, John Arquilla, David Ronfeldt and Michele Zanini, 7–38. Santa Monica, CA: RAND.

5. See, for example, Zimbardo, Philip. 2007. *The Lucifer Effect: Understanding How Good People Turn Evil*. New York: Random House; Arendt, Hannah. 2006. *Eichmann in Jerusalem: A Report on the Banality of Evil*. New York: Penguin Classics.

6. Arendt, Hannah. 2006. *Eichmann in Jerusalem: A Report on the Banality of Evil* New York: Penguin Classics.

7. Zimbardo, Philip. 2007. *The Lucifer Effect: Understanding How Good People Turn Evil*. New York: Random House.

8. Jefferis, Jennifer. 2010. *Religion and Political Violence: Sacred Protest in the Modern World*. New York: Routledge, 94.

9. Krebs, Valdis. 2002. "Uncloaking Terrorist Networks." *First Monday* 7, no. 4.

10. Arquilla, John and David Ronfeldt. 1996. *The Advent of Netwar*. Santa Monica, CA: RAND.

11. Arquilla, John and David Ronfeldt. 1996. *The Advent of Netwar*. Santa Monica, CA: RAND.

12. Robb, John. "Mapping Terrorist Networks." http://globalguerrillas.typepad.com/globalguerrillas/2004/04/mapping_terrori.html.

13. Zanini, Michele. 1999. "Middle Eastern Terrorism and Netwar." *Studies in Conflict and Terrorism* 22: 247–256, 247.

14. Beam describes this "journal" as a quarterly journal of seditionist thought.

15. Beam, Louis. 1992. "Leaderless Resistance." *The Seditionist* 12. http://www.louisbeam.com/leaderless.htm.

16. Beam, Louis. 1992. "Leaderless Resistance." *The Seditionist* 12. http://www.louisbeam.com/leaderless.htm.

17. Beam, Louis. 1992. "Leaderless Resistance." *The Seditionist* 12. http://www.louisbeam.com/leaderless.htm.

18. "As he looked up, Jesus saw the rich putting their gifts into the temple treasury. He also saw a poor widow put in two very small copper coins. 'I tell you the truth,' he

said, 'this poor widow has put in more than all the others. All these people gave their gifts out of their wealth; but she out her poverty put in all she had to live on.'" (Luke 21:1–4)

19. See Nelson, Joan M. 1979. *Access to Power: Politics and the Urban Poor in Developing Nations*. Princeton, NJ: Princeton University Press; Bowen, Don and Ted Robert Gurr. 1968. "Deprivation, Mobility and Orientation toward Protest of the Urban Poor." *American Behavioral Scientist*, March–April: 20–24; Norris, Pippa and Ronald Inglehart. 2004. *Sacred and Secular: Religion and Politics Worldwide*. Cambridge: Cambridge University Press.

20. Kirby, Aiden. 2007. "The London Bombers as 'Self Starters': A Case Study in Indigenous Radicalization and the Emergence of Autonomous Cliques." *Studies in Conflict and Terrorism* 30: 415–428.

21. Kirby, Aiden. 2007. "The London Bombers as 'Self Starters': A Case Study in Indigenous Radicalization and the Emergence of Autonomous Cliques." *Studies in Conflict and Terrorism* 30: 415–428, 416.

22. Kirby, Aiden. 2007. "The London Bombers as 'Self Starters': A Case Study in Indigenous Radicalization and the Emergence of Autonomous Cliques." *Studies in Conflict and Terrorism* 30: 415–428, 419.

23. Stinchcombe, Arthur. 2000. "Social Structure and Organizations." In *Economic Meets Sociology in Strategic Management*, ed. Joel Baum, 17. Bingley, UK: Emerald Publishing.

24. Author phone interview with Donald Spitz, 2010.

25. Horsley, Neal. 2003. "Exploding the Myth of the Army of God." *Christian Gallery News Service*, November 14. http://www.christiangallery.com/ExplodingArmyof GodMyth.htm.

26. See Lesser, Ian O., Bruce Hoffman, John Arquilla, David Ronfeldt, Michele Zanini and Brian Michael Jenkins. 1999. *Countering the New Terrorism*. Santa Monica, CA: RAND.

1

───⊗∞⊗───

In the Arena

The introduction to this book argued that the Army of God is an important, if perplexing, organization because of the model it offers for the future of terrorism. The introduction pointed out that the issues driving the Army of God are quite different from those driving many other terrorist organizations operating today, but the lessons to be learned from the Army of God are still relevant. This chapter will endeavor to provide a context for the issues most important to the Army of God and the ideals that shape their agenda. This chapter will show that while the Army of God grew out of a broader debate about the meaning of life, the organization has narrowly defined the parameters of the issue for their own purposes.

The quest to form an accurate contextual frame for the development of antiabortion terrorism is rife with challenges, in part because few other issues in American politics are so inherently polarizing. While one may feel strongly about the appropriate size of government, the necessary rate of taxation, the proper distribution of health care, or the role of homosexuals in the military, it is abortion that stands out as an issue that moves beyond quality-of-life arguments to arguments about life itself. Many involved in pro-life politics are quick to characterize abortion as murder—thereby condemning supporters of the practice as murderers. In contrast, those involved in pro-choice politics frequently suggest that pro-lifers are sexist chauvinists in favor of keeping women trapped in their kitchens rather than active in pursuit of equal rights.[1] Such characterizations leave little room for neutral, middle ground, and the existence of this polarity is dramatically evident not just in the actions of activists, but also in the narrative of history that defines the context of each movement. Although both sides of the abortion movement examine the same historical timeline, utterly divergent interpretations of history influence the state of the movement.

Such varied narratives can develop because there is very little known about legal statutes or social mores regarding abortion. Only a few references to the practice appear in legislative records, and even these don't emerge until the turn of the 19th century. And even then, cases were few and far between. Pro-life advocates suggest that laws were not necessary for something that was almost universally recognized as an abhorrent act—social pressure and structure was sufficient to limit the practice of abortion.[2] But pro-choice advocates argue that there are relatively few records of abortion because it was widely practiced—and accepted.[3] This chapter will not endeavor to "set the record straight" for either interpretation. Rather it will offer an overview of the different interpretations through the lens of history.

HISTORICAL DEVELOPMENT OF CONTENTION

With that in mind, it is appropriate to begin with John Noonan's book, published by Harvard University Press in 1970. Although Noonan was writing three years before *Roe v. Wade* would be decided, abortion was already a highly controversial and highly publicized issue. In his introduction, Noonan writes with concern about the "shift in influential sentiment" he sees in American positions on abortion. He says "Respectable, serious, committed persons have contended that the planned termination of pregnancy has a social utility and humane character not appreciated by earlier generations. Response to these contentions among groups likely to determine attitudes towards abortion has ranged from benevolent tolerance to passionate conviction. Abortion, once regarded as a secret and loathsome crime, a medical disaster or a tragic manifestation of human weakness, has been justified by the draftsmen of the American Law Institute, defended by the American Medical Association, applauded by Planned Parenthood—World Population and publicized by the New York Times."[4]

Noonan presciently observes that while at the time of his writing abortion was a moral issue, "moral issues become legal issues, and legal issues become constitutional issues" because "What is right must be legal and what is wrong must be unconstitutional."[5] Noonan contends that before abortion became a legal issue, it would be necessary to understand its roots as a moral one, and to this end, he examines the value of life through the lens of a moral history.

Noonan begins with the Old Testament. According to Noonan, while the Old Testament does not reference abortion directly, Hellenic Jews in the Diaspora interpreted the text of Exodus 21:22[6] to imply that the unborn were equated by God as fully human and equal in value to other humans. There are records in the early Christian church suggesting that church elders condemned abortion as early as A.D. 100,[7] and Noonan argues that Christians during A.D. 50–450 were the definitive voice in the abortion discussion: "Where some wise men had raised voices in defense of early life so that the question was in the air and not yet authoritatively decided, where even the wisest presented hesitant and divided counsel, where other authorities defended abortion, the Christians proposed a rule which was certain, comprehensive and absolute."[8] Noonan argues that Christian teaching on abortion was clear even in the earliest days of the religion. He argues that the emphasis in both the Old and New Testament to love God and love one's neighbor is indicative of a value placed on God-given life in any form. Further, he suggests that when Paul depicted certain behaviors that violated God's call to love one's neighbor, Paul deliberately used the term *pharmakeia*, which translates to the use of drugs "with occult properties"[9] to induce abortion. Noonan argues that numerous later writings supported this reading of Galatians, including one written in Syria around A.D. 100 that specifically states, "You shall not practice medicine (pharmakeia). You shall not slay the child by abortions (phthora)."[10]

However, this is not to say that the practice did not occur—on the contrary, Greco-Roman physician Soranos of Ephesus (A.D. 98–138) articulated several different methods of inducing abortions—and kept records indicating three primary reasons to practice abortion: to hide the evidence of adulterous relationships; to maintain the female figure; the health of the mother.[11] There are several other instances of well-known Christian leaders condemning the practice in the following centuries, with more formalized positions evolving between A.D. 450 and 1450.

Indeed, as Christianity evolved from a religious sect to a legal religion closely tied to the third-century state, antiabortion legislation began to take shape. Councils in Ancyra and Elvira established statutes to excommunicate women who knowingly had abortions.[12] As time went on, some church leaders began to wonder whether abortion was against the will of God prior to "ensoulment" or the moment that the fetus was formed with a soul, given by God. Nonetheless, according to Noonan, "all the writers agreed that abortion was a violation of the love owed to one's neighbor. Some saw it as a special failure of maternal love. Many saw it also as a failure to have reverence for the work of God the creator. The culture had accepted abortion. The Christians, men of this Greco-Roman world and the gospel condemned it. Ancient authorities and contemporary moralists had approved, hesitated, made exceptions: the Christian rule was certain."[13]

The question of ensoulment continued to be found in discussions of abortion, from the start of the Christian church and for many centuries after. While Augustine's definitive judgment that all abortion was murder played a prominent role in the Gratian canons, Gratian also included his own variation on Augustine's theme by suggesting that abortion was not a crime until it resulted in the destruction of a soul. Gratian's interpretation was implicitly accepted by Pope Innocent III (1160–1216) when he judged a monk guilty of homicide if he caused his mistress to abort only if the fetus that had been aborted was "vivified."[14]

In 1620, a physician named Thomas Fienus published a work titled "A Book on the Formation of the Fetus in Which it is Shown that the Rational Soul is Infused on the Third day."[15] Another physician built on Fienus's thesis a year later, arguing that the only reasonable explanation for ensoulment revolved around the existence of a soul from the moment of conception. The thesis resonated with Pope Innocent X, who then appointed its author to the role of "General Proto-Physician of the Whole Roman Ecclesiastical State."[16]

Noonan argues that the period between 1621 and 1965 reflects a heightening of the Catholic Church's understanding of ensoulment and a consequential tightening position on abortion. Scientific discovery undergirded these developments, beginning with Karl Ernest von Baer's 1827 discovery of the ovum and the 1875 discovery of the relationship between sperm and ovum in conception. Noonan argues that "a change in organism was seen to occur at the moment of fertilization which distinguished the resultant from the components" and "it was easier to mark it than it was to mark it off from the living elements which had preceded it than it was to mark it off from some later stage of its organic growth in the uterus."[17]

But where Noonan judges the church to have clearly and firmly denounced abortion as a grave sin, numerous other academics see history in a very different light. Most academic histories address several related questions about how abortion went from being virtually nonexistent in records of American history to being one of the most detailed and discussed medical procedures in the legal realm, all in a space of less than 100 years. But as will become clear in the pages that follow, it is here that the similarities of accounts end.

There are two pillars of abortion history in the United States: James C. Mohr and Marvin Olasky. Mohr is a historian at the University of Oregon and is well known for his works on medical history. He wrote *Abortion in America: The Origins and Evolution of National Policy* in 1978, and virtually all books written on the history of abortion since that time heavily reference Mohr's seminal work. Marvin Olasky has a PhD in American Culture from Yale University and is a professor of journalism at the University of Texas. Olasky's book, *Abortion Rites: A Social History of Abortion in America*, was written in 1992 to serve as a contrast to Mohr's.

According to Mohr, "In 1800, no jurisdiction in the United States had enacted any statute whatsoever on the subject of abortion; most forms of abortion were not illegal and those American women who wished to practice abortion did so."[18] Mohr argues that prior to quickening (the first movement felt from the fetus in the womb—usually around the fourth or fifth month), abortion was typically seen as little more than restoring the woman's regular cycle, and a wide variety of methods were available toward this end. Abortion after quickening was recognized as a crime, but one that Mohr says was "qualitatively different from the destruction of a human being, however, and punished less harshly."[19]

When the first law against abortion prior to quickening was published in 1803 in Britain, American court rulings indicated that prior to quickening pregnancy was impossible to prove and thus outside the purview of the courts. Mohr argues that *Commonwealth v. Bangs,* in which this issue was decided, was the precedent that resulted in few indictments for abortion prior to quickening ever being brought before American courts in the first half of the 19th century. "Every time the issue arose prior to 1850, the same conclusion was sustained; the interruption of a suspected pregnancy prior to quickening was not a crime in itself."[20]

Mohr points to the easy availability of abortifacient information in home medical literature as evidence of the prominence of abortion in the early 19th century. Leslie Reagan suggests that the term *abortion* is not entirely appropriate to represent the actions of women during the 18th and 19th centuries. She notes that in the few records that exist, women refer to the process as being "fixed up,"[21] or the restoration of menses, where the early condition of pregnancy was often perceived as the obstruction of menstruation—a condition that necessitated medical intervention.[22] This intervention usually took the form of home remedies involving herbs used to induce vomiting and the flushing of the fetus.

Records go back to as early as 1742 indicating abortion was referred to in the vernacular as "taking the trade,"[23] a phrase history professor Leslie Reagan interprets to have been widely used and recognized by women in the 18th century. There is some dispute in this narrative about who was most likely to seek an early-term abortion in the 18th and 19th century.

Reagan argues that abortion in the latter half of the 19th century was an open secret among women and doctors. She argues that the absence of cases in which women were brought before courts for abortion proves that under common law, abortion was legal.[24]

Mohr suggests that abortions were most frequently sought by unmarried women seeking to hide illicit relationships, and only rarely pursued by married women seeking to limit their fertility.[25] But Reagan suggests that "early 20th century women's use of abortion was part of a long tradition among women to control and limit their child-bearing."[26] She argues that abortion was most popular among married women until after World War II, when abortions by single women began to increase.

While Reagan and Mohr differ over who was most likely to seek an abortion during the early years of American history, they are in agreement that the practice was widely available and rarely condemned. Olasky disagrees. Whereas Blanchard, Mohr, and Reagan, among others, look at the small number of abortions brought before criminal courts as evidence of the ubiquity of its practice, Olasky argues that the same absence indicates its condemnation in society at large. He sees the absence of laws not as an acceptance of the practice of abortion, but as the absence of a need for laws to regulate something that virtually never occurred.

In the introduction to *Abortion Rites*, Olasky pays homage to Mohr's influential history but aims to highlight its limitations. Olasky says, "Mohr in the 1970s walked bravely into the darkness of old and hard-to-find records. Like all historians, he had a sheaf of assumptions in one hand and a flashlight in the other. Mohr's book shows his assumptions: that abortion before 'quickening' . . . was acceptable in America at least until the mid-nineteenth century; that abortion was widely diffused throughout the population in the nineteenth century; that anti-abortion laws passed during that century were an aberration in American history; and that the legalization of abortion over the past two decades thus represents a return to the true American consensus, rather than a sudden deviation from past practice."[27] Olasky goes on to argue that Mohr had been armed with his thesis that the American Medical Association was to blame for the sharp change in American abortion policy at the turn of the century. And Olasky suggests that "Mohr walked only one straight path and presented only one simple thesis."[28] In contrast, Olasky claims to examine the "curved paths" of abortion history.

This curvy path takes Olasky deep into a social understanding of abortion at the time of the American colonies. Olasky argues that abortion records are hard to find not because—as Mohr and others suggest—abortion was so readily available as to not be worth noting, but because abortion itself was infrequent. Olasky contends that records prove that "repeatedly, the women involved in the crimes were not only unwed, but among the minority of the pregnant unmarried who fell outside the informal and legal society safety nets."[29] Olasky concludes that the growing occurrence of abortion in America was the result of the urbanization that loosened the ties within and between families. As a result, the cracks in which unwed women could fall widened, and abortion became a more expedient option.

Olasky also disputes Mohr's contention that abortion was "neither morally nor legally wrong in the eyes of the vast majority of Americans, provided it was accomplished before quickening."[30] Olasky argues that far from being mainstream, the majority of those abortions that did take place were related to prostitution. Olasky describes prostitution as a "muddy stream rather than a mainstream of American life" and argues that it is central to discussions of morality—not unrelated, as Mohr suggests.

It is interesting to note that although Olasky's book was written to challenge the history Mohr firmly established in 1978, it is Mohr's work that is most often cited in other works on the subject. Nearly every book about abortion used as a reference toward the writing of this work cites Mohr's work when providing the history of abortion in America. Only one cites

Olasky's.[31] Mohr's thesis is generally regarded as indisputably correct, though few of these works delve into sources that date back further than Mohr's.[32] The point here is not whether or not either Olasky or Mohr have solved the mystery of abortion's history, so much as the continued status of uncertainty surrounding it.

DRAWING THE LINES OF A LEGAL BATTLE

By 1910, all states in the United States had laws on the books limiting the practice of abortion. However, whether one prefers Olasky's or Mohr's narrative of abortion history, none dispute the social changes that kept the issue of abortion on the table. As urbanization swept the country, more and more families were moving away from the country into very different city living situations. Where families living on farms could benefit from the help of many growing hands, in the squalor that characterized big-city living, new hands could not offset the seemingly insurmountable costs of new stomachs that each child brought. Consequently, at the same time that abortion awareness and legislative oversight grew, conditions making control over family size valuable increased as well.

At the same time that living conditions were changing dramatically, the ubiquity of Charles Darwin's argument regarding evolution and natural selection was increasing. Concerned that the Church was not responding adequately to the striking changes occurring rapidly in society and worried that secularism was eroding central tenets of scripture, a group of American Protestants began publishing pamphlets laying out the elements of Christianity that they considered essential. The Fundamentals, as these publications came to be called, detailed the centrality of certain elements of scripture to the Christian community. Included in these key tenets were the inerrancy of scripture and the denunciation of more liberal beliefs.

The publication of these Fundamentals served as an important function in what would become, many decades later, the antiabortion movement. The Fundamentalists (the individuals who agreed with the doctrine identified in the Fundamentals) came to see themselves as necessarily set apart from the evolving secularization of society. The Scopes Monkey fiasco that developed as a result of the debate between William Jennings Bryan and Clarence Darrow over John Scopes's effort to teach Darwinism in public schools reinforced this manner of thinking. Fundamentalists began to see themselves as at odds with the greater secular community (and even much of the non-Fundamentalist Christian community) and endeavored to withdraw from active participation in politics. This effort was undergirded by the Fundamentalist adherence to the premillennial dispensationalist understanding of scripture, which predicts an impending Armageddon from which true believers will be excused, by means of the rapture before

Jesus's return to earth. The practical consequence of this theological understanding was to remove themselves from active involvement in social and
political life, as the end times were near and efforts to impact society would
be ultimately wasted.

At the same time that the Fundamentalists were withdrawing from society, the Great Depression was spurring a greater demand for abortion
among women. Leslie Reagan boldly states that "women had abortions on a
massive scale"[33] due to the increased expenses that would result from more
children for families already suffering extreme poverty. Indeed, in 1936 the
New York Times ran a story about hundreds of women in New Jersey that
had purchased "abortion insurance," which ensured their care in the event
of an unwanted pregnancy.[34] However, because abortion was ubiquitously
illegal during this time, precise records about abortion services and usage
are not available.

As the 20th century progressed, the debate about abortion remained
heated, though well outside the official political sphere. Therapeutic abortion (abortions performed to protect the health of the mother) was legal,
and some doctors were known to carefully navigate the line between legal therapeutic abortions and illegal abortions. Other doctors were less
circumspect in their opinions and opened clinics specifically designed to
provide abortions. However, these clinics were shrouded with secrecy and
referrals were challenging to obtain.

In the 1940s and 1950s, abortion became less common as medical practitioners banded together to prevent its practice. The line between therapeutic and illegal abortions was more actively defended by the medical
community through the formation of hospital oversight committees that
could rule on the appropriation of the practice. Criminal proceedings were
undertaken more frequently against physicians willing to offer abortions,
and the news media carried stories of illegal abortions, effectively increasing social opposition to those who would practice it.

Reagan argues that the increased attention paid to abortion in political, medical, and legal communities led not to decreased numbers of abortions, but to an increased reliance on secrecy. She contends that well-to-do
white women had greater access to therapeutic abortions, while women
of lesser means or different ethnicities were forced to suffer at the hands
of ill-qualified practitioners.[35] Also during this period, the conditions that
formerly were believed to threaten the health of the mother to the extent
that a therapeutic abortion would be legally condoned had been largely
addressed by the medical community. In the 1950s the dangers of tuber-
culosis, excessive vomiting, and cardiovascular disease had been met with
viable treatment other than abortion. As a result, the line between the therapeutic and illegal abortions became clearer.[36]

Some scholars credit this deepening of the divide between legal and obviously illegal abortions with being the catalyst for the birth of the pro-choice

movement.[37] When opportunities for therapeutic abortion abounded, the American medical community could remain united in their formal opposition to the practice of illegal abortions. However, as fewer situations arose in which therapeutic abortions could be judged as necessary, doctors lost their discretionary authority to distinguish between necessary and unnecessary. Instead, doctors had to come down on one side of the argument or the other—and fissures began to develop within the community. Luker argues that these fissures were the necessary opportunity for women's groups to burst onto the scene of pro-choice politics.[38]

During this same period, middle-class, married mother-of-four Sherri Finkbine also became indelibly imprinted on the public's consciousness. In 1962, Finkbine became pregnant. Anxious about the impending birth of her fifth child, Finkbine took a tranquilizer called thalidomide. Later in her pregnancy, Finkbine learned that thalidomide could produce severe birth defects. Her doctor recommended she have an abortion despite the fact that Arizona laws were clear that abortions could only be condoned when the health of the mother was at risk. Before having the abortion, Finkbine contacted a reporter, in an effort to spread awareness about the dangers of thalidomide. The article was published on the front page of the *Arizona Republic* the same day that Finkbine's abortion was scheduled. Fearful of negative publicity, the hospital canceled the procedure and Finkbine eventually went to Sweden to have the abortion.[39]

Finkbine's case propelled abortion to the forefront of national consciousness, because she defied the stereotypes traditionally associated with the issue. Whereas previously abortion was understood to be something practiced by and for the irresponsible and immoral, Finkbine was a respected mother seen to be in a tough situation. Over the following 10 years, 14 states changed their legislation toward abortion by extending the definition of therapeutic abortion to include the mental health of the mother.

Moreover, the use of birth control continued to rise, and women's movements gained greater traction every year. Women began to view their roles differently, as issues of gender equality in the workforce began to take precedence over the prominence of women being functionally and exclusively viewed as wives and mothers.[40] In 1969, the National Association for the Repeal of Abortion Laws was formed, and public views toward abortion began to shift. Between 1965 and 1969, public support for abortion in the first trimester for any reason jumped from 8 percent to 40 percent.[41]

By 1970, the abortion law repeal movement had gone national—and the organizations pushing for reform were not exclusively secular. Numerous Protestant organizations promoted abortion rights, and the American Medical Association began advocating for revisions to the extensive restrictions placed on the practice of abortion. Hawaii, Alaska, and New York led the states in legislative change, being the first to legalize abortion upon request.

In 1973, all states were required to follow suit, when on January 22, the Supreme Court ruled that no state could legally restrict a woman's right to abortion in the first trimester of pregnancy. In the second trimester, the state has some authority to restrict abortions, and in the third trimester, the state's oversight increases further.

While most debates about abortion center around the impact of pregnancy on a woman, Supreme Court Justice Harry A. Blackmun's majority opinion on *Roe v. Wade* embedded the rights of women in the context of the same issues that had plagued the abortion debate since Roman times: the issue of when life begins. Blackmun essentially argued that the answer to when life begins is outside the purview of the state or the courts. Until this question could be satisfactorily resolved by someone capable of doing so, the issue of privacy had to outweigh the possibility of life. But Blackmun made clear that his decision hinged on the state's inability to prove the fetus was a human being. Were they to do so, the "case, of course, collapses, for the fetus' right to life would then be guaranteed specifically by the [Fourteenth] amendment."[42]

Blackmun's comment is hugely significant for anyone seeking to understand the environment in which the antiabortion movement in general, and the Army of God in particular, developed. For supporters of the pro-life movement, the question that Blackmun considered outside the purview of the state had already been answered time and again. Thus the state, even in its most limited form, was obligated to protect the life that they saw so clearly in existence. Abortion was not about privacy, any more than killing one's child should be, and the same urgency that would naturally inspire action in the case of the latter fueled the fires of action in the former.

STIRRINGS OF PROTEST

The reaction to *Roe v. Wade* was immediate and jarring. Many current opponents of the fateful Supreme Court decision recall being shocked that an American court could issue a decision so contrary to their values.[43] Leaders in the antiabortion movement speak bitterly of the power the Court assumed in that decision—and argue that such a decision was a violation of the representative nature of American politics.[44] The Court decision was scandalous to abortion opponents—few of whom had yet organized themselves into anything close to a movement. But after the decision was rendered, the movement coalesced fairly quickly.

The first organized antiabortion protest took place on the first anniversary of *Roe v. Wade*. Six thousand demonstrators gathered on Capitol Hill to express their support for Senator James Buckley (a Republican from New York) who had proposed a constitutional amendment outlawing abortion.[45] Smaller protests took place the same day all over the country.

Interestingly, the first organizers of the antiabortion movement were not experienced political operators. On the contrary, the early movement was characterized by Catholic mothers. Craig and O'Brien argue that the demographic characteristics of the early movement played a significant role in its gradual success. Noting that whereas 94 percent of pro-choice women worked outside the home and only 37 percent of pro-life women did, the pro-life movement was staffed by members with more flexibility in their schedules and more availability to participate in protests, letter-writing campaigns, and the like.[46]

Whether or not one accepts Craig and O'Brien's dubious characterization of the easy lifestyle of stay-at-home mothers in contrast to their employed counterparts, and the advantageous consequence Craig and O'Brien see as a result, it is useful to realize that the antiabortion movement was never a professional endeavor—it has instead been characterized by individuals who may not have entered the arena of protest for any other issue.

Whatever the early movement supporters lacked in experience, they made up for in intensity. Abortion quickly became a central issue in many political campaigns, and pro-life advocates sought to make abortion a litmus test for anyone running for any office.[47]

Every year, the numbers gathering to protest *Roe v. Wade* on the anniversary of the decision grew—and by 1980, organizers estimated 100,000 individuals gathered in the Capitol. While the movement was not successful in achieving any sweeping legislative or judicial rulings against abortion, they did have measured success in chipping away at the issue from other directions, including the Hyde Amendment, which limited federal funding of abortions.

A MOVEMENT AT ODDS

But even as the movement demonstrated its ability to launch large rallies, organizations within the movement were coming to realize that the Right to Life movement had a limited number of options to pursue in their quest to end abortion in the United States: They could attempt to take the issue back to the courts and pursue an overturn of *Roe v. Wade*; they could pursue a constitutional amendment that would make abortion illegal; they could influence the social environment and try to make the practice of abortion a social taboo.[48] The question plaguing the burgeoning movement was how to accomplish any or all of these objectives.

Coming as it was on the tail-end of the Vietnam era, the early days of anti-abortion protest mimicked many of the protest techniques common to the period. Young Catholic, anti–Vietnam War protestor John O'Keefe didn't fit well with the developing movement. O'Keefe had been an active participant in many nonviolent Vietnam War protests and lamented the absence of commitment in the pro-life movement. O'Keefe believed that the pro-life movement would do well to employ the same civil disobedience tactics that had impacted the fight for civil rights in the 1960s, but the largely suburban Catholic body of the pro-life movement were horrified at the thought of participating in illegal protest.

It was through O'Keefe's understanding of nonviolent protest politics that the antiabortion sit in strategy developed. O'Keefe joined with a few like-minded individuals, who persuaded Quaker peace activist Charles Fager to lead seminars on civil disobedience and its potential for the pro-life movement. Fager said that the civil rights movement was successful because the nonviolent movement stood in sharp contrast to the actions of the general public and the American state. He argued that "when blacks marched peacefully . . . only to be clubbed and beaten by Alabama state troopers on national television, their suffering served as a wake-up call to America."[49] Fager further "said that anti-abortion protesters could engage in similar acts of civil disobedience by entering clinics before abortions were underway and peacefully intervening, demanding that the 'violence would be visited on me, not the unborn.'"[50]

O'Keefe believed that there was a logical connection between the anti-war and nonnuclear proliferation movements of which he had been a part in the 1960s, and the pro-life movement he was trying to build in the 1970s. O'Keefe saw logical parallels between the efforts to protect life through the renunciation of war, the condemnation of nuclear weapons, and the rejection of abortion. However, supporters of the three distinct movements were not so quick to see the parallels O'Keefe observed. In fact, Vietnam and nonproliferation protests had merged with feminist organizations into a broad and diverse "liberal" social movement that was inevitably at odds with the antiabortion movement. Whereas O'Keefe and most antiabortion movement supporters focused on the threat to life that abortion presented, most liberal social movements' supporters emphasized the role of women in society. In this way, the two movements consistently found conversation almost impossible, because the vernacular of each was entirely foreign to the other.

This consequence of vocabulary is evident even in the works of scholars looking back on events of the 1970s from the social safety of the new millennium. Consider Kristin Luker's explanation of the difference between the two objectives:

> The abortion debate has become a debate among women, women with different values in the social world, different experiences of it, and different resources with which to cope with it. . . . While on the surface it is the embryo's fate that seems to be at stake, the abortion debate is actually about the meaning of women's lives. . . . To attribute personhood to the embryo is to make the social statement that pregnancy is valuable and that women should

subordinate other parts of their lives to that central aspect of their social and biological selves. Conversely, if the embryo is held to be a fetus, then it becomes socially permissible for women to subordinate their reproductive roles to other roles; particularly in the paid work force.[51]

Luker successfully identifies competing value sets—but ironically goes on to situate both of the value sets in the structure of the feminist argument. She sees the issue of life as something that can give value to the issue of this kind of conservative feminism (women alone can fulfill the function of pregnancy). But even Henry Blackmun's argument in defending the Court's decision in *Roe v. Wade* acknowledged that the issue of life was dependent on the issue of privacy only so long as the existence of life at a particular stage could not be conclusively proved. If it is recognized that within the minds of pro-life advocates, this issue of life *has* been conclusively proved, then Luker's argument is frivolous.

This same reasoning applies to the challenges inherent in O'Keefe's efforts to merge liberal movements with the pro-life cause. Neither side could abide by the values they saw the other as denouncing. As a result, the pro-life movement began to flounder. Fortunately for O'Keefe, and others who supported the pro-life cause, a countercultural movement was afoot in Protestant Christian circles. The Catholic Church was the logical spearhead of the early pro-life movement; however, concerns regarding the appropriate separation of church and state made this arrangement less than ideal, and so the National Community for a Human Life Amendment was formed. But over time, it became evident that the antiabortion sentiment was not universal among Catholics, nor limited to their ranks. In fact, the abortion controversy was sufficient to prod Protestant Fundamentalists out of their antipolitical slumber.

This development would eventually propel the pro-life movement to firm footing on a central and national stage. In fact, the Fundamentalist Christians that had been so involved in politics at the turn of the 20th century had successfully retreated from society for the 50-plus years between the Scopes Monkey Trial and the decision of *Roe v. Wade*. But they came back in force in the late 1970s, thanks in large part to the al theo-philosophy of Presbyterian evangelist Francis Schaeffer. Schaeffer rejected the Fundamentalist argument that political participation was worthless owing to the impending rapture, and instead argued that the political isolation of Christians had allowed a ruthless enemy to prowl unchallenged across American social terrain. Secular humanism, which Schaeffer defined as acts or truths conducted or derived separate from God, had taken hold of American society—and the legalization of abortion was the fruit of its reign.

Schaeffer adamantly opposed the predominant Christian doctrine of the time, which suggested that Christians and secular humanists could live in harmony. Instead, Schaeffer insisted that moral depravity is not simply an alternative to morality—but rather is its most ardent enemy. He believed that efforts of Christians to live peacefully next to secular humanists, without challenging the destruction of morality they preached, was to join in a fight against God. Schaeffer saw abortion as the embodiment of his argument, noting that in a single century, Americans had gone from considering life to be the penultimate expression of value, to being something that could be cast for destruction on the altar of convenience.[52] Schaeffer saw this as a clear indication that "the consensus of our society no longer rests on a Judeo Christian base, but rather on a humanistic one."[53]

Schaeffer's call to action was heard throughout hundreds of slumbering churches, and Fundamentalists across the country began to organize a memorable political fight. Randall Terry, the founder of Operation Rescue, clearly alludes to Schaeffer's call in Terry's own antiabortion manifesto, "99 Ways to Stop Abortion." In this work, Terry admonishes his readers to awake from complacency and to rise up in a way that will make future generations of Christians proud: "What will the Lord Jesus say when he looks at our lives? How will your children and grandchildren view your response to this current holocaust? Will they see your example of courage, sacrifice and love for your neighbor? Will you be remembered as the one who helped end abortion and turn America back to God? Or will you just be another face in a sea of self-centered Christians who stood by while millions of children were killed and our nation collapsed into hell?"[54]

In this way, Schaeffer, Terry, and other leaders of the movement linked the critical element of life with the protection of their Christianity. In Christianity, the death of Jesus Christ is paramount because it was it was completed in defense of the life of God's children. Thus abortion—and the murder of defenseless children—can be seen as the ultimate antithesis of God's gracious plan for humanity. It is for this reason that the Christian pro-life movement places such an emphasis on life in the attack against abortion. Destruction of life is tantamount to the attempted destruction of God—and this raises the stakes far higher than most other political issues.

THE EMERGENCE OF OPERATION RESCUE

Terry did not just use his pen to spur Christians to action, though neither did he use the pen's greatest rival either. Terry was a master of equivocation and found the middle ground between the pen and the sword to be a very loud bullhorn. Using his communication tool of choice, Terry applied his considerable organizational and inspiration skills to developing a sustained abortion opposition organization. Operation Rescue was modeled after the nonviolent civil disobedience tactics of Mahatma Gandhi and Martin Luther King Jr. Protestors were instructed to crawl toward abortion clinic entrances and to go limp when approached by police, so as to intensify the contrast between violence and nonviolence in the newsreels destined to catch the approach. The first large-scale operation launched by Terry took place in Atlanta, Georgia, in the summer of 1988. Twelve hundred demonstrators blocked entrances to abortion clinics all over the city during the Democratic presidential convention. But far more impressive than the 1,200 volunteers Terry's tactics generated was the $60,000 in revenue that began pouring into Operation Rescue's coffers after the protest was nationally televised.

In 1989, Operation Rescue boasted membership rosters of more than 35,000 members all over the United States,[55] and several more large-scale demonstrations had taken place, with hundreds of arrests of protestors taking place. However, the impressive membership numbers and consequential monthly donations were not sufficient to cover the legal bills leading members of the organization accrued because of their frequent arrests. Terry himself was fined repeatedly for his actions, with expenses ranging from $500 to $50,000.[56] In 1990, Terry announced that Operation Rescue had run out of money and would be closing its doors permanently. The physical protest strategy that Terry had spearheaded, however, was not dependent on the existence of Operation Rescue, and accordingly it continued to be present in the movement.

As powerful as Terry's bullhorn was, Operation Rescue may not have seen the level of success it did, were other critical events not occurring in other sections of the conservative political arena. In 1978 the scope of the debate changed dramatically with the entrance of the Moral Majority on the right of American politics. The Moral Majority held a unique status in American politics, because it only loosely unified a plethora of political interests. The organization focused on sharpening the influence of existing religious and conservative organizations by teaching supporters how to fight meaningfully on a political level.

Francis Schaeffer approached Jerry Falwell, an Evangelical Baptist pastor, and urged him to unify the disparate denominations of politically aware Christians under a single umbrella of political action. Falwell joined forces with Terry Dolan, Richard Vinguerie, Paul Weyrich, and Howard Phillips to organize the "moral majority" that was underutilized in the American political process. McKeegan said, "The purpose of the Majority was to undermine the boundaries that separated secular Republicans, Fundamentalists, ordinary Protestants and Catholics by tying them all together under the banner of a commitment to 'pro-family' values."[57]

The emerging organization did not have to choose between moral altruism and political expediency when determining the cause that would spearhead the movement. Rather, the founders of the Moral Majority quickly recognized that by making abortion an issue irrevocably tied to the Republican Party, they could create a significant gap between the traditionally Democrat-voting Catholics and the issue most dear to their hearts. In fact, McKeegan argues that the promotion of antiabortion politics by the Moral Majority was not born of moral interests at all—but rather that the interests were entirely political. McKeegan demonstrates that the end of Nixon's presidency left a traditional Republican base of only 30 percent of the electorate. The Christian right did not fit well with either party, and it promised a 20 percent voting bloc that was yet entirely untapped. If Republicans adopted the antiabortion fight, they stood to lose 4 percent of their traditional base (hovering at 30%) but stood to gain at least eight percent from the social conservatives. The 4 percent net gain was alluring to Weyrich and his cohort, and a marriage between the Republicans and the Moral Majority presented an opportunity to secure it.[58]

Whether born of political expediency or commitment to life, the marriage between social conservatives and Republicans proved to be an effective one in the 1980 presidential elections. The religious influence of the Moral Majority was presented in the belief that all issues could be filtered down to a right and a wrong position. The key was to frame the issue in such a way that a larger portion of the voting bloc wanted to be on the side that was defined as "right."

The Moral Majority had actively promoted the election of Ronald Reagan and were successful in seeing him elected. However, the predominant issue in the mind of the social conservatives was not as evidently successful. Whereas the abortion opponents had anticipated dramatic rollbacks in abortion rights thanks to the Reagan presidency, the facts on the ground were quite different. While Reagan considered himself to be among the ranks of the pro-life, his strategy of implementation was politically incremental. Reagan's choice of Supreme Court justices did little to allay concerns of the pro-lifers and many in the movement began calling for more sweeping changes.

THE ENTRANCE OF THE ARMY OF GOD

When such changes were not pursued at the political level, a new element of the antiabortion movement emerged. In 1982, Dr. Hector Zevallos and his wife Rosalee Jean were kidnapped by two men claiming to be from an organization called the Army of God. And the fight against abortion turned violent.

Though several of the individuals who would later make up the Army of God found their start in Operation Rescue, or other branches within the pro-life movement, the Army of God was a movement unto itself from the beginning. Some members of Operation Rescue struggled to evaluate the appropriate response to the first clinic bombings as they occurred,[59] but most appear to have come down conclusively one way or another on the issue and have distinguished themselves both publicly and privately. In the early days of the use of force, some future members of the Army of

God worked closely with nonviolent rescue efforts, but as these individuals began to chafe at the restrictions placed on what they saw as a life and death struggle, cleavages formed between the two movements.[60]

In many ways, these distinctions were possible because of the ambiguous organization of the emerging Army of God. Because the group has rarely been organized along anything other than ideological lines, the distinctions between members are at once clearer and harder to define. They are clearer to the individuals themselves, as belief is the primary marker of membership in the organization. If one does not support the use of deadly force to stop abortion, then there is no membership.

On the other hand, this ambiguity makes legal distinctions much harder. In order to prosecute "membership" in an organization structured by belief, one has to first be able to prove belief, then determine how to prosecute it—something that is an anathema to rights thought to be unalienable. Consequently, law enforcement usually looks to evidence of belief rather than belief itself—but in so doing is forced to seek out organizational ties that do not necessarily exist.

This chapter has attempted to show the historical context of the Army of God and the polarized debate concerning abortion in the United States. It has argued that the Army of God is at once a part of and distinct from the antiabortion groups that have emerged since the passing of *Roe v. Wade* in 1973. The following chapter will cover the consequence of this emergence through the acts attributed to and claimed by the Army of God.

NOTES

1. Blanchard, Dallas A. 1994. *The Anti-Abortion Movement and the Rise of the Religious Right*. New York: Twayne Publishers.

2. Olasky, Marvin. 1992. *Abortion Rites: A Social History of Abortion in America*. Washington, DC: Regnery Publishing.

3. Blanchard, Dallas A. 1994. *The Anti-Abortion Movement and the Rise of the Religious Right*. New York: Twayne Publishers; Mohr, James. 1978. *Abortion in America: The Origins and Evolution of National Policy*. Oxford: Oxford University Press; Reagan, Leslie. 1997. *When Abortion Was a Crime: Women, Medicine and the Law in the United States, 1867–1963*. Berkeley: University of California Press.

4. Noonan, John T., ed. 1970. *The Morality of Abortion: Legal and Historical Perspectives*. Cambridge, MA: Harvard University Press, ix.

5. Noonan, John T., ed. 1970. *The Morality of Abortion: Legal and Historical Perspectives*. Cambridge, MA: Harvard University Press, ix.

6. "And if men struggle with each other and strike a woman with child so that she has a miscarriage, yet there is no [further] injury, he shall surely be fined as the woman's husband may demand of him; and he shall pay as the judges decide. But if there is any [further] injury, then you shall appoint as a penalty life for life, eye for eye, tooth for tooth, hand for hand, foot for foot, burn for burn, wound for wound, bruise for bruise." American Standard Version.

7. Blanchard, Dallas A. 1994. *The Anti-Abortion Movement and the Rise of the Religious Right*. New York: Twayne Publishers.

8. Noonan, John T., ed. 1970. *The Morality of Abortion: Legal and Historical Perspectives*. Cambridge, MA: Harvard University Press.

9. Noonan, John T., ed. 1970. *The Morality of Abortion: Legal and Historical Perspectives*. Cambridge, MA: Harvard University Press, 8.

10. Noonan, John T., ed. 1970. *The Morality of Abortion: Legal and Historical Perspectives*. Cambridge, MA: Harvard University Press, 9.

11. Noonan, John T., ed. 1970. *The Morality of Abortion: Legal and Historical Perspectives*. Cambridge, MA: Harvard University Press, 4.

12. Noonan, John T., ed. 1970. *The Morality of Abortion: Legal and Historical Perspectives*. Cambridge, MA: Harvard University Press.

13. Noonan, John T., ed. 1970. *The Morality of Abortion: Legal and Historical Perspectives*. Cambridge, MA: Harvard University Press, 18.

14. Noonan, John T., ed. 1970. *The Morality of Abortion: Legal and Historical Perspectives*. Cambridge, MA: Harvard University Press, 21.

15. Noonan, John T., ed. 1970. *The Morality of Abortion: Legal and Historical Perspectives*. Cambridge, MA: Harvard University Press, 33.

16. Noonan, John T., ed. 1970. *The Morality of Abortion: Legal and Historical Perspectives*. Cambridge, MA: Harvard University Press.

17. Noonan, John T., ed. 1970. *The Morality of Abortion: Legal and Historical Perspectives*. Cambridge, MA: Harvard University Press, 38.

18. Mohr, James. 1978. *Abortion in America: The Origins and Evolution of National Policy*. Oxford: Oxford University Press, vii.

19. Mohr, James. 1978. *Abortion in America: The Origins and Evolution of National Policy*. Oxford: Oxford University Press, 3–4.

20. Mohr, James. 1978. *Abortion in America: The Origins and Evolution of National Policy*. Oxford: Oxford University Press, 6.

21. Reagan, Leslie. 1997. *When Abortion Was a Crime: Women, Medicine and the Law in the United States, 1867–1963*. Berkeley: University of California Press, 24.

22. Reagan, Leslie. 1997. *When Abortion Was a Crime: Women, Medicine and the Law in the United States, 1867–1963*. Berkeley: University of California Press, 9.

23. Freedman, Lawrence. 2008. *A Choice of Enemies: America Confronts the Middle East*. New York: Public Affairs.

24. Reagan, Leslie. 1997. *When Abortion Was a Crime: Women, Medicine and the Law in the United States, 1867–1963*. Berkeley: University of California Press.

25. Mohr, James. 1978. *Abortion in America: The Origins and Evolution of National Policy*. Oxford: Oxford University Press, 17.

26. Reagan, Leslie. 1997. *When Abortion Was a Crime: Women, Medicine and the Law in the United States, 1867–1963*. Berkeley: University of California Press, 20.

27. Olasky, Marvin. 1992. *Abortion Rites: A Social History of Abortion in America*. Washington, DC: Regnery Publishing, xiii.

28. Olasky, Marvin. 1992. *Abortion Rites: A Social History of Abortion in America*. Washington, DC: Regnery Publishing, vxi.

29. Olasky, Marvin. 1992. *Abortion Rites: A Social History of Abortion in America*. Washington, DC: Regnery Publishing, 37.

30. Mohr, James. 1978. *Abortion in America: The Origins and Evolution of National Policy*. Oxford: Oxford University Press, 16.

31. See Risen, James and Judy Thomas. 1998. *Wrath of Angels: The American Abortion War*. New York: Basic Books.

32. Leslie Reagan's work is a notable exception—though even her book does not go deeply into the period before 1867 in the United States. See Reagan, Leslie. 1997. *When Abortion Was a Crime: Women, Medicine and the Law in the United States, 1867–1963.* Berkeley: University of California Press.

33. Reagan, Leslie. 1997. *When Abortion Was a Crime: Women, Medicine and the Law in the United States, 1867–1963.* Berkeley: University of California Press, 130.

34. "Birth Control 'Club' Exposed." 1936. *New York Times,* October 13, 3. Cited in Reagan, Leslie. 1997. *When Abortion Was a Crime: Women, Medicine and the Law in the United States, 1867–1963.* Berkeley: University of California Press, 134.

35. Reagan, Leslie. 1997. *When Abortion Was a Crime: Women, Medicine and the Law in the United States, 1867–1963.* Berkeley: University of California Press.

36. Ginsburg, Faye 1989. *Contested Lives: The Abortion Debate in an American Community.* Berkeley: University of California Press.

37. Ginsburg, Faye 1989. *Contested Lives: The Abortion Debate in an American Community.* Berkeley: University of California Press; Luker. 1984. *Abortion and the Politics of Motherhood.* Berkeley: University of California Press.

38. Luker. 1984. *Abortion and the Politics of Motherhood.* Berkeley: University of California Press.

39. Ginsburg, Faye. 1989. *Contested Lives: The Abortion Debate in an American Community.* Berkeley: University of California Press.

40. Jefferis, Jennifer. 2010. *Religion and Political Violence: Sacred Protest in the Modern World.* New York: Routledge.

41. Jefferis, Jennifer. 2010. *Religion and Political Violence: Sacred Protest in the Modern World.* New York: Routledge.

42. Risen, James and Judy Thomas. 1998. *Wrath of Angels: The American Abortion War.* New York: Basic Books, 38.

43. Luker. 1984. *Abortion and the Politics of Motherhood.* Berkeley: University of California Press.

44. Author interview with Pat Robertson, 2006, Virginia Beach, VA.

45. Craig, Barbara Hinkson and David M. O'Brien. 1993. *Abortion and American Politics.* Chatham, NJ Chatham House Publishers, 45.

46. Craig, Barbara Hinkson and David M. O'Brien. 1993. *Abortion and American Politics.* Chatham, NJ: Chatham House Publishers, 46.

47. Craig, Barbara Hinkson and David M. O'Brien. 1993. *Abortion and American Politics.* Chatham, NJ: Chatham House Publishers, 48.

48. Craig, Barbara Hinkson and David M. O'Brien. 1993. *Abortion and American Politics.* Chatham, NJ: Chatham House Publishers.

49. Risen, James and Judy Thomas. 1998. *Wrath of Angels: The American Abortion War.* New York: Basic Books, 64.

50. Risen, James and Judy Thomas. 1998. *Wrath of Angels: The American Abortion War.* New York: Basic Books, 60.

51. Luker. 1984. *Abortion and the Politics of Motherhood.* Berkeley: University of California Press, 46.

52. Schaeffer, Francis and Everett Koop. 1978. *Whatever Happened to the Human Race?* Old Tappan, NJ: Fleming H. Revell Company.

53. Schaeffer, Francis, and Everett Koop. 1978. *Whatever Happened to the Human Race?* Old Tappan, NJ: Fleming H. Revell Company.

54. Scheidler, Joseph. 1982. *Closed: 99 Ways to Stop Abortion.* Charlotte, NC: Tan Books and Publisher.

55. Craig, Barbara Hinkson and David M. O'Brien. 1993. *Abortion and American Politics*. Chatham, NJ: Chatham House Publishers.

56. Craig, Barbara Hinkson and David M. O'Brien. 1993. *Abortion and American Politics*. Chatham, NJ: Chatham House Publishers.

57. Jefferis, Jennifer. 2010. *Religion and Political Violence: Sacred Protest in the Modern World*. New York: Routledge, 36.

58. McKeegan, Michele. 1992. *Abortion Politics: Mutiny in the Ranks of the Right*. New York: The Free Press.

59. See letter from John O'Keefe to Joseph Scheidler in Risen, James and Judy Thomas. 1998. *Wrath of Angels: The American Abortion War*. New York: Basic Books, 75.

60. The Army of God lists comments made by pro-life groups condemning their use of force on the Army of God website. The Army identifies Christians who make condemnatory comments as traitors.

2

⟡

Choose Your Weapon

Because the Army of God is a loose network at best, its existence is in many ways defined by the acts members of the organization have undertaken on its behalf. Indeed, if declaration of sympathy is counted as an action, membership in the organization is entirely based on the actions of these loosely connected individuals. Donald Spitz, manager of the Army of God website, says he knows "most" of the people he posts about, but acknowledges that he's "pretty liberal" about what goes up on the site: "If a friend feels strongly about honoring someone on the Army's site, I'll put them on, even if I don't know much about them."[1] While Spitz says he knows and is in regular contact with just about everyone listed on the site, he is willing to take the word of his friends to vouch that some of his honorees are actually "deserving" of that honor.

All this is to say that intent made evident by action matters to the Army of God. For this reason, understanding the tactics of the organization is crucial to understanding the organization itself. This chapter will provide a history of the acts undertaken and endorsed by the Army of God. It will draw on the primary methods and means used by the organization to project their position in an effort to illuminate the evolution of the organization and highlight its significance in American politics today.

EVOLUTION OF FORCE

The Army of God is notorious for a manual—of which no one in the group claims authorship—that surfaced after Shelley Shannon was arrested for shooting George Tiller. Parts of the third edition of the manual are available online, and the preface can be viewed in the appendix to this volume. The book serves as a 100-page "inspirational" tutorial that offers ideas of how to destroy abortion clinics. Interestingly, much like the chronological trajectory of the group itself, the manual begins with nonlethal methods for shutting down clinics (using syringes to inject foul-smelling substances in the walls, pouring concrete over machinery, etc.). The next section is preceded by a cautionary word:

> The Appendix that follows is intended for the serious and committed covert activist. If you decide to read and use the information in the following appendix, be careful, be thorough, and remember, as far as men are concerned, you are on your own. But what we do, we do for the babies, and God knows and God helps. God bless.

The section that follows this admonition depicts for the reader how to destroy cars and commit more serious acts of vandalism. The final section of the manual identifies itself as being only for those with "Terminal Courage." Here readers are told

> Not everyone will be blessed with this opportunity. With family ties, it would be most difficult. . . . You may not be afraid to die. You are afraid of a lifetime living in bonds. Understandable. Yet, you have faith. You look forward to meeting our Lord face to face. The time has come. . . . It would only take a few activists practicing terminal courage to drive the entire killing industry underground. Maybe the Spirit of God has been hounding you to take certain actions on behalf of his children and you have not obeyed. Here is your last chance.

The history of the Army of God has followed a similar path. Initially, members embarked on acts, though dangerous, that proved not to be lethal. Over time, members began comfortably using terms such as "collateral damage" and became less careful about who could be harmed. Eventually, members began deliberately killing doctors.

ANTIABORTION VIOLENCE IN THE 1970s

Fires, bombings, petty vandalism, and felonious destruction of property have plagued abortion clinics since the late 1970s. While numbers differ depending on the source (Army of God affiliates cite more cases but argue that the police deliberately keep them out of the news so as not to encourage other members), nearly 2,000 cases of antiabortion violence have been tracked in the last 30 years. One of the first known antiabortion acts occurred in 1976, when Joseph Stockett set fire to a Planned Parenthood office in Eugene, Oregon. Stockett believed that his girlfriend's IUD had caused her to have an abortion.[2] Stockett had not affiliated himself in any way with the Army of God or any other antiabortion group.

Two years later, in 1978, the Concerned Women's Clinic in Cleveland, Ohio, was bombed while patients were inside, though no one was hurt as a result. Then in 1979, a clinic in Hempstead, New York, was bombed, while 50 patients were inside. According to one report, 21-year-old Peter Burkin entered the clinic carrying a torch and a gallon of gasoline. He yelled, "Nobody move; this place is going up. In the name of God I'm going to cleanse Bill Baird's soul by fire!" before throwing the gas and the torch in a room where a doctor was performing an abortion.[3] Though Burkin allegedly alluded to his religious intentions as he threw the torch, the Army of God had not yet been recognized on the national scene, and Burkin has no known connection to it.

ANTIABORTION VIOLENCE IN THE 1980s

The antiabortion scene changed in 1982, when the first reference to the Army was discovered. Believed to be the first members and perpetrators to claim Army of God allegiance, Don Benny Anderson, along with his nephews, Matthew and Wayne Moore, kidnapped Dr. Hector Zevallos and his wife, Jean, at gunpoint and, during their eight days of captivity, pressured them to close their abortion clinic and write letters to then president Ronald Reagan, urging him to take a stronger stance against abortion. Anderson and the Moores also issued directives intended for President Reagan, in which they called for him to issue a firm statement against abortion. If he refused, they threatened to kill their captives.[4]

During their captivity, the Zevallos were kept in an abandoned bunker in Illinois. Anderson claimed he received orders directly from God and the archangel Michael about the fight against abortion. The Zevallos said that Anderson and the Moores called themselves the Army of God, claiming that God had instructed them to "fight abortion to the death."[5]

According to a letter received by the Secret Service from the Moore brothers two weeks after the Zevallos were released, the trio had been planning to kill their captives: "We all agreed that the will of God would be carried out if they were executed, and we were planning for the procedure."[6] Fortunately for the Zevallos, God allegedly corrected this belief at the last minute, and the Zevallos were released instead.

Don Benny Anderson is recognized as a hero on the Army of God website, and while kidnapping was never adopted as a favored tactic of members of the organization, the ubiquity of justification before, during, and after the event certainly has been. While holding the Zevallos captive, Anderson and the Moores wrote a 44-page letter detailing their motivation for kidnapping the Zevallos, taped it to a gas station restroom wall, and then called the FBI to alert them to its existence. The letter spoke, in some places, from God's perspective and stated that those who truly loved God would "kill the baby killers."[7]

Anderson was charged with "attempting and conspiring to obstruct interstate commerce through threats or violence"[8] and used his trial to call attention to his opposition to abortion. Anderson's lawyer, Wayne Schoeneberg, emphasized the men's commitment to the abortion issue in his opening statement: "These three men had a very, very strong belief that abortion was wrong and abortion in this country should end. Their purpose in going in there was to kidnap Dr. Zevallos and his wife and hold them to gain public sentiment to end abortion,"[9]

Dr. Zevallos told the court that Anderson believed he was receiving revelations from God about embarking on an antiabortion crusade. Anderson also allegedly told Zevallos that he and the Moore brothers had bombed several abortion clinics, a claim that was supported by their subsequent conviction for setting fire to two Florida clinics, one in Clearwater and the other in St. Petersburg A Florida television station received a letter the night the fires were set in which the Army of God was credited with the bombing—and a band of angels was ascribed to have protected the perpetrators. Anderson was also convicted for throwing a pipe bomb at a Virginia clinic. The Moore brothers later admitted to robbing multiple clinics to finance their activities. They collected $4,300.[10]

While their financial success is disputable, that Anderson and the Moore brothers unleashed a new and violent commitment to ending abortion is certainly not. Anderson's commitment to justifying his acts according to his belief in God impacted the antiabortion movement from periphery to core. Perhaps the most chilling example is found in John O'Keefe—the veritable father of the antiabortion movement. It was O'Keefe who had promoted nonviolent protest so convincingly—arguing that the use of violence would destroy the contrast the movement needed to cultivate between the violence of the law and the innocence of aborted children. And yet, O'Keefe questioned his own instructions when faced with the alternative presented by Anderson.

Journalists James Risen and Judy Thomas published a letter written by O'Keefe to Joseph Scheidler after the kidnapping. In it O'Keefe revealed his uncertainty about the use of force:

> I have been in touch with Don Anderson (though not as much as I should have been). I have two arguments with what I heard about the Army of God. The first argument is one I have with almost everybody in the pro-life movement. I think that non-violence is an urgent necessity. But to be sure, I'm not going to hold it against anybody that they disagree with me about that. So while it was a criticism I had of Anderson's work, it was not the most important one. The

second problem I had was that the Army of God let Zevallos go. I consider that inexcusable, and in my thinking it destroyed the credibility of their effort altogether. In the just war theory—which I reject, but respect—it is of course legitimate to take somebody by force and hold them by force if that will protect lives. . . . Life is a higher value than freedom.[11]

Though O'Keefe did not make his evolving thoughts public, he began to avoid condemning the use of force in the media. At this time, one could clearly identify the fulcrum of the antiabortion movement as it marked the decrease in perceived effectiveness of those unwilling to use violence and the impatience of those who would.

The remainder of the 1980s was categorized by dozens of abortion-clinic bombings. On May 26, 1983, Joseph Grace burned a women's clinic in Norfolk, Virginia, though police believe his act had more to do with his mental instability than his religious ideology. He claimed to have set fire to the clinic while leaving the area to avoid an impending nuclear holocaust.[12]

The National Abortion Federation identifies 30 incidents of arson or bombing in 1984, exceeding the previous seven years combined. The series of bombings included, but was not limited to, the offices of the National Abortion Federation (NAF) and the American Civil Liberties Union in Washington, D.C., as well as abortion clinics in Virginia, Maryland, and Delaware. A signature of the Army of God (AOG) was also found at a subsequent clinic bombing in Sarasota, Florida.

Three clinics were set on fire in Delaware, Washington, D.C., and Virginia, acts for which Michael Bray, Thomas Spinks, and Kenneth Shields were later convicted. The trio were accused of using homemade firebombs for their series of attacks and allegedly left notes from the Army of God in the clinic ruins. In June, a Pensacola Ladies' Center was bombed, causing $40,000 in damage, and in December of the same year, three other Pensacola clinics were bombed.

Abortion activist John Burt is linked to the bombings on the Army of God website; however, Matt Goldsby, Kaye Wiggins, and Jimmy and Kathy Simmons were found guilty of the act. Goldsby and Jimmy Simmons confessed to the crime, telling federal agents that the three clinics bombed on Christmas were a gift for baby Jesus.[13] Whether actually involved in the bombings or not, Burt was a well-known figure outside the courthouse during the trial, where he walked around with an aborted fetus in a jar, trying to impress upon witnesses the horror of abortion. Burt is lauded as a "Prisoner of Christ" on the Army of God website, and a timeline from the same source puts him in frequent contact with other members of the organization.

In addition to the numerous acts of arson, bombing, and vandalism in 1984, threats were made against the Supreme Court as well. Supreme Court Justice and author of the *Roe v. Wade* decision, Harry Blackmun, received a death threat signed by the Army of God, and on January 14, Thomas Spinks is credited with placing a "Declaration of War" outside of the U.S. Supreme Court building. The Army of God blog proudly touts that this declaration was made legitimate shortly thereafter when Spinks embarked on a multistate bombing spree. Eventually, he began strapping 20-pound liquid propane tanks to his homemade gunpowder bombs and using these to destroy abortion clinics.

The year 1984 was important in the fight against abortion for several reasons. Not only did it represent the most violent year (as measured by numbers of bombings or acts of arson) in the 20th century, it was also transformational in the way the government looked at antiabortion violence. Ronald Reagan was regarded as a pro-life president, and whether out of political expediency or personal belief, Reagan was slow to condemn the attacks in the first years of his presidency. A *Time* magazine article published in 1985 quoted Reagan's FBI director William Webster as saying that "the violence was not the result of a conspiracy and thus did not constitute a form of political terrorism that his agency could investigate."[14] However, after the succession of 3 bombings in Pensacola on Christmas, running the total for a four-month period to 15, Reagan spoke out forcefully against the violence.

The number of clinic bombings and destruction by fire decreased slightly in 1985, from the previous year's 30 down to 22. However, when vandalism (which includes things as relatively innocuous as spray paint, as well as the more creative acts suggested in the Army of God manual, such as pouring concrete over heat pumps, or using syringes to inject foul-smelling butyric acid into the walls of clinics) is taken in to account, the number of incidents rises from 131 in 1984 to 149 in 1985.[15]

In January 1985, Thomas Spinks and Kenneth Shields were implicated in the bombing of an abortion clinic in Washington, D.C. In February, John Burt, along with two other antiabortion activists, entered an abortion clinic to talk to patients awaiting abortions. All three were arrested and received probation.[16] In March, Burt attempted to show an aborted fetus on live television to create public awareness of the "reality and horror of abortion."[17] In May, Burt, along with other activists, protested outside of the courthouse where Goldsby and Simmons were to receive their sentencing.

Toward the end of the year, Dennis Malvasi allegedly bombed two New York women's clinics—the Eastern Women's Clinic in Queens and the Planned Parenthood Margaret Sanger Center in Manhattan. No one was killed in the first attack at the Eastern Women's Clinic, though two people standing near the clinic when the blast occurred were hurt by flying glass. At the Planned Parenthood Center, Malvasi attempted to use a homemade bomb consisting of "15 sticks of dynamite and a blasting-cap detonator,"[18] a method described in the Army of God manual. Although the bomb did not explode, the attempt caused $30,000 in damage.

Malvasi later informed agents of the Bureau of Alcohol, Tobacco, Firearms, and Explosives (BATF) of the location and stock of his weapon supply, which included "seventy-eight dynamite sticks, black powder, electric detonating plastic caps, and another undefined explosive in a mini-storage locker."[19] Malvasi is listed as a Prisoner of Christ on the Army of God website and was celebrated as a hero at the White Rose Banquet in both 2001 and 2002. In 2002, he sent a letter to the leaders of the banquet, which was read aloud. In it he expressed his continued passion for ending abortion in the United States:

> Since September 11, all I've been hearing is "God Bless America" . . . "God Bless America." Mr. President, if you want to get rid of terrorism in the world—please, I beseech you, start right here. Rid our country of the terrorist who slaughter over 4,500 innocent babies every day. Abortionists who, just like the terrorists at the World Trade Center, butchered and shredded thousands of innocent people into tiny pieces in a matter of minutes. And, Mr. President, let's not forget to go after those who support, aid and harbor these terrorists, they should be easy to find, as they often wear blue wind breakers with big bright yellow letters saying; FBI, US MARSHAL, and JUSTICE DEPT. Mr. President, please, I beseech you, if there was ever a Just War that cries out to heaven to be fought, it is the war against the unjust killing of thousands of babies every day in this country. Mr. President, if you want to "rid the world of evil," please, I implore you, start here with these ungodly evil laws of our nation that enable and support the baby killing industries in our country. Until we get rid of the state sponsored terrorists in this country, GOD WILL NOT BLESS THIS COUNTRY. GOD WILL FLUSH THIS COUNTRY.[20]

Though the total number of incidences decreased from 1985 to 1986, the Army of God was still busy. In March, John Burt was accused of entering the Pensacola Ladies' Center with his daughter and four other activists and causing damage. He was charged with burglary, battery, and resisting arrest, but was later released on probation. In April of the same year, Burt was arrested for illegal protesting.[21]

James Kopp, who would soon escalate beyond vandalism, was arrested for several blockades on abortion clinics, including one at the Ladies' Center in Pensacola, Florida. The same clinic would later be the site of the first assassination of an abortion provider. Kopp was arrested for these blockades because of their illegal methods. For example, in the "lock and block technique" (a method Kopp receives credit for inventing) activists chained themselves to each other, blocking the entrances of abortion clinics. Kopp was also arrested for illegally protesting the sentencing of Joan Andrews Bell, who was his longtime friend and employee. Bell was charged with invasion and burglary of several abortion clinics throughout the mid-1980s. She would later become a signer of the Army's "justifiable homicide" document, released after the killing of John Britton.

At the time of the 1988 Democratic National Convention, Shelley Shannon, James Kopp, John Arena, Randall Terry, Norman Weslin, and Regina Dinwiddie were arrested in Atlanta, Georgia, for an Operation Rescue "siege."[22] The National Abortion Federation suggests it was during this time in jail that the small group officially formed the AOG, creating aliases and writing another edition of the AOG manual.[23] It should be noted, however, that several of these individuals (Randall Terry among them) have consistently condemned the use of force to stop abortion and have publicly denounced the violent methods of the Army of God. There are no records to suggest what conversations may or may not have taken place in that jail.

There were no recorded bombings in 1987 or 1988 (though there were eight thwarted attempts in 1987 and three attempts thwarted in 1988), and successful clinic fires decreased to four in both years. Vandalism declined by nearly 25 percent and assaults declined by half.[24] The numbers went up again in 1989, with two successful bombings, six incidents of arson, and 12 cases of assault.

ANTIABORTION VIOLENCE IN THE 1990s

The 1990s were ushered in with similar tactics—coordinated by regular contributors to Army of God literature resources. Dan Holman began his antiabortion campaign, which included picketing clinics, neighborhoods, and abortion supporters with graphic signs of aborted fetuses.[25] Holman would also contribute at least 20 articles to the Army of God website throughout his campaign.[26] Donald Spitz was sentenced for blockading an abortion clinic in Norfolk, Virginia. Michael Bray began and would continue editing and publishing a 12-page newsletter called *Capital Area Christian News* until 2000. The newsletters would later inform the "radical fringe" on the status and successes of Army of God members, such as Hill, Shannon, Brockhoeft, and other antiabortion activists. It kept track of government actions over abortion laws and natural deaths or retirements of abortion providers.[27]

Paul DeParrie became editor-in-chief of *Life Advocate*, a magazine that reported news concerning abortion. This included national perspectives on both the anti- and pro-choice campaigns, judicial decisions on abortion cases, including lawsuits on activists, and the like. The magazine had a commentary, feature section, and contact columns that gave voice to "prestigious" activists, of whom many were closely affiliated with the antiabortion movement. Each of these sources made extensive use of graphic signs showing aborted fetuses. A discussion forum was available on the website while the magazine was still active. It has since been deactivated.

In June 1991, John Burt purchased land next to the Pensacola Ladies' Center, in an effort to give protestors a close and legal place from which to protest, and in August, Burt and two others were arrested after attempting to cut down a fence that separated the Ladies' Center and his new land. He claimed the fence was on his property. Paul DeParrie was arrested and fined for an operation against a clinic in Lovejoy, Oregon, which included over $350,000 in damages.[28] Regina Dinwiddie was arrested at a Kansas City abortion clinic, where she was accused of yelling threats at both clinic patients and staff, including a threat to the director stating, "Patty, you have not seen violence yet until you see what we do to you!"[29]

In the same year, Shelley Shannon ended her nonviolent protest against abortion clinics and began a violent campaign through four states. This included seven recorded arsons and three attacks using butyric acid, or AVON. The first acid attack was in Ashland, Oregon, the second in Reno, Nevada. Shannon frequently pretended to be a potential patient in order to gain access to clinics. In Reno, she asked to use the restroom and "made a hole in the wall with an ice pick and emptied four hypos of butyric acid," a method depicted in detail in the Army of God manual.[30] The third acid attack was in Chico, California, where Shannon described the damage as similar to Reno. In her journal entry, she described following the Army of God manual's instructions on using syringes to "deliver the acid into building walls."[31] She describes struggling to rid herself of the smell of the acid by using baking soda mixed with water and then trying Lysol or perfume. None of these worked. Shannon is accused of committing three butyric acid attacks in three different states within three consecutive days.[32]

According to court records, Shannon's first arson attempt was on April 11 at the Catalina Medical Clinic and the offices of Dr. Willard L. Brown in Ashland; the second was on June 6 at the Feminist Women's Health Center in Redding, causing $70,000 in property damage; the third was on August 1 at the Lovejoy Surgicenter in Portland; the fourth and fifth were both on August 18 at the Feminist Women's Health Center in Sacramento (though Shannon accidentally set fire to the chiropractic office next door to the clinic instead) and the West End Women's Health Group in Reno, Nevada; the sixth was on September 16 at the Feminist Women's Health Center in Eugene; and the seventh was on November 28 at the Pregnancy Consultation Center in Sacramento, which caused more than $175, 000 in damage.[33] Shannon used a variety of resources for her spree, ranging from five-gallon gasoline cans and plastic milk containers with "pop-off tops," to napalm, and acetylene gas.[34]

According to the National Abortion Federation Violence and Disruption Statistics (NAFVDS), 1992 is still dated as the year with the highest committed arsons as well as the highest arson and bomb attempts by any antiabortion campaign, including the AOG. It was also the second of four years in which no actual bombings were reported.[35]

However, 1992 was also the year in which an epilogue was added to the AOG manual. Whereas the manual up to this point had emphasized tactics

for destroying clinics and resources, the new epilogue introduced the justification for attacking human beings:

> No longer! All of the options have expired. Our Most Dread Sovereign Lord
> God requires that whosoever sheds man's blood, by man shall his blood be
> shed. Not out of hatred for you, but out of love for the persons you exter-
> minate, we are forced to take arms against you. Our life for yours—a simple
> equation. Dreadful. Sad. Reality, nonetheless. You shall not be tortured at
> our hands. Vengeance belongs to God only. However, execution is rarely
> gentle.[36]

The introduction to the epilogue suggests that acceptance of violence
against abortion providers and their staff had already begun prior to the epilogue's publication, and an interview given by Michael and Jayne Bray to the
Washington Post in 1991 supports this line of reasoning. Hints of the change
in tactics were revealed by the Brays within the interview. The *Washington
Post* reporter recounted the following exchange between the Brays: "'Is there
a legitimate use of force on behalf of the unborn?' Bray asks rhetorically. 'I
say yes, it is justified to destroy the abortion facilities. And yes, it is justified
to . . . what kind of word should I use here?' 'Well, they use terminate a pregnancy,' Jayne Bray says. 'Yeah, terminate an abortionist,' he says."[37]

The author(s) of the Army of God Manual state that around the time of
publication, an abortion provider in Houston, Douglas Karpan, was shot
in a parking garage along with two "accomplices, a clinic receptionist and
building owner, in Springfield, Missouri The manual implicitly claims credit: "All three of the above survived, and no activists were credited for the
shootings. David Gunn was the first 'direct hit' attributed to us."[38]

UNDERSTANDING A SHIFT IN TACTICS

Why did the tactics of the Army change so dramatically at this time? Sociologist Dallas Blanchard argues that there is a cause and effect relationship between the political context and the level of antiabortion violence. He
points to the intensity of clinic bombings in 1984 as coinciding with Reagan's "two year silence on the violence despite well-publicized requests that
he speak out firmly against it."[39] Blanchard argues that the violent movement believed themselves to have the endorsement of President Reagan—
pointing to the decline in bombings after Reagan condemned the tactic in
January 1985.

There are problems with this explanation, not the least of which is that
all of the targeted killings of abortion providers have been undertaken during the presidencies of leaders on the record as favoring a woman's right to
choose abortion. Neither President Clinton nor President Obama could be
argued to have given approval, implicit or otherwise, toward arsonists or

sharpshooters. Further, the supporters of force have been consistently clear in their explanations that the issue of abortion exceeds the law—and are consequently in no way bound by it. In other words, their decision to act essentially circumvents whoever may hold office, because they believe that God Himself condemns the practice unequivocally.

In fact, the activists themselves explain the shift from a different perspective. Though the justification for the escalation of force will be explored in more detail in the following chapter, it is useful to note here that the state and federal responses to the violence of the 1980s more stringently limited opportunities for lawful protest outside abortion clinics and looked with greater scrutiny at the relationships between perpetrators.

As a result, charges of conspiracy were frequently levied against affiliates who were also supportive of the use of force, and the government began looking at abortion clinic attacks as terrorist attacks rather than individual cases of vandalism. Proponents of the use of force contend that these changes altered the stakes of the very real game they were playing. They argue that if the government is going to prevent them from protecting babies peacefully, they have little choice but to do so using force. In an interview with the *Washington Post,* John Burt said, "There's talk of making protesting abortion clinics a felony. If you start talking about that, people are just going to find other ways of dealing with it."[40]

Michael Griffin was the first to "find another way" on March 10, 1993, when he shot and killed Dr. David Gunn. Gunn was walking from his car to his clinic when Griffin shot him in the back three times. Griffin and Gunn had met days earlier by chance at a gas station, and during the encounter Griffin told Gunn that God wanted him to stop performing abortions. Gunn ignored Griffin and drove away. The following Sunday, Griffin asked the congregation at his church to pray that Gunn would repent.

The ramifications of Griffin's act were immediate and significant. Shelley Shannon began mulling over her own effectiveness in the use of force and began plotting to shoot Dr. George Tiller. Paul Hill, a man who—until Griffin's act—had spent much of his time picketing outside women's clinics in Pensacola, Florida, exploded onto the national scene with his argument that Griffin's act was justified. In a matter of days, Hill was a guest on numerous national television shows, from which he publicized his platform in support of Griffin's decision.

Michael Hirsh, then a student of law and public policy at Regent University, was also impacted by Griffin's decision, writing a thesis justifying Griffin's deed under Florida and biblical law. He dedicated the thesis to Michael Bray.

In January 1993, Shelley Shannon wrote to *Life Advocate* magazine concerning recent attacks on abortion clinics, most of which she had just committed. In the article, she philosophized about what could have happened had anyone been in the clinics at the time of the attacks and concluded that any injuries that were sustained were justified as collateral damage. The antiabortion campaign was indeed a war, Shannon reasoned: "I'm sure the bombers are acting in the will of God, and doubt they would or should stop if a guilty bystander or innocent person is hurt. If they don't act, a lot of people will be killed. Let's pray no one gets hurt, but this is war and we have to be realistic."[41]

THE SHOOTINGS CONTINUE

In March, Angela Shannon, daughter of Shelly Shannon, allegedly mailed a death threat to abortion provider George Woodward in Milwaukee, Wisconsin. The letter warned him that if he did not stop performing abortions, she would stalk and kill him and his wife: "The letter included specific information that enhanced the credibility of the threat, such as a description of the doctor's car, a description of the building in which he worked, his home address, the fact that he sang in his church choir, and the fact that he had a 'habit of stopping at McDonalds on Wisconsin Ave.' before going to work."[42]

In May, Paul Hill, Spitz, and Burt joined others in protest at a memorial for David Gunn outside Pensacola Women's Medical Services. Later the same month, Shannon set fire to the Women's Health Care Center in Boise, Idaho.[43]

On August 19, Shannon shot Dr. George Tiller with a .25 semiautomatic pistol. Shannon had entered the clinic posing as a patient and then left after deciding to attack Tiller when he left for the day. Shannon spoke with some of the protestors and then waited inside her car until the clinic closed at 7:00 P.M. Her car was parked in front of Dr. Tiller's, and when he pulled his car out she turned around, shot several times, and sped off. Tiller suffered wounds on both arms from the six shots Shannon fired. She would later be charged for also pointing a gun at a clinic employee.[44]

During the summer, Hill organized a "Defensive Action" campaign that defended Griffin's actions, calling it "justifiable homicide."[45] Hill wrote a declaration, the "Defensive Action Statement," and began to circulate a petition that advocated violence against abortion doctors. Hill, Bray, and others described Gunn's death as "justifiable homicide," and Fr. David Trosch would later produce a newspaper advertisement showing a caricature of a man killing an abortion provider followed by a caption proclaiming "JUSTIFIABLE HOMICIDE."[46]

In October, James Kopp was arrested for trespassing and damaging property on Dobbs Ferry clinic in San Jose, California.[47] In the same month, Joshua Graff was accused of setting fire to a Houston abortion clinic, and he may have been involved in 60 other clinic arsons throughout the country.[48]

Even as the use of force was becoming more varied, the Army of God maintained their commitment to explain the justification of their actions.

The Brockhoeft Report, a series of letters written by John Brockhoeft while incarcerated, described in considerable detail arsons he committed during his antiabortion campaign and his justifications for them. Before Shannon was arrested for shooting Dr. Tiller, she edited the report for Brockhoeft and helped format it into a newsletter. After her trial, Dave Leach, signer of the "Justifiable Homicide" document publisher of the Army of God manual, and self-proclaimed "secretary-general" of the Army of God, published and continued to edit the report in the *Prayer & Action News*, a magazine promoting justifiable homicide. There are 16 letters within the report. The first four were published in December 1993.[49]

In April of 1994, Hill protested several times in front of a Pensacola abortion clinic with signs and yelled statements accusing workers and volunteers of being accessories to murder. In June, a month before he would kill an abortion provider, Hill yelled, "Please don't kill me" and "God hates murderers" outside the waiting room of the Pensacola clinic. He was subsequently arrested.

In July, Hill used a shotgun to kill both Dr. John Britton and James Barrett, a volunteer escort, at a Pensacola Clinic. James Barrett's wife, June Barrett, was wounded on the arm. As Griffin had a year earlier, Hill calmly laid down his gun after shooting Britton and Barrett, raised his hands in the air, and turned himself in to the police.[50] He was soon listed as a Prisoner of Christ on the Army of God website.[51]

In December, John Salvi III walked into two women's' clinics in Brookline, Massachusetts, and with a .22 caliber rifle, shot and killed Shannon Lowney and Leanne Nichols and wounded five others. The clinics, Planned Parenthood Clinic of Greater Boston and Pre-term Health Services, were about two miles apart. After the shootings, Salvi traveled to Hillcrest Clinic in Norfolk, Virginias, and fired 22 shots outside because he could not get in. This clinic was often picketed by Spitz and was allegedly bombed by Bray in the 1980s.

At his trial, the district attorney argued that Salvi had regular interaction and extensive connection to Army of God affiliates. The *Washington Post* reported that "Assistant District Attorney John Kivlan portrayed Salvi as a cunning antiabortion zealot, a 'terrorist' who plotted the murders, then evaded an elaborate police manhunt."[52] However, the jury did not acknowledge any links to a conspiracy.[53]

Salvi is listed on the second Prisoners of Christ list on the Army of God website, which webmaster Donald Spitz says is "reflective of his own knowledge of the individual." In other words, Spitz did not know Salvi personally but was encouraged to post his name on the site by others who knew and/ or admired him.

Spitz does add his own colorful commentary about Salvi nonetheless: "John Salvi actions resulted in the death of babykilling abortion mill workers Shannon Lowney and Leanne Nichols, plus the wounding of five others.

These evil people were part of the hit team that murder helpless unborn children in Massachusetts. They reaped what they sowed. Were their lives worth more than the lives of the helpless babies they helped murder? I don't think so."

In 1994, Michael Bray published *A Time to Kill*, which articulately defends Christians' right to use force to prevent and end abortion. The same year, Donald Spitz launched a message board on the Army of God website in support of Paul Hill. Dozens of supporters have written to Spitz, and he faithfully posts their messages on the board. Most extol Hill's courage in killing John Britton: "Thank you Rev. Hill for your uncompromised courage in the face of death. I hope you are an example for many others to follow." The comment is left unsigned. Others are more open in their support. Dan Holman, self-identified "missionary to the pre-born," says "Some day, I hope I will have the courage to be as much as a man as he was." Shortly thereafter, a "Second Defense Action Statement" was crafted in support of Hill. Both statements were posted on the Army of God website.[54]

Also in 1994, a group called the American Coalition of Life Activists (ACLA), composed of several alleged Army of God members, published a poster titled "The Daily Dozen," which featured 12 abortion providers nationwide. Some members claimed that they confronted some abortion providers on their family vacations and warned them that they were put on a "hit list," as the government had come to label the poster. Members expressed appreciation for the government's publicity of the poster, which enhanced awareness for the ACLA's project.[55] The ACLA would eventually face a tenacious lawsuit by Planned Parenthood of Willamette County, which will be discussed in greater detail in chapter 5 of this book.

While the ACLA was publishing the wanted posters, someone was using a sniper rifle to shoot abortion providers through the windows of their homes. In 1994, Dr. Garson Romalis of Vancouver was hit in the leg. In 1995, Dr. Hugh Short of Ancaster, Ontario, was shot in the elbow, and in 1997, Dr. Jack Fainman was shot in the shoulder in Winnipeg. In 1998, Dr. Barnett Slepian was shot and killed by a sniper while he was at his home in upstate New York. James Kopp was arrested for the Slepian slaying after spending three years on the run. Kopp is widely believed to be responsible for the other three shootings as well. Kopp revealed to reporters that Slepian was not a primary target. He happened to be the easiest because he had back windows that faced the woods.[56] Kopp is listed as a Prisoner of Christ on the Army of God website. Robert Ferguson, one of the Army of God's "Heroes of the Faith," stated that the murder of Dr. Slepian was "justifiable homicide—'a legitimate spiritual practice.'"[57]

From 1995 to 1996, DeParrie organized a SHAME campaign for the Advocate for Life in which activists protested abortion clinics and handed out pro-life leaflets throughout neighborhoods.[58]

In February 1995, Vincent Whitaker allegedly mailed death threats from his jail cell to Wisconsin abortion providers Elizabeth Karlin and Dennis Christenson: "In them the writer threatened to blow Dr. Karlin's head off and kill her family, and kill Dr. Christenson and his family. According to an account posted on the Army of God Prisoners of Christ page, Whitaker also wrote and mailed a letter to President Clinton at the White House, threatening to kill him when Whitaker got out of jail. The letters to Christenson and Clinton concluded with the threat, 'I'm not joking.'"[59] Whitaker is listed as a Prisoner of Christ on the AOG website.

In January 1996, the first White Rose Banquet was held in the D.C. area. This event, named after a German secret society that opposed Hitler in World War II, was founded by Michael Bray and coordinated by the ACLA to honor the Prisoners of Christ who were convicted of antiabortion violence. Future White Rose Banquets would be held on January 21, the eve of the *Roe v. Wade* anniversary. Bray was a guest speaker for the first banquet and would host several others.[60]

At this first banquet, Rev. Bray reportedly called for the dismissal of homicide charges against John Salvi, stating Salvi was as mentally stable as Ted Kennedy, regardless of the tactic undertaken by Salvi's lawyers at the trial. It was also at the White Rose Banquet that the "Nuremberg File Project" was first unveiled. The Nuremberg File Project was a "secret archive" of information on both abortion providers and workers, later posted on a website by Neal Horsley, creator and manager of multiple websites that featured videos and pictures of people entering and exiting abortion clinics. The project provided very detailed information, including photos, addresses, and phone numbers of abortion providers. The information was not limited to abortion doctors either—clinic staff and security were considered fair game. A *Baltimore Sun* article would later describe the website as another level of Internet war and intimidation, stating that it "marks the first time the World Wide Web site has broken down by state the more than 200 providers and clinics."[61]

The White Rose Banquet was also the launching point for the notorious Wanted posters that would plague Bray for years to come. A financial reward was offered for any act that would lead to the continuation of the group's aims: "For every doctor they convince to stop providing abortions, a $500 reward is presented by ACLA. If a clinic is closed, the reward is $1,000."[62]

At the fourth banquet, held on the 26th anniversary of *Roe v. Wade,* Bray reportedly "read a prepared position statement for the media," in which he summarized the consensus of the Army of God: "The key points in his thesis included these: 1) The Supreme Court exceeded its constitutional powers in issuing Roe, and the other branches of the federal government failed to fulfill their responsibility—under the constitutional system of checks and balances of power—to negate such illegitimate action; 2) The "retained rights" provision of the Tenth Amendment makes clear that abortion regulation is beyond the scope of federal control, and thus the States' anti-abortion laws have not been nullified, are still intact, and should be enforced."[63]

According to *Life Advocate* magazine, "Bray's paper called upon governors, legislatures and civil authorities in all states to 'Free those in your prisons who have been prosecuted for defending the innocent Unborn children . . . ,' 'enforce your own laws which prohibit abortion, and close down the facilities of childslaughter . . . ,' and 'perfect your laws with the recognition that the killing of children in the womb is murder, a capital crime punishable by death: execute abortionists.'"[64]

LEGAL PENALTY FOR IDEOLOGICAL TIES?

According to a page dedicated to John Burt within the Army of God website, in July 1996, the family of David Gunn, the abortion provider killed by Michael Griffin, successfully sued Burt for his involvement in a violent conspiracy that resulted in Gunn's death. The family blamed Burt for inciting Griffin before the murder by showing him the abortion in a jar. According to the web page, the Gunn family was awarded the property Burt had purchased next to the clinic in 1991, and this case marks an interesting beginning in the Army of God's history.

Though the Army of God is careful to ridicule any suggestion of conspiracy between members, they are willing to acknowledge that the acts of some greatly influenced and even define the acts of others. For example, while Burt may not have had much success as a sidewalk (or in the case of his February 1985 arrest, bedside) counselor, he did have a significant impact on the future of the movement. John Brockhoeft, who spent years in prison for 1985 bombings conducted against clinics in Ohio, recounts with perfect clarity the first time that Burt showed him an "abortion in a jar." Michael Griffin recounts the same experience as the moment he decided to stop abortion at any cost: "Since January of 1993 (when I first met John BG and I saw for the first time an abortion in a jar) I had tried endlessly to express how outraged I was at this and the thousands like that happen every day."[65]

The case brought by Gunn's family indicates a growing intolerance among American legal institutions for any correlation between supporters of the antiabortion fight. Burt's influence was not proven to have extended beyond the influence of an idea, and yet he was held legally, if implicitly responsible for Griffin's actions.

ERIC RUDOLPH AND THE ARMY OF GOD

More notoriously, in July 1996, Eric Rudolph[66] detonated a series of bombs throughout the Centennial Olympic Park, killing a woman and injuring over 100 people. Rudolph admitted to using five different bombs with timed explosives that he set off remotely. Officials called the bombs "knapsack bombs" because they contained a mixture of nails and screws that ripped through the stadium's crowds. Rudolph said, "The purpose of the attack on July 27th at Centennial Park was to confound, anger and embarrass the Washington government in the eyes of the world for its abominable sanctioning of abortion on demand."[67]

Though Rudolph claimed to be remorseful about the consequence of his Olympic attack, it was only his first of several attacks over the next few years. In January 1997, Eric Rudolph bombed an abortion clinic in Atlanta. Shortly after, a second bomb exploded in a nearby dumpster. This one was presumed to be aimed at law enforcement. The entire incident injured seven people. A month later, Rudolph bombed an Atlanta gay nightclub leaving six wounded. In an adjacent parking lot, police found a second bomb in a backpack and safely detonated it. All four bombs in both incidents were packed with nails and dynamite.[68]

Rudolph says he lay low for a while after these attacks, surfacing a year later to "send yet another message to the killers and those who protected them."[69] Rudolph detonated a bomb at the New Women All Women Health Care Clinic in Birmingham, Alabama. As nurse Emily Lyons and off-duty police officer Robert Sanderson opened the clinic, a remote-controlled bomb detonated. Sanderson was immediately killed, while Lyons was pelted with hundreds of nails and pieces of shrapnel, ripping her face and body. She lost her right eye as a result of severe injuries. This was the first fatal bombing of an abortion clinic.[70]

Rudolph explained his actions as expedient: "Birmingham and that particular abortion mill were chosen purely for tactical reasons. The city was a sufficient distance away from any location I was known to have frequented. Three abortion mills were looked at in Birmingham, none of which I truly liked for a target. New Woman All Women was tactically the least objectionable."[71] He goes on to justify his attack:

> This facility routinely kills and mutilates an average of 50 human beings every week. Every employee is a knowing participant in this gruesome trade. The security guard is instrumental in protecting these murderers and their facility from those who would intervene to stop this bloody practice, and therefore he is on the front lines of this fight. The object was to target the doctor-killer, but because the device was prematurely discovered by the security guard, it had to be detonated with only the assistant-killers in the target area. A protester was across the street, and customers waiting to have their child killed were in the parking lot just yards away, but because of the focused nature of the device and being command-detonated, only the killers were caught in the blast zone. I had nothing personal against Lyons and Sanderson. They were targeted for what they did, not who they were as individuals.[72]

After the bombings, letters crediting the Army of God were subsequently mailed to media outlets and officials.[73]

When Rudolph was later convicted of the four bombings, he revealed where he hid 250 pounds of dynamite: "You may not appreciate how much dynamite 250 pounds is until you realize that Rudolph's bombs that caused so much devastation in Atlanta and Birmingham each contained only 5 pounds to 15 pounds of dynamite," U.S. attorney David Nahmias stated.[74] Rudolph also revealed that he learned to make bombs with his commander while assigned to the 327th Infantry Air Assault Regiment at Fort Campbell, Kentucky. The commander "taught him how to make explosives with objects discarded around the base."[75] Federal officials reported one of the Atlanta bombings "employed high explosives in a military ammunition can."[76]

In 1996, reports placed Scott Roeder picketing in front of a Kansas City Planned Parenthood. Fellow picketer Regina Dinwiddie recalls that Roeder walked into the clinic and asked for abortion provider Robert Crist. When the doctor came out, Roeder "'stared at him for approximately 45 seconds [. . . then said], 'I've seen you now.' Then he turned his back and walked away, and they were scared to death.'"[77] While Roeder did nothing more at the time, the doctor's fears proved justified 13 years later when Roeder shot and killed abortion provider George Tiller.

In 1998, the third annual White Rose Banquet honored Don and Thea Spitz. Letters from imprisoned activists Hill, Beseda, Sperle, and others were read to the attendees, and an auction was conducted, which raised and disbursed money to the families of imprisoned members. One of the auction items was Shelley Shannon's "fanny pack," which carried the pistol used to shoot Tiller.[78] Proof of authenticity was offered for the suspicious.

Most of the remaining events in 1998 involved releasing butyric acid into clinics all over the United States, a technique that is described in precise detail in the Army of God manual. In May, a group suspected to be affiliated with the Army of God poured butyric acid through holes into 10 Florida clinics. The group traveled to Orlando, Daytona Beach, St. Petersburg, Clearwater, and Miami for their attacks. Three injuries were reported. Then in July, 5 New Orleans clinics were vandalized when butyric acid was poured through the mail slot.[79] Two days later, a group suspected to be affiliated with the Army of God drilled several holes through 4 Houston clinic doors and sprayed in several gallons of butyric acid. No fatalities were recorded but over 10 people were injured.

In September 1999, Clayton Waagner was arrested while driving a stolen vehicle into Illinois with his family. Police found four handguns under the driver's seat, which were later reported stolen. Waagner reportedly admitted that he was on his way to Seattle to shoot an abortion provider and would have shot the arresting police officer had his family not been in the car at the time. Waagner had a criminal history of armed robbery and weapon charges before becoming active in the antiabortion campaign.[80]

TACTICS FOR THE NEW MILLENNIUM

In 2000, Scott Roeder was accused of super-gluing the locks of a Kansas City clinic two weekends in a row, a tactic detailed in the Army of God manual. Surveillance video recorded the perpetrator, but law enforcement said the images were too blurry for a conviction.

The rest of 2000 was less eventful than previous years had been on the antiabortion front. There were no bombings at all during the year, and most of the correspondence published through the various websites and newsletters depicts discussions about the best way to graphically portray the horror of abortion. Bob Lokey placed a 16-by-40-inch billboard of an aborted fetus in his yard that said "The US Supreme Court Murders Babies like This." In addition, Dan Holman was credited for inventing a more effective and efficient way of using billboards: "By raising the signs (one per side) on a high pole, and adding an arrow, he is able to hold the signs with one hand, freeing the other to pass out information to passersby. The arrow draws attention to the location of the abortionist, and the overall height of the sign makes it much more visible to motorists. Way to go, Dan!"[81]

Bob Lokey created a page in Horsley's Nuremberg Files titled "Save the Babies." He compares his purpose to the Army of God website and states, "There are people that I'm absolutely certain have read my Web site and have gone and killed somebody or hurt somebody. That was my intention."[82]

In 2001, Bray was presented with an honorary plaque at the year's White Rose Banquet. It read

> In recognition of your faithful and true commitment and support of the underground soldiers and saints of the Army of God. And for your unyielding and uncompromising spirit when confronted with the hedonistic pagan forces currently dominating our government and society. We do this day, January 21, 2001 A.D., establish and ordain Rev. Michael Bray, a lifetime chaplain in the Army of God.[83]

He was also given a gasoline can that was reportedly used by an AOG member to attack a clinic.[84] Among the guest speakers was Chuck Spingola, an emphatic supporter of the antiabortion movement, well known for his activism on behalf of James Kopp following the killing of abortion provider Barnett Slepian. Spingola picketed in front of the courthouse where Kopp was being tried and handed out "pro-Kopp" literature to passersby. He also occasionally was seen holding up a large sign that read "Praise Jesus! Jim Kopp popped and stopped a baby butchering 'doc.'"[85] Spingola also wrote an article for the Army of God website called "Thanks be to God and the Christian Terrorist," in which he happily accepts the description of Kopp, Rudolph, and himself as Christian terrorists. He says:

> Considering what Romans chapter 13 has to say about rulers it could logically be concluded that the Christian terrorists Waagner, Rudolph, Kopp etc. qualify as "minister(s) of God" more so than America's Department of "Justice" and its subsequent agencies. Indeed the wicked should be terrified of good men. Impenitent baby murderers, sodomites, adulterers, man stealers, pedophiles, rapists, etc. should indeed cringe in the shadows at the presence of a God fearing man even as they would cringe before Jesus because they are to act as his body on earth, receiving Him as their Governor. I have heard it said that Christian terrorist Clay Waagner, did some things wrong before and during his 10 month reign of terror. It has been said that he does not deserve hero status or recognition because he is a bank robber and car thief. Perhaps it should also be noted that this bank robbing, car thieving, terrorist is directly responsible for saving the lives of 5,000 innocent babies. His reward will most likely be life without the possibility of parole. Waagner's response is, "A small price to pay". So what have brother Clay Waagner detractors done so great as to qualify them to stand in judgment of his deeds? Prudence would suggest we leave his war time actions for God to judge, and give honor to whom honor is due. Chalk up another Halleluia and a hip hip hooray for the Christian who terrorized the entire nation's abortion industry without firing a shot.[86]

In June, Waagner wrote a two-part message on the Army of God message board and on the Nuremberg Files website. The U.S. Marshal's office immediately warned abortion clinics, as Waagner proclaimed his mission to kill clinic workers: "So the abortionists don't get the wrong idea, I don't plan on talking them to death. I'm going to kill as many of them as I can. . . . It doesn't matter to me if you're a nurse, receptionist, bookkeeper, or janitor; if you work for the murderous abortionist I'm going to kill you."[87]

In July 2001, John Burt was charged with noise violation when he protested outside the Community Healthcare Center of Pensacola (formerly known as Ladies' Center). He was ordered not to go near the clinic again.[88] He is listed as a Prisoner of Christ on the Army of God website.

In the same month, though on a different continent, Peter James Knight allegedly entered the Fertility Control Clinic in Melbourne, Australia, with a rifle and shot and killed a security guard after the guard resisted Knight. He then pointed the rifle at a female patient but was tackled by two men before any other fatalities could occur. Police later searched Knight and found 16 liters of "kerosene, three cigarette lighters, foam rubber 'torches', gags for binding the staff and clients, metal devices for sealing the clinic doors, and a note to post outside, reading, 'As a result of a fatal accident of one of the staff, we have been forced to cancel all appointments today.'"[89] Knight is listed as a Prisoner of Christ on the Army of God website.

In late 2001, following the national hysteria sparked by the destruction of the Twin Towers, Clay Waagner brought the Army of God to national awareness thanks to a nationwide anthrax hoax. Between October and November 2001, Waagner sent out approximately 800 envelopes containing fake anthrax with a signature of the Army of God to various Planned Parenthood clinics throughout 17 states and Washington, D.C. Waagner mixed flour and Monsanto, an insecticide that can produce a chemical containing a biological makeup similar to anthrax, called BT. As a result, the powdery substance tested positive, though it had caused no harmful physical effects.[90] Some of the envelopes were sent from Ohio, Tennessee, and Georgia via postal mail labeled "Time Sensitive," or they included claims that there were "Urgent Security Notices Enclosed"; others used government addresses for the return address line. The rest of the envelopes were later sent via FED-EX services. The messages were consistent, stating "You have chosen a profession which profits from the senseless murder of millions of innocent children each year. . . . We are going to kill you. This is your notice. Stop or die."[91] Apart from the anthrax hoax, Waagner would also be charged for robbery, auto theft, and possession of weapons. He was charged with 53 counts of terrorism. Waagner would later write his autobiography while in prison. *Fighting the Great American Holocaust* is sold on the AOG website with the proceeds going to Mrs. Waagner.[92]

Following Waagner's foiled anthrax campaign, the new millennium demonstrated a steep drop in violent antiabortion activities. The Army of God still regularly denounced abortion and those who aid in its provision, but few successful attacks were undertaken between 2002 and 2009. Nonetheless, the Army of God highlights many of the acts undertaken during this time—whether successful or not—and extols their felled masterminds on the Army of God Prisoners of Christ list.

Many of the events of the next several years were more verbal than physical. Starting off the New Year in 2002, the Army of God (Donald Spitz and Michael Bray in particular) celebrated Saudi Arabia's beheading of three homosexuals. Spitz created two new sections on the Army of God website, attaching links that covered the beheading as well as other activities within the gay community.[93] Bray was the most vocally supportive of Saudi Arabia's beheadings, posting the following to his Army of God page:

> While the Christians among us Westerners would decline to emulate our Muslim friends in many ways we can appreciate the justice they advocate regarding sodomy. Might these fellows also consider an embryonic jihad? Let us welcome these tools of purification. Open the borders! Bring in some agents of cleansing. In the meantime, let us pray for justice: that the heads of adulterers, sodomites, murderers, child murderers (abortionists), witches, traitors, and kidnappers roll.[94]

For the first time since they had begun, Bray canceled the annual White Rose Banquet.

Between October and November 2002, activist Dan Holman was seen in the neighborhoods surrounding the Emma Goldman clinic in Iowa City, standing or sitting with signs displaying aborted fetuses, yards away from his van, which also displayed graphic signs and statements such as "Abortion Causes Breast Cancer." According to NAFVDS, 2002 was the only year with neither bombing nor arson attempts.[95]

In January 2003, Michael Bray again canceled the annual White Rose Banquet and organized a rally in support of James Kopp on the 30th anniversary of *Roe v. Wade*. In August, Hill's book, *Mix My Blood with the Blood of the Unborn*, was published.[96] In September, Dan Holman, along with several Hill supporters, picketed outside Florida State Prison in Starke. They held signs that stated, "Killing Baby Killers is Justifiable Homicide," "Extremism in Defense of Life Is Not Extreme," and "Dead Doctors Can't Kill."

In November 2003, Stephen Jordi was arrested for attempting to bomb several abortion clinics in Florida and Georgia. According to the Army of God's depiction of the event, which largely correlates with Jordi's own account, Jordi and an undercover FBI agent "bought gasoline cans, flares, starter fluid and propane tanks—including a large one filled with propane gas. . . . The source also provided Jordi a .45-caliber pistol, silencer and empty magazines in exchange for $200. . . . Jordi had discussed with an FBI source possibly using C-4 plastic explosives, propane tank bombs or pipe bombs and had studied bombing methods throughout the fall."[97] Jordi is listed as a Prisoner of Christ on the AOG website.

In June 2006, Robert F. Weiler Jr. was arrested for plotting a bomb attack on an abortion clinic in Greenbelt, Maryland. Weiler was accused of building a pipe bomb and hiding it in a friend's house. It later exploded when a bomb technician attempted to diffuse it.[98] No fatalities or injuries were reported but the house caught fire. A loaded .40 caliber and ammunition was later found in Weiler's car and he confessed his plan to use the gun to kill abortion providers. Weiler is listed as a Prisoner of Christ on the Army of God website.

A few months later, in September 2006, David Robert McMenemy positioned his car in front of Edgerton Women's Health Center in Davenport, Michigan, and drove it into the clinic's lobby. He expected the car to burst into flames, and when it didn't he poured a bottle full of gasoline all over the interior of the car and set it on fire. Little damage was done to the clinic, as the sprinkler system was immediately activated. McMenemy mistakenly believed the clinic provided abortions. He surrendered himself at the scene.[99] McMenemy is also listed as a Prisoner of Christ on the Army of God website

In April, Paul Ross Evans was accused of placing a homemade bomb in a bag outside the Austin Women's Health Center. An employee discovered the bag and the bomb squad quickly came to safely detonate the device. The bomb contained two pounds of nails and an explosive powder and had a destruction capability of 100 feet.[100] Evans is listed as a Prisoner of Christ on the AOG website.

According to an article posted on the Operation Rescue website, Dan Holman joined several protestors in Iowa displaying graphic signs that compared "Hitler's holocaust" to "Hillary's Holocaust." The signs show an open grave filled with dead bodies of the holocaust next to an aborted fetus.[101]

In May 2008, Canadian antiabortion activist Linda Gibbons was arrested for illegal protesting outside a Toronto abortion clinic. She held a sign with a picture of a baby and a caption that read "Why, Mom? When I have so much love to give."[102] She distributed pamphlets and had "strewn a number of plastic fetuses along the sidewalk in front of the abortuary."[103] She also dumped approximately 100 headless plastic baby dolls on the steps of the clinic. Workers watched Gibbons pace in silence in front of the clinic. She is listed as a Prisoner of Christ on the Army of God website.

THE ARMY KILLS AGAIN

But circumstances changed in 2009, a year in which the Army of God was repeatedly thrust into the headlines again. In January 2009, Matthew Derosia drove his car into the entrance of an abortion clinic in St. Paul. He proceeded to hold up a crucifix while reciting Bible verses and shouting, "Close down the Auschwitz Death Camp!" Derosia continued to shout until he was arrested. The Army of God, Spitz in particular, quickly came to Derosia's defense as Brian Gibson, executive director of a pro-life organization, condemned Derosia's actions. Spitz posted his e-mail to Gibson on the AOG website:

> Brian Gibson why did you condemn Matthew Derosia who only drove a van into a babykilling facility, yet accept women who actually murder their own children by abortion and have the blood of their own children on their hands? What is more important to the LORD Jesus Christ, to save babies about to be murdered in a babykilling abortion mill or the facade of that babykilling abortion mill?[104]

Derosia's mother also defended him, stating, "Derosia was only doing the Lord's work."[105] She went on to say, "I agree he needs help and we are getting him the help he needs but without your help he will be lost to everyone forever. With Gods [sic] love we can get justice for this poor boy who was only doing what God asked him to do."[106]

In May 2009, Scott Roeder attempted to pour epoxy—a very strong chemical adhesive—into a Wichita clinic's locks a day before he would shoot abortion provider Dr. George Tiller. The clinic's security cameras recorded his actions, while some workers chased him off the property and recorded his license plate number. A worker reported the incident, as well as Roeder's information, to the FBI, who in return said the evidence was not enough for any kind of conviction and "nothing could be done with the information until a federal grand jury convened."[107]

The next day, Roeder went to Dr. Tiller's Reformation Lutheran Church, where he shot and killed the doctor.[108] Roeder is listed as a Prisoner of Christ on the Army of God website.[109] Roeder communicates with several Army of God members, some of whom have admitted writing and talking to Roeder, as well as sending him antiabortion literature, including Hill's pamphlets, Bray's *A Time to Kill*, and Holman's "The Just End to a Violent, Wicked Man," an article that defends Roeder's actions.[110] "We talk about defending the unborn with the use of force, but we don't talk about his particular case," said Spitz.[111] Roeder sent some of Hill's pamphlets and copies of Holman's article to several people, including his ex-wife. The literature advocates "justifiable homicide." Roeder was a subscriber of Leach's *Prayer and Action News*.[112] Leach published several of Roeder's writings in his magazine, while Army of God members have posted several statements or articles on the Army of God website in support of Roeder.[113]

A COMMON IDEOLOGICAL FLAME

The acts undertaken by and attributed to the Army of God are as varied as the individuals who make up the organization. And yet there are trends clearly evident throughout the 30-year history. The organization has never hesitated to loudly express their belief that abortion is murder; however, in the earlier years of the organization's history, there was an aversion to the use of deadly force evident among most members. While it is true that any act of arson or fire-bombing could lead to fatalities, most of the attacks were undertaken at night when no one was in or around the location of the attack. But as more individuals began taking part in the campaign, the intensity of anger at the murder of unborn babies intensified.

As a result, it is possible to trace the escalation of violence that traverses the 30-year history of the organization. It is also evident that violence begat violence: Michael Griffin's killing of David Gunn escalated the rhetoric, and then shortly thereafter, the actions of the antiabortion campaigners. Griffin's act challenged other activists to put their belief into action and can be seen to have influenced, if not inspired, the subsequent acts of Shelley Shannon, Paul Hill, and others. But who is culpable for influence or inspiration? It has been mentioned previously in this volume that "members" of the Army of God do not take or issue orders from or to one another. Shelley Shannon knew Michael Griffin—and he likely encouraged her passions on the subject of abortion, but he did not help her plan her act to shoot George Tiller. Is Griffin still responsible for Shannon's actions?

This author has argued elsewhere that the Army of God successfully constructed an ideological frame that wrapped the members as tightly in it as any organizational hierarchy could have.[114] "In other words, while structure has traditionally been accredited with the most comprehensive explanation for the development of violence, the ideological frame of religious belief can act as an intangible alternative to the violence-inducing elements of structure. This is most clearly seen when the ideological frame of the organization casts violence as a responsibility, rather than a right, and makes questioning or the rejection of violence the questioning and rejection of God."[115]

The Army of God has always coupled their action with rhetoric explaining why they do the things they do, and this rhetoric forms the tie that binds members together. While the assignment of culpability remains elusive, the next chapter of this book will attempt to shed light on how the events we examined in this chapter are justified by those who brought them about.

NOTES

1. Phone interview with Donald Spitz, 2010.

2. Horne, Terry. 2003. "Man Questioned in Museum Fire: Ex-Convict Who Had Set Fire to an Office of Planned Parenthood Denies Being Involved." *Indianapolis Star*, November 26. http://www.docstoc.com/docs/46593682/Man-questioned-in-museum-fire.

3. Scott, Joni. 1999. "From Hate Rhetoric to Hate Crime: A Link Acknowledged Too Late—Anti-Abortionists Alleged Crimes Not Investigated." *The Humanist*, January/February. http://www.thehumanist.org/humanist/articles/scott.html.

4. Blanchard, Dallas A. and Terry J. Prewitt. 1993. *Religious Violence and Abortion*. Edited by the Gideon Project. Gainesville: University Press of Florida.

5. Blanchard, Dallas A. and Terry J. Prewitt. 1993. *Religious Violence and Abortion*. Edited by the Gideon Project. Gainesville: University Press of Florida, 289.

6. Blanchard, Dallas A. and Terry J. Prewitt. 1993. *Religious Violence and Abortion*. Edited by the Gideon Project. Gainesville: University Press of Florida.

7. Blanchard, Dallas A. and Terry J. Prewitt. 1993. *Religious Violence and Abortion*. Edited by the Gideon Project. Gainesville: University Press of Florida, 189.

8. "Abortion Opposition Stressed in Kidnapping Trial in Illinois." 1983. *New York Times*, January 26. http://www.nytimes.com/1983/01/26/us/abortion-opposition-stressed-in-kidnapping-trial-in-illinois.html.

9. "Abortion Opposition Stressed in Kidnapping Trial in Illinois." 1983. *New York Times*, January 26. http://www.nytimes.com/1983/01/26/us/abortion-opposition-stressed-in-kidnapping-trial-in-illinois.html.

10. Blanchard, Dallas A. and Terry J. Prewitt. 1993. *Religious Violence and Abortion*. Edited by the Gideon Project. Gainesville: University Press of Florida.

11. Risen, James and Judy Thomas. 1998. *Wrath of Angels: The American Abortion War*. New York: Basic Books, 75.

12. Blanchard, Dallas A. and Terry J. Prewitt. 1993. *Religious Violence and Abortion*. Edited by the Gideon Project. Gainesville: University Press of Florida.

13. Blanchard, Dallas A. and Terry J. Prewitt. 1993. *Religious Violence and Abortion*. Edited by the Gideon Project. Gainesville: University Press of Florida.

14. Magnuson, Ed, Patricia Delaney and B. Russell Leavitt. 1985. "Explosions over Abortion." *Time*, Monday, January 14. http://www.time.com/time/magazine/article/0,9171,962698,00.html.

15. Blanchard, Dallas A. 1994. *The Anti-Abortion Movement and the Rise of the Religious Right*. New York: Twayne Publishers, 56.

16. National Abortion Federation. "A History of the Army of God." http://www.prochoice.org/about_abortion/violence/army_god.html.

17. "John Burt." http://www.armyofgod.com/JohnBurt.html.

18. Blanchard, Dallas A. and Terry J. Prewitt. 1993. *Religious Violence and Abortion*. Edited by the Gideon Project. Gainesville: University Press of Florida, 197.

19. Blanchard, Dallas A. and Terry J. Prewitt. 1993. *Religious Violence and Abortion*. Edited by the Gideon Project. Gainesville: University Press of Florida, 197.

20. "John Malvasi." http://www.armyofgod.com/MalvasiMarraPic.html.

21. "John Burt." http://www.armyofgod.com/JohnBurt.html.

22. Operation Rescue (OR) is a pro-life organization that advocates *nonviolent* means of protest, particularly sit-ins and graphic sign displays of aborted fetuses. Many members of the AOG first became involved in the pro-life movement through OR. Although most of these members, including Shannon, DeParrie, and Holman, justify the use of violence against abortion providers, the nonviolent OR has written articles in remembrance of certain AOG members as well as allowed members to post messages throughout their website. The AOG would later vehemently and consistently use graphic signs as a major means of protest.

23. The Army of God website states that the first AOG manual was available in the early 1980s. The manual found in 1993, which contained an epilogue endorsing violence against abortion providers and their staff, was the third and last known edition: http://www.armyofgod.com/AOGhistory.html.

24. Blanchard, Dallas A. 1994. *The Anti-Abortion Movement and the Rise of the Religious Right*. New York: Twayne Publishers, 56.

25. Jordan, Erin. 2002. "Abortion Foe Punched." *Cedar Rapids Gazette*, November 27;

26. "Dan Holman." 2010. http://www.armyofgod.com/DanHolmanIndex.html.

27. Bray, Michael. 1994. *Capitol Area Christian News*. http://www.christiangallery.com/bray.html.

28. DeParrie, Paul. "Biography—Editor in Chief Paul de Parrie." *Life Advocate*. http://www.lifeadvocate.org/bio/paul/biopaul.htm.

29. Robb, Amanda. 2010. "Not a Lone Wolf: Scott Roeder Is Now Serving a Life Term for Murdering Abortion Doctor George Tiller. But Did He Really Act Alone?" *MS. Magazine*, Spring. http://www.msmagazine.com/spring2010/lonewolf.asp.

30. "The Mad Gluer Interviews the Army of God." http://armyofgod.blogspot.com/. Part I Section N, "Avon Calling."

31. Bower, Anne. 1996. "Soldier in the Army of God." *Albion Monitor*, February 19. http://www.albionmonitor.com/abortion/abortionsoldier.html.

32. "Woman Gets 20 Year Term for Abortion Clinic Fires." 1995. *Orlando Sentinel*, September 9. http://articles.orlandosentinel.com/1995-09-09/news/9509090557_1_abortion-redden-firebombing; the eighth arson was committed on May 27, 1993; the number of arsons credited to Shannon continue to vary. For example, NAF records credit her for six arsons. Nonetheless, the Justice Department as well as court records from both Oregon and California credit and have sentenced Shannon for several counts of arson, arson attempts, butyric acid attacks, and napalm usage totaling 10 incidents at 9 different abortion clinics on the West Coast. See also "Guilty Plea Expected in Fires at Clinics." 1995. *New York Times*, June 4. http://www.nytimes.com/1995/06/04/

us/guilty-plea-expected-in-fires-at-clinics.html; Bower, Anne. 1996. "Soldier in the Army of God." *Albion Monitor*, February 19. http://www.albionmonitor.com/abortion/abortionsoldier.html; Shannon, Shelley. "Who Is Shelley Shannon." *Army of God*; and "Woman Who Firebombed Abortion Clinics Is Sentenced." 1995. *Los Angeles Times*, September   9.   http://articles.latimes.com/1995-09-09/news/mn-44016_1_abortion-clinic. Although she may have been involved in more arsons, there is a maximum count for sentencing; thus, there is a contradiction between what Shannon admits to committing and what the courts have claimed to count for sentencing. The *Washington Post* records charges for both arsons and butyric acid attacks at 10, as cited from the Justice Department: "Antiabortion Extremist Indicted in Attacks on Clinics in West." 1994. *Washington Post.* http://www.washingtonpost.com/wpsrv/national/longterm/abortviolence/stories/shannon.htm.

33. Justice Department. 1994. *Oregon Woman Charged in Arson, Acid and Napalm Attacks on Nine Abortion Clinics.* www.justice.gov/opa/pr/Pre_96/October94/607.txt.html. The AOG website, *Albion Monitor*'s Anne Bower, and NAF credit this arson as Shannon's last and the most successful at causing damage; nonetheless, court records indicate this was not her last arson.

34. Shannon, Shelley. "Who Is Shelley Shannon." *Army of God.* www.armyofgod.com/ShelleyWhois.html; the use of napalm carries a heavy sentence (1 count = 30 years) because of its destructiveness; acetylene gas is also a volatile chemical as it is a destructive incendiary that can be used on any kind of surface. This gas, frequently employed by the AOG, causes the most violent explosions in comparison to other fuels. See: Mine Safety and Health Administration. "Safety Hazards of Acetylene." *United States Department of Labor.* http://www.msha.gov/alerts/hazardsofacetylene.htm.

35. Nineteen arsons and 13 arson and bomb attempts against clinics were reported.

36. "The Army of God: Epilogue," extracted from AOG manual cited in Shannon, Shelley, "Who Is Shelley Shannon." *Army of God.*

37. Quoted in Robb, Amanda. 2010. "Not a Lone Wolf: Scott Roeder Is Now Serving a Life Term for Murdering Abortion Doctor George Tiller. But Did He Really Act Alone?" *MS. Magazine*, Spring. http://www.msmagazine.com/spring2010/lonewolf.asp.

38. Baird-Windle, Patricia and Eleanor J. Bader. 2001. *Targets of Hatred: Anti-Abortion Terrorism.* New York: Palgrave, 170.

39. Blanchard, Dallas A. and Terry J. Prewitt. 1993. *Religious Violence and Abortion.* Edited by the Gideon Project. Gainesville: University Press of Florida.

40. Booth, William. 1993. "Doctor Killed during Abortion Protest." *Washington Post*, March 11, A01.

41. Shannon, Shelley. "Who Is Shelley Shannon." *Army of God.* www.armyofgod.com/ShelleyWhois.html.

42. *United States v. Shannon; United States of America, Plaintiff-Appellee, v. Angela Dawn Shannon, Defendant-Appellant.* 1998. United States Court of Appeals, 9th Circuit.

43. Justice Department. 1994. *Oregon Woman Charged in Arson, Acid and Napalm Attacks on Nine Abortion Clinics.* www.justice.gov/opa/pr/Pre_96/October94/607.txt.html.

44. Risen, James, and Ronald J. Ostrow. 1994. "U.S. to Act in 10 Abortion Clinic Attacks Indictments: Charges Are Expected Against an Extremist in Prison for Attempted Murder. Authorities Hope Action Will Lead to Names of Others. *Los Angeles Times*, October 23. http://articles.latimes.com/1994-10-23/news/mn-53887_1_abortion-clinic-attacks. See also "Abortion Foe Who Shot a Doctor Is Convicted of Attempted Murder." 1994. *New York Times*, March 26. http://www.nytimes.com/1994/03/26/us/abortion-foe-who-shot-a-doctor-is-convicted-of-attempted-murder.html. Bower,

Anne. 1996. "Soldier in the Army of God." *Albion Monitor,* February 19. http://www.al bionmonitor.com/abortion/abortionsoldier.html. Risen, James and Judy Thomas. 1998. *Wrath of Angels: The American Abortion War.* New York: Basic Books, 356.

45.   Diamond, Sara. 2000. *Not By Politics Alone: The Enduring Influence of the Christian Right.* New York: Guilford Press, 146.

46.   Simpson, Victor. "John Paul II Issues Strong Rebuke of 'False Morality.'" http://www.trosch.org/tro/mpr-7h15.htm; Sturgis, Sue. 2009. "Abortion Doctor a Killer in Terrorist 'Army of God'?" *Facing South.* http://www.southernstudies.org/2009/06/abortion-doctor-killer-a-soldier-in-terrorist-army-of-god.html

47.   Lou, Michel and Dan Herbeck. 2002. "Kopp May Have Risked Capture to See Ill Girlfriend." *Buffalo News,* August 18. www.freerepublic.com/focus/news/735244/posts.

48.   "Teen-Ager Admits He Set Fire to Texas Abortion Clinic." 1993. *Los Angeles Times,* October 15. http://articles.latimes.com/1993-10-15/news/mn-45991_1_abortion-clinic.

49   Barkun, Michael. 1996. *Millenialism and Violence.* London: Routledge.

50.   Bower, Anne. 1996. "Soldier in the Army of God." *Albion Monitor,* February 19.

51.   "Prisoners of Christ." *Army of God.* http://www.armyofgod.com/POClist.html.

52.   Daly, Christopher. 1996. "Salvi Convicted of Murder in Shootings." *Washington Post,* March 19, A01.

53.   Daly, Christopher. 1996. "Salvi Convicted of Murder in Shootings." *Washington Post,* March 19, A01.

54.   "The Second Defensive Action Statement." *Army of God.* http://www.armyof god.com/defense2.html.

55.   Porteous, Skipp. 1996. "Banquet of the White Rose." *Albion Monitor,* February 18. http://www.monitor.net/monitor/abortion/whiterose.html.

56.   National Abortion Federation. "A History of The Army of God." http://www.prochoice.org/about_abortion/violence/army_god.html.

57.   Don the Dingo: "Phil Kline's Special Prosecutor Linked to Antiabortion Terrorism." http://www.talk2action.org/story/2006/12/29/235039/90.

58.   http://www.lifeadvocate.org/bio/paul/biopaul.htm.

59.   *NOTICE: Seventh Circuit Rule 53(b)(2) states unpublished orders shall not be cited or used as precedent except to support a claim of res judicata, collateral estoppel or law of the case in any federal court within the circuit. UNITED STATES of America, Plaintiff-Appellee, v. Vincent D. WHITAKER, Defendant-Appellant. 1996. United States Court of Appeals Seventh Circuit.*

60.   Domingo, Roger. 1999. "Media Zeroes in on White Rose Banquet." *Life Advocate* 13, no. 5. http://www.lifeadvocate.org/3_99/nation3.htm.

61.   Thomson, Candus. 1999. "Site Targets State's Clinics." *Baltimore Sun,* February 4. http://articles.baltimoresun.com/1999-02-04/news/9902040143_1_abortion-mary land-listing-clinics.

62.   Porteous, Skipp. 1996. "Banquet of the White Rose." *Albion Monitor,* February 18. http://www.monitor.net/monitor/abortion/whiterose.html.

63.   Domingo, Roger. 1999. "Media Zeroes in on White Rose Banquet." *Life Advocate* 13 no. 5. http://www.lifeadvocate.org/3_99/nation3.htm.

64.   Domingo, Roger. 1999. "Media Zeroes in on White Rose Banquet." *Life Advocate* 13 no. 5. http://www.lifeadvocate.org/3_99/nation3.htm.

65.   Griffin, Michael. *Army of God.* www.armyofgod.com/MichaelGriffin.html.

66.   For more information about Eric Rudolph please see Davis, Danny. 2010. *The Phinehas Priesthood: Violent Vanguard of the Christian Identity Movement.* Westport, CT: Praeger.

67. "Eric Rudolph Statement." http://www.armyofgod.com/EricRudolphAtlanta CourtStatement.html. For a description of the event see "Rudolph Reveals Motives: Pleads Guilty to Four Attacks, Including 1996 Olympic Blast." 2005. *CNN*, April 19. http://edition.cnn.com/2005/LAW/04/13/eric.rudolph/index.html; and "Rudolph Pleads Guilty to Clinic, Olympic Park Bombings." 2005. *Washington Post*, April 14. http://www.washingtonpost.com/ac2/wp-dyn/A49309-2005Apr13?language=printer.

68. "Similarities Mount in Atlanta Bombings." 1997. *CNN*, February 24. http://articles.cnn.com/1997-02-24/us/9702_24_atlanta.bombing_1_jay-spadafore-clinic-bombings-atlanta-bombings?_s=PM:US.

69. "Eric Rudolph Statement." http://www.armyofgod.com/EricRudolphStatement.html.

70. "Army of God Letters Claim Responsibility for Clinic Bombing." 1998. *CNN*, February 2. http://edition.cnn.com/US/9802/02/clinic.bomb.late/index.html.

71. "Eric Rudolph Statement." http://www.armyofgod.com/EricRudolphStatement.html.

72. "Eric Rudolph Statement." http://www.armyofgod.com/EricRudolphStatement.html.

73. "Eric Rudolph Statement." http://www.armyofgod.com/EricRudolphStatement.html; "Terror from the Right." http://www.splcenter.org/get-informed/publications/terror-from-the-right; "Similarities Mount in Atlanta Bombings." 1997. *CNN*, February 24. http://articles.cnn.com/1997-02-24/us/9702_24_atlanta.bombing_1_jay-spadafore-clinic-bombings-atlanta-bombings?_s=PM:US; Potok, Mark. 2009. *Terror from the Right: 75 Plots, Conspiracies, and Racist Rampages Since Oklahoma City.* Southern Poverty Law Center. www.splcenter.org/get-informed/publications/terror-from-the-right.

74. "Rudolph Reveals Motives: Pleads Guilty to Four Attacks, Including 1996 Olympic Blast. 2005. *CNN*, April 19. http://edition.cnn.com/2005/LAW/04/13/eric.rudolph/index.html.

75. Stein, Jeff. 1998. "A Day to Remember?" *Salon News Real.* www.salon.com/news/1998/11/11news.html.

76. Stein, Jeff. 1998. "A Day to Remember?" *Salon News Real.* www.salon.com/news/1998/11/11news.html.

77. Thomas, Judy. 2009. "Suspect in Tiller's Death Supported Killing Abortion Providers, Friends Say." *Wichita Eagle*, June 1, A01.

78. "Bray Conducts Third Annual White Rose Banquet." 1998. *Life Advocate* 7, no. 11 (March/April), http://www.lifeadvocate.org/3_98/nation.htm.

79. Cole, Benjamin and Nadine Gurr. 2002. "Terrorism in the USA Involving Weapons of Mass Destruction." In *The New Face of Terrorism: Threats from Weapons of Mass Destruction.* London: I. B. Tauris; "Project Noah—the Waters Below." http://armyofgod.blogspot.com/. Part I, Section H.

80. National Abortion Federation. "A History of The Army of God." http://www.prochoice.org/about_abortion/violence/army_god.html.

81. http://www.antiabortionsigns.com/signsinaction.html.

82. Altum, Justin. 2003. "Anti-Abortion Extremism: The Army of God." *Chrestomathy: Annual Review of Undergraduate Research at the College of Charleston* 2: 1–12, 4.

83. Yewell. 2001. "Straight Shooters." *Life Advocate.* January 24. http://www.lifeadvocate.org/3_98/nation.htm.

84. Yewell. 2001. "Straight Shooters." *Life Advocate.* January 24. http://www.lifeadvocate.org/3_98/nation.htm.

85. "Message from Chuck Spingola." *Army of God.* http://www.armyofgod.com/ChuckSpingola.html.

86. "Message from Chuck Spingola." *Army of God.* http://www.armyofgod.com/ChuckSpingola.html.

87. "Clayton Waagner's Message to the United States." *Army of God.* http://www.armyofgod.com/Claytonsmessage.html.

88. "John Burt." *Army of God.* http://www.armyofgod.com/JohnBurt.html.

89. Pro-Choice Action Network. 2002.

90. Ellen Beck. "Anthrax Scare Sweeps Capital, Nation." 2001http://www.upi.com/Science_News/2001/10/17/Anthrax-scare-sweeps-Capitol-nation/UPI-21511003363300/.

91. Ronson, John. 2002. "Hoax!" *The Guardian,* October 5. http://www.armyofgod.com/ClaytonBook.html.

92. National Abortion Federation. "A History of The Army of God." http://www.prochoice.org/about_abortion/violence/army_god.html.

93. Waagner, Clay. 2003. *Fighting the Great American Holocaust.* Kearney, NE: Morris Publishing; Clarkson, Frederick. 2003. "The Quiet Fall of an American Terrorist." *Salon.* http://www.salon.com/news/feature/2003/12/10/waagner.

94. http://www.armyofgod.com/Leviticus.html.

95. Berkowitz, Bill. 2002. "Army of God Declares Solidarity with Muslim Extremists." *Albion Monitor,* March 24. http://www.albionmonitor.com/0203a/copyright/armyofgod2.html.

96. Arthur, Joyce. 2003. "Where Is the Anti-Choice Movement Headed?" *The Pro-Choice Action Network,* Summer. http://www.prochoiceactionnetwork-canada.org/prochoicepress/03summer.shtml.

97. Hill, Paul. 2003. *Mix My Blood with the Blood of the Unborn.* http://www.armyofgod.com/PHillBookForward.html.

98. Murphy, Jarrett. 2003. "FBI: Abortion Bomb Plot Thwarted: Suspect Leapt into Biscayne Bay to Avoid Arrest." *CBS News,* November 13. http://www.cbsnews.com/stories/2003/11/13/national/main583390.shtml.

99. "Man Arrested for Plotting Attack on Abortion Clinic." 2006. *Associated Press,* June 8. http://www.foxnews.com/story/0,2933,198791,00.html.

100. Baker, Deirdre Cox. 2006. "Man Believed Clinic Performed Abortions." *Quad City Times,* September 13. http://qctimes.com/news/local/article_13f05e10-3a6d-550d-bf9f-e3f278c2bf59.html.

101. Shannon, Kelley. 2007. "Arrest Made in Bomb at Texas Clinic." *Washington Post,* April 28. http://www.washingtonpost.com/wp-dyn/content/article/2007/04/27/AR2007042701882.html.

102. Operation Rescue. 2007. "Pro-Lifer Attacked with Club, Threatened with Arrest during Clinton Protest." http://www.operationrescue.org/archives/pro-lifer-attacked-with-club-threatened-with-arrest-during-clinton-protest/.

103. Gosgnach, Tony. 2008. "Pro-Life Heroine Linda Gibbons Sentenced to Only One Additional Day in Prison." *Canada Free Press,* July 29. http://canadafreepress.com/index.php/article/4187.

104. Gosgnach, Tony. 2008. "Pro-Life Heroine Linda Gibbons Sentenced to Only One Additional Day in Prison." *Canada Free Press,* July 29. http://canadafreepress.com/index.php/article/4187.

105. Matthew Derosia. *Army of God.* http://www.armyofgod.com/POCMatthewDerosiaWebPage1.html.

106. Birkey, Andy. 2009. "Family, Army of God Defend Man Who Drove Car into Abortion Clinic." *Minnesota Independent,* May 21. http://www.tcdailyplanet.net/article/2009/05/20/family-army-god-defend-man-who-drove-car-abortion-clinic.html?mini=eventcalendar/2009/06/all.

107. Birkey, Andy. 2009. "Family, Army of God Defend Man Who Drove Car into Abortion Clinic." *Minnesota Independent,* May 21. http://www.tcdailyplanet.net/article/2009/05/20/family-army-god-defend-man-who-drove-car-abortion-clinic.html?mini=eventcalendar/2009/06/all.

108. Griffin, Drew, Randi Kaye, Kathleen Johnston, Paul Vercammen, Ashley Fantz and Matt Smith. 2009. "Clinic Worker Chased Off Suspect before Doctor's Slaying." *CNN,* June 1. http://edition.cnn.com/2009/CRIME/06/01/kansas.doctor.killed.charges/.

109. Robb, Amanda. 2010. "Not a Lone Wolf: Scott Roeder Is Now Serving a Life Term for Murdering Abortion Doctor George Tiller. But Did He Really Act Alone?" *MS Magazine,* Spring. http://www.msmagazine.com/spring2010/lonewolf.asp.

110. Thomas, Judy. 2009. "FBI's Investigation of Tiller Killing Looks at Roeder's Jail Visitors." *Kansas City Star,* August 10. http://www.kansascity.com/637/story/1373179.html.

111. Thomas, Judy. 2009. "FBI's Investigation of Tiller Killing Looks at Roeder's Jail Visitors." *Kansas City Star,* August 10. http://www.kansascity.com/637/story/1373179.html.

112. Thomas, Judy. 2009. "Suspect in Tiller's Death Supported Killing Abortion Providers, Friends Say." *Kansas City Star,* June 1, A01.

113. "Scott Roeder." *Army of God.* http://www.armyofgod.com/POCScottRoederIndexPage.html.

114. Jefferis, Jennifer. 2010. *Religion and Political Violence: Sacred Protest in the Modern World.* New York: Routledge.

115. Jefferis, Jennifer. 2010. *Religion and Political Violence: Sacred Protest in the Modern World.* New York: Routledge, 136–137.

3

⸺✣⸺

Just War?

Understanding the ideology of the Army of God is a critical step toward understanding the group itself. While within the literature of terrorism, social movements, and organizational theories, ideology is not always considered a key component of groups, the members of the Army of God are linked by little else. As was mentioned in the introduction to this book, there are those both outside and inside the organization that question whether it is even appropriate to call it an organization at all based on the fact that some of the members have never even met one another. And yet, this book argues that as technology advances on both the terror and counterterror sides of the equation, organization will come to mean something very different in the years to come. While certainly structure is still important, the role of ideas—and their power to link individuals even just conceptually—will matter far more, particularly in matters of terrorism.

Edward Said has famously lamented that amateur scholars of Islam have a tendency to fall into two divergent camps, the first of which views Islam as the natural adversary of modernization and democratization, and the second that sees Islam as an unparalleled foundation for peace and development.[1] Said's point characterizes the broader discussion of religion and violence equally as effectively. Many academic discussions of religion tend to view religions' often exclusive doctrines as potential, if not inevitable, catalysts for violent conflict,[2] while others tend to ignore the significance of religion all together, lumping it instead into the category of a misunderstood variables by another name.[3] But if one can take nothing else from the study of religion in politics, at least the value of ideas must be considered. While other variables may well contribute to decision-making processes, religion—as an idea or set thereof—still offers critical explanatory power. And as will be seen in the pages that follow, this is particularly true in the case of the Army of God.

The Army of God refers to itself as a real army with God as the general, a turn of phrase that refers to both the ideology and the structure of the organization. The Army does not formally recruit members or put prospects through any form of boot camp. Individuals are recruited based on the compatibility of their worldview and its relation to the ideology espoused by the organization, largely over the Internet. One of the consequences of this informal structure is the absence of a formal theological doctrine to define the organization, as one might expect from other religious organizations. The Army of God has no creed. Instead, it has dozens of documents (some attributed, others not) articulating the individual views of supporters. While these all contain certain core elements (the belief that abortion is murder and violent resistance is a valiant act) there are divergent perspectives about appropriate methods and some differences in theology.

Reverend Donald Spitz, the director of the Army of God website, speaks proudly of the religious diversity that characterizes the group. He points out that Paul Hill—the Presbyterian minister executed by the State of Florida for killing Dr. John Britton—was his best friend for 12 years, though Spitz is a Charismatic. Spitz informed this author that "We just kind of ignored it. Hill was a Super-Calvinist, but we got along great. Early on we made a deal. If he wouldn't lecture me about pre-destination, I wouldn't lecture him about speaking in tongues."[4] Spitz went on to confirm that all Army of God affiliates share "basic Christian beliefs" about who Jesus is and what He did for mankind, but he emphasizes that beyond these core elements, there is no required doctrine.

Perhaps owing to the loose nature of the organization, members are not assigned a role within the organization that they are arbitrarily expected to fill. Instead, individuals speak of being drawn to the doctrine or the methods and then, through the encouragement of other members, are mentored to find how their unique skills can be put to use. The result is an organic diffusion of strengths and interests that have the added benefit (to the organization) of making connections between members harder to trace. While the next chapter will discuss in greater detail the distribution of labor by individual, for the purposes of this chapter, it is useful to note that the justification of the actions of soldiers in the Army of God also reflects the unique attributes of the participating individuals. It is beyond the scope of this book to argue causality between personality and ideological justification or vice versa, but it is helpful to recognize that most members fall into one of four categories of justification when making their case for violence: theological, strategic, personal, and legal. These categories are not mutually exclusive, and thus they naturally overlap from time to time, but they are appropriate nonetheless to serve as parameters for understanding the ideology of the organization.

THEOLOGY

While the writings of the Army of God are extensive, there are arguably two seminal works that have come to serve as the foundation for theological arguments in favor of the use of force to stop abortion. In 1994, Reverend Michael Bray published *A Time to Kill*, in order to expand the pro-life debate to "include a vigorous discussion of intervention, without ignoring the use of Godly force."[5] Nine years later, shortly before he was executed by the State of Florida for the killing of John Britton, Paul Hill wrote *Mix My Blood with the Blood of the Unborn*, a book "to maintain the defensive duties of the Moral Law, as it applies to the unborn."[6] Hill describes the book as an act of "obedience to this divine call."[7] These two works, both written by ordained ministers, situate the discussion of the use of force to stop abortion in (what they call) a biblical context.

Bray and Hill both carefully distinguish between moral and immoral force. Both point out that Scripture clearly allows killing in some situations, including capital punishment (Deuteronomy 19:12 and Genesis 9:6), war (Deuteronomy 20–21) and self-defense (Exodus 22:2). Hill argues that of these, the killing of abortion providers is covered under the third justification (self-defense).

The same distinction is made by Dan Holman in an article he wrote in response to Scott Roeder's killing of George Tiller. In "The Just End to a Violent, Wicked Man," Holman specifies that "some argue that the killing of Tiller or any other abortionist is a vigilante act. They confuse vengeance with defensive action. It would be vigilantism to avenge the deaths of those whom someone has killed; it is acting in defense of others to protect the living."[8] Holman, who calls himself a missionary to the preborn, goes on to say, "In Tiller's case it does not matter what the shooter's motive was. Tiller was a predictable serial killer. I do not believe it is possible to murder a murderer, especially when he is an active killer. Tiller would have gone on murdering children with the cooperation of the state as long as he desired. The state is a party to Tiller's crimes. The state has a fiduciary duty to protect all human life within its jurisdiction. The state has chosen to cooperate in murdering the most helpless of its human inhabitants by denying him his God given Right to Life."[9]

Bray contends that in Hebrew there is no specific word for murder. Instead, there is a word that refers both to murder (which Bray argues is unlawful) and killing (which Bray says is lawful). The distinction is found in the purpose of the act. Bray argues that properly translated, the sixth commandment does not caution against killing, but against committing murder. Bray suggests that the former is amoral, while the latter is immoral. Practically speaking, the difference is manifest in the purpose of the act committed. An individual who kills to save a life has not committed murder, but has in fact, prevented it.[10]

Hill expands on this principle by identifying what he calls the Moral Law, present in both the Old and New Testament and evident throughout history. Hill contends that the Moral Law requires the defense of the innocent—of which unborn children are clearly classified. Hill argues that "not only does the Moral Law require the means necessary for defending the innocent; this duty comes directly from God and cannot be removed by any human government. The duty to defend your own or your neighbor's child is thus inalienable. When the government forbids this defense the people must obey God rather than men (Acts 5:29b). The Scriptures teach that when the government requires a sin of omission (as it has by forbidding the defense of our unborn children) we must obey God rather than the government. As a consequence, you do not need the state's permission before defending your unborn child. No man-made law can remove the individual's duty to defend his own or his neighbor's child."[11]

Hill is clearly arguing that not only is force justified in the prevention of abortion, but, if proven to be the only effective means of stopping it, it is required. Throughout his book, Hill references the concept of sins of omission: thus every commandment has an inverse commandment along with it. In other words, "thou shall not kill" requires not only the absence of killing, but the prevention of others being allowed to do so. Moral Law then demands the prevention of killing, according to Hill's understanding of the sixth commandment. By this same reasoning, Hill says "Not only does the Moral Law require the means necessary for defending the innocent, the Moral Law also requires that this duty be upheld in no uncertain terms. The Ninth Commandment ('You shall not bear false witness against your neighbor' Exodus 20:16) not only forbids lying, it also requires the maintaining and promoting of truth, including the defensive duties of the Moral Law."[12]

By making the distinction between moral and immoral force, Bray and Hill force the acknowledgement that, absent the adjectives, force is amoral. Doing so compels other pro-life advocates to move beyond the argument that force is inherently wrong and instead changes the discussion to what type of force is used. This rhetorical strategy is present in the careful way that Army of God members avoid using the term violence at all—except when describing what aborted babies go through. In an e-mail to this author, Donald Spitz says, "we do not use the term violence as that word indicates an illegitimate use of force or defensive force."[13]

But having established the amoral nature of force, if not violence, Bray and Hill effectively argue that force is present throughout the Scriptures, and the job of a good Christian is to seek out the distinction between the force that God demands, that which He allows, and that which He condemns. Bray offers numerous examples of contending types of force—in which moral force is compelled to put a stop to immoral force. He reminds his reader that the Bible is full of examples of God using force and demanding His followers to do so as well. There are portions of Old Testament law that prescribe community participation in the use of force—for the prevention of evil. Bray cites the example of the Israelites' reaction to child sacrifice in Leviticus 20:2–4. When this occurred, the entire community was to participate in the stoning of the perpetrator.[14]

Bray is referring to the third book of the Old Testament, in which God lays down the very detailed Law for Moses to give the people of Israel. In Leviticus, God's commands range from how to treat infectious skin diseases to, in the case to which Bray refers, how the Israelites should deal with child sacrifice, a practice of some of the non-Israelites living in Israel. The Scripture reads "Then the Lord spoke to Moses, saying 'Again your shall say to the children of Israel, or of the strangers who dwell in Israel, who gives any of his descendants to Molech, he shall surely be put to death. The people of the land shall stone him with stones. I will set My face against that man, and will cut him off from his people, because he has given some of his descendants to Molech, to defile My sanctuary and profane My holy name. And if the people of the land should in any way hide their eyes from the man when he gives some of his descendants to Molech, and they do not kill him, then I will set My face against that man and against his family and I will cut him off from his people and all who prostitute themselves with him to commit harlotry with Molech.'" Bray argues that this example clearly shows death is considered by God to be a suitable punishment for killing innocent people. He uses this to conclude that the use of force to protect the innocent must be equally permissible.[15]

Bray also references Hebrews 11, a chapter of the New Testament devoted to praising great heroes of the faith. Bray notes that several of the heroes mentioned were applauded for their use of moral force. Samson killed hundreds (and eventually himself) as part of God's plan for Israel. Gideon led a small but lethal army to protect Israel from enemies, and David successfully claimed and defended Jerusalem as the capital of Israel.

As Bray points out,

"By faith" it is said they "conquered kingdoms" and "became mighty in war" (vv.33,34). All these, it is said, "gained approval through their faith" (vv 2,39). They applied force faithfully and according to the good pleasure of the One who teaches the hands of His faithful "to war" (Ps. 144:1). When the Lord Jesus was transfigured before His disciples He appeared in His glory in the presence of two giants among the saints of Old: Moses and Elijah. Moses: that deliverer of God's people at whose hands great violence brought upon the oppressors of God's people. Elijah's finest hour was his bloody victory at Mt. Carmel where to the glory of God, he put hundreds of false prophets to death with his sword. Jesus shunned no man of righteous force.[16]

Bray later cites numerous examples of God's wrath taking the form of physical force, noting in particular God's use of pestilence to punish His people
when they rejected him (1 Chronicles 21:2–16).[17]

Bray argues that Jesus was fully aware and accepting of the necessity of
force for the defense and protection of justice. Bray distinguishes between
Jesus' passivity in regards to His own life (which was necessarily sacrificed
for justice) and His intolerance of injustice when He encountered it. Bray
explains that when Jesus first called his disciples, He commissioned them
to engage in productive ministries including healing the sick and raising
the dead and advised them to take very little with them. Bray contrasts
this to Jesus' advice to the disciples at the end of his ministry just before
his death, wherein he urged that "him who has no sword sell his robe and
buy one" (Luke 22:36). Bray interprets this to mean that Jesus expected
evangelists to encounter danger and injustice, and that the sword was an
appropriate measure of defense. Bray posits that the justice and mercy that
characterized Jesus' ministry were never intended to interdict the use of
force to protect the innocent. Bray understands the theme of love present
in the New Testament to make the (forceful) preservation of justice and
mercy all the more important. He argues that love is manifest in the actions
of God's followers. Those who would stand by as God's law is violated are
not manifesting love for God.[18]

Bray highlights the many examples in which God is extolled in the Bible
as a warrior. He notes that one frequently used title for God is the "Lord
of Hosts" which literally means "Lord of Armies." Bray cites Deuteronomy
20:16–17, in which God instructs the Israelites to destroy the Hittites, the
Amorites, the Canaanites, the Perizzites, the Hivites, and the Jebusites, by
leaving not "alive anything that breathes."[19]

In *A Time to Kill*, Bray endeavors to vanquish the dominant Christian argument that Jesus did not, could not, and would not use violence to achieve
His ends and intended this rejection to serve as an example for Christians
for all time. Instead, Bray suggests that Jesus had a specific mission unique
unto Himself. His mission was predicated on the absence of force, but only
so that what He accomplished could then be spread to the ends of the earth.
In the pursuit of these ends, force may be necessary.

Thus Bray proposes changing the dominant question from "what would
Jesus do?" to "what would Jesus approve?" Bray argues that Jesus, as the
Son of God, is not a change from the God of war present throughout the
Old Testament. If one accepts the idea of the trinitarian nature of God,
then the acts of God in the Old Testament—including God's physical
wrath in the form of plagues, famines, and pestilence—must be reconciled
against the themes of love and mercy in the New Testament. One does
not supersede the other, because according to Bray, "the One who uses
force and consecrates others to do the same does not have a problem with
it." Bray warns that Christians have taken the imagery of sacrifice present

in Christ's death and mistakenly concluded that this is the standard for all Christians. By doing this, Bray laments that Christians have identified one narrow element of God and falsely expanded it to represent his entire character. He says, "We have taken His one role as suffering servant as our example without regard for His eternal and present role as Almighty Ruler and Judge of the Universe. And we have defined His nature on the narrow mission of Christ on earth."[20]

It is interesting to note that Bray's argument about Jesus as a unique example of the use of nonviolence is present also in the structure of the Army of God. Just as Bray believes that Jesus' mission was communicated by God for the Christ alone, the Army of God is structured to enable the same sentiment to guide the actions of its members. In other words, while the Army of God is structured to facilitate the use of force against abortion providers, individual action is commanded only by the individual's understanding of God's calling for them. Several members speak of deep admiration for those who use force, while making clear (if sounding wistful) that God had not (yet) called them to the same path.[21] But it should be made clear that neither Bray, nor most others in the Army, wait passively for others to be called. They do not order the action of would-be members, but they strongly exhort, encourage, and goad them to move in the righteous direction.

For example, Bray titles one of the sections of A Time to Kill "An Emasculated Church." Using the tongue-in-cheek style that characterizes most of his writing, Bray writes "There is one other impediment, we believe, which prejudices one against giving the doctrine of godly force fair consideration. It is not a doctrinal problem of the head, but a duct problem of the phallus. Or, to use the modern (albeit less poetic) metaphor, it is a problem of testosterone deficiency, if not emasculation of American males."[22] Bray is disdainful of the misplaced manhood of American men. At one point he declares his disdain for the "law-abiding John Q. Public" who sits passively by in the face of abortion, saying he prefers thieves and murderers to this.[23]

Interestingly, Hill lays down a similar challenge, though he challenges one's spiritual strength, rather than his testosterone. He says:

> The more we love the Lord, the greater will be our affection for His word, including the defensive duties required by the Sixth Commandment. David, in Psalm 119:97 cried out "Oh, how I love Thy law. It is my meditation all the day." His affection for God's law certainly included the duty to defend innocent people. We should have a similar fervor for this neglected but essential aspect of God's word. As believers meditate on this aspect of God's law, as it applies to the plight of the unborn, His Spirit will give us great ardor for proclaiming and maintaining this duty throughout the world.[24]

Hill goes further to argue that the absence of force in the prevention of abortion reflects a dead faith on the part of the Christian. Integrating a verse from the New Testament (James 2:17—Thus also faith by itself, if it does not have works, is dead.), Hill says "the faith that abortion is murder is dead unless it is put to work by upholding the duty to resist this murderous force with force. How can you show your faith that abortion is murder as long as you neglect the duty to intervene in defense of these children? You believe the unborn are human. You do well; many who support abortion also believe this, but they don't act like it. 'But are you willing to recognize, you foolish fellow, that faith without works is useless?' (James 2:20)."[25]

Hill continues to argue that not only is the use of force justified, but the absence of force is sinful. He contends that the unwillingness to forcibly protect the unborn is Satanic, and carries with it the dangers therein.

> The influence of Satan, our sinful nature, and the world's system have combined to blind us to the defensive duties of the Moral Law. Sin has a searing and stupefying effect on the heart that blinds it to the offense in question. One of the punishments for tolerating mass murder is the inability to recognize the duty to resist this lethal force with force. Our only hope is that the Spirit of God will quicken the word of God to our consciences and awake us to the magnitude of our neglect.[26]

In both cases, while neither minister is ordering action, each is suggesting that a deficiency (whether of character, manliness, or spirituality) is what prevents the use of force to stop abortion. In so doing, the standard of spiritual and masculine excellence becomes one who uses force. And one who rejects the use of force is nullified either as a wimp or someone who does not love God.

The consequence of this, according to Hill, is condemnation from God. He says "Any movement that is based on ignoring the duty to love and defend your neighbor, as millions are being slaughtered, is fatally flawed and cannot hope to enjoy God's blessing."[27]

In this way, Bray and Hill have created (or as they would argue, returned to) a different standard of right and wrong, in which the man (or woman) who does not prevent abortion in any way possible must justify himself, rather than he (or she) who does. Bray refers to this shifting of terms in an article he wrote in response to a book on abortion by journalist Judy Thomas.[28] He says

> Thomas slanders anti-abortionists by intentionally associating them with racists and labeling them "terrorists." She advances the propaganda of pro-aborts who charge anti-abortionists with criminal "conspiracy" and "leaderless resistance" and what terrorist experts call a "lone wolf strategy" by which anti-abortionists encourage one another by their praise rather than condemnation of those who terminate abortionists. Indeed, Hern and his comrades are annoyed by the fact that the "pro-choice" rhetoric can be turned around! (Hoisted on their own petard, alas!) The fact is that many good citizens, on the issue of terminating abortionists are not advocates, but simply *pro-choice*

on the subject. They have to believe that the decision to abort an abortionist is a *good* thing because such action saves *real* lives—a truth that they cannot deny unless they deny what is patently true: that which is produced in the womb of humans through human reproduction is another human being—worthy of life and worthy of protection.[29]

The influence of this shift on the rest of the Army of God is evident in their own rhetoric. Jonathan O'Toole, a recognized proponent of the use of force, posted a letter written to the man who, in 2009, killed abortion provider George Tiller:

> Dear Scott,
>   You have acted in righteousness and mercy. Who among those who believe the Truth can deny the obvious good use you made by the Lord of Hosts as you sought to deliver the innocents from the knife of a baby murderer. . . . The congregation of Reformation Lutheran Church which Tiller was serving as an usher at the time of his termination was properly indicted by your actions. Tiller's blood is on their heads for tolerating his murders and refusing to correct him (Rev 2:20) Such a "church" is not a church, but a Synagogue of Satan (Rev. 3:9).[30]

Bray echoed these sentiments in the letter he wrote following Tiller's death:

> Of all the places where the blood of Tiller ought to be shed, it was most appropriate that it spill in full view of his "brothers" and "sisters" who allowed him to continue in his sin-filled, blind life. May his death serve as a wake-up call so that others may repent and mend their ways. May God spare the nation the judgment it so richly deserves.[31]

Another member makes a similar argument in an article titled "A Biblical and Common Sense Refute to Gregg Cunningham's "Killing George Tiller": "There are NO Christian babykillers (Revelations 21:8). If abortion is murder, then Tiller is a murderer, [and] his so-called 'church' consists of collaborators, and accomplices to murder. Tiller was ushering them and himself into hell."[32]

Donald Spitz, the webmaster of the organization, uses similar reasoning in a letter he wrote to the pastors of Reformation Lutheran Church, the place where Scott Roeder shot George Tiller:

> Dear Pastors:
>   Why would you allow a babykilling abortionist like George Tiller to serve as an usher in your church without informing him his eternal soul was at stake for the sins he was committing?
>   As ministers of the Lord Jesus Christ, you have failed in your responsibility towards the position He has placed in you and have brought damnation onto yourselves.

I urge you to repent of your sins and accept the responsibility to be holy and preach holiness.

1Peter 1:16 Because it is written, Be ye holy; for I am holy.

Hebrews 12:14 Follow peace with all men, and holiness, without which no man can see the Lord:

Sincerely in the hope you repent of your sins,

Reverend Donald Spitz[33]

Finally, Shelley Shannon, who is currently serving time in prison for shooting George Tiller (the same George Tiller shot and killed by Scott Roeder years later), said of her attempt to maim him by shooting him in both arms, "I am not denying I shot Tiller. But I deny that it was wrong. It was the most holy, most righteous thing I've ever done. I have no regrets."[34] Shannon has also argued that preserving the child in the womb is akin to preserving belief in God, because children are made in God's image. She says, "From the perspective of the child in the womb, and as a fundamental matter of ethics, there could be no denying the justifiability of the use of force. To condemn it would be to deny the humanity of the child. This defensive action truth was essential to maintaining the doctrine of imago Dei—the very "image of God" inherent in the child in the womb."[35]

Bray expands on this principle in an essay he titles "The Restoration of Fatherhood." In it, Bray expounds on the idea that the real sin, in the fight against abortion, is not the use of force, but its absence:

Temperance of justice may be afforded the offender by the injured party in the case of civil wrongs: e.g. one may forgive a personal debt and thus extend godly grace. But the case of first degree murder is another matter. There is to be no mercy shown. No Judge has the right to reduce the sentence to prison time or flogging or fine. Because human beings are created in the image of God, those who murder them must forfeit their lives. (Genesis 9:6)[36]

Holman echoes the concept of the duty-bound protector of justice. "As a missionary, a representative and an advocate for the pre-born, it is my duty to speak up for them as they have no voice, but it is not my duty alone. We all have a duty to love our neighbors as ourselves. The pre-born child is our neighbor in need. Would we refuse the use of force to save our life? Why deny it to the preborn? We who say that abortion is murder should act like it is murder."[37]

In an interview from prison following his killing of George Tiller, Scott Roeder demonstrates that he shares this line of thinking. He notes that someone quoted him after the shooting as having said "My God forgive me," but he insists he did not. In fact he says, "Obviously I did not do anything wrong, so I do not have to ask for forgiveness." Roeder goes on to say "The attacker, the perpetrator, loses their rights when they're trying to take life."[38] He describes abortion methods in great detail to highlight the contrast between his defense act and George Tiller's "blood thirsty" nature.

Attorney Michael Hirsh extends the blame even further. "In many respects, the pro-abortion contingent had more to do with his death than the pro-life community ever could have. . . . To my counterparts in the pro-abortion camp, I say, you did this, you brought this on, if David Gunn's blood is on anyone's hands, it is on yours. . . . Michael Griffin called your bet and raised you one. But this paper won't convince you of much of anything; except, perhaps that there might be a price for you to pay later on."[39]

It is clear that a fundamental shift has taken place that distinguishes the Army of God from other antiabortion groups, and certainly from pro-choice organizations. The Army of God does not justify the use of force—rather they demand opponents of force justify its absence. Paul Hill calls for this on the basis of the Moral Law, and Bray does so based on his interpretation of biblical and historical precedent. According to this reasoning, force is not a sinful act justified by necessity. Rather the absence of a forceful act is a sin condemned by God.

Answering the common objection that Christians are obligated to obey their governments[40] Bray argues "the people of God are never enjoined to unconditional submission. When tyrants ruled, God sent deliverers to the people. The Scriptures are full of examples of righteous disobedience and revolution."[41] Bray points out that Gideon was not recognized to have civil authority until after he had overthrown the Midianite government (Judges 6:35), Samson was denied legitimacy by the Israelites themselves for his opposition to the Philistines ruling over them (Judges 15:11). Bray concludes "If Scripture justifies revolution, how much more does it justify the defense of an innocent individual? If the assassination of a godless tyrant can be justified, how much more the forceful rescue of an innocent child from his assailant?"[42]

The verses from Romans 13 are the source of another distinction that Bray and Hill both make to distinguish between retributive and preventive force. They argue that killing abortion providers is not intended to be a substitute for capital punishment, as this would be usurping authority that rests with God or those to whom he delegates it (as cautioned against in Romans 13). They do not consider soldiers in the Army of God to be the hand of God's vengeance, but rather the defensive hand of protection over unborn children.

And though there are at least one or two Army of God affiliates that advocate revolution,[43] Bray's argument is deliberately positing revolution as a far more extreme option than that which the Army has chosen for themselves. Bray identifies what he sees as an irony in the fact that Christians can celebrate revolutions, but be appalled by the idea of killing an abortion provider: "We wonder at the Christian who reacts with horror at the use of force to save a child, and yet heartily waves the flag on the Fourth of July in celebration of revolution against a long-standing Christian government. Where is the theological beef?"[44] He goes on to say that revolution may be justified, but must be considered very carefully. The implicit argument being made then is that while revolution (which he considers to be far more justifiable in present times given circumstances surrounding the separation of church and state and the use of American tax dollars to provide abortions) must be very carefully weighed and is not definitively right, violent efforts to end abortion are obviously justified. Shortly thereafter, Bray shifts to suggest that his reasons for not advocating revolution have less to do with the moral quandary surrounding its justice and more to do with the "testosteronally challenged" Christians in America. "American Christians are too morally apathetic to carry out such an enterprise at this time. And the theological infancy of the 'Bible believing' community is such that it has no vision for administration of government by the Almighty's standards."[45]

A LEGAL DEFENSE

While all members of the Army of God situate themselves firmly in the biblical context of their ideology, there have also been efforts made to translate this into formal legal defenses of the actions of their members. When Michael Griffin killed abortion provider David Gunn in 1993, a Regent University law and public policy student fulfilled his thesis requirement by applying Florida statues and cases to defend Griffin's action as "defense of an innocent third party."[46] After graduation, Hirsh wrote an article for the Regent University Law Review on the same subject. The article was withdrawn before publication.

Hirsh's thesis is dedicated to Michael Bray, whom he calls a "Defender of the Unborn, Soldier of the Cross, Hero of the Faith."[47] The strategy that Hirsh proposes in the thesis is not entirely new—the necessity defense was successfully used in the 1970s and 1980s in Virginia and St. Louis by other antiabortion organizations. In these cases, however, the defendants were not on trial for murder but rather for illegal protest. Even so, courts allowed expert medical testimonies in these cases in which doctors argued that life began at conception, thereby allowing the attorneys to argue that protest to protect that life was necessary and legal. Over time, fewer courts have been willing to entertain the necessity defense.

Hirsh's thesis is written as an opposition brief to the State's motion in limine.[48] Hirsh based his justification on the Florida law that states, "The use of deadly force is justifiable when a person is resisting any attempt to murder such person or to commit any felony upon him or in any dwelling house in which the person shall be."[49] He contends that the State's motion in limine prevents the presentation of the danger to the unborn and Griffin's desire to protect them. As a result, Hirsh says that "the State's motion seeks to preclude this evidence and interfere with a just verdict."[50]

In his thesis, Hirsh argues that "when the claim is self-defense, the duty to retreat is applied to the accused. For the defense of another, the duty to retreat analysis is applied to the one being protected, not the intervener. Preborn children 'dwell' in their mother's womb. Though Michael Griffin could have fled for his own safety, the children he protected could not flee and had their backs to the wall—the uterine wall."[51]

Hirsh argues that "A person . . . is justified in the use of deadly force only if he reasonably believes that such force is necessary to prevent imminent death or great bodily harm to himself or to another."[52] He applies this to the case of Michael Griffin in three points: First the accused must reasonably believe that the use of force is necessary—"Evidence of Gunn's reputation for violence and Michael Griffin's knowledge of that reputation is one factor indicating that Michael Griffin acted reasonably."[53] Hirsh argues that Gunn's reputation as an abortion provider was well known, and Griffin's belief that abortion was murder made Griffin's belief that Gunn was a murderer reasonable. Thus the importance of the second part of the statue becomes apparent. If Griffin's analysis was reasonable, then the extent of force became (according to Hirsh) the main issue. Michael Griffin had monitored the antiabortion scene for years and had seen that picketing, blockades, and the like were not effective in stopping Gunn from practicing his occupation. Further, because Griffin shot Gunn as Gunn was heading to his place of work, harm to the unborn was imminent. Thus, according to Hirsh's thesis, Griffin's actions were justified according to Florida law.

The crux of Hirsh's argument lies with his contention that when Griffin killed Gunn, he was acting in (justified) defense of another human being. Hirsh quotes numerous examples of the principle that "a defendant who acts in justifiable defense of himself or of a third person when he commits homicide is not guilty of murder"[54] and then provides numerous examples of cases in which a fetus had been treated by the courts as a person with rights (individuals can be charged with wrongful death when a child dies as a result of an action committed against the mother; states have recognized unborn children as equal to born children in determining welfare aid for the mother; one woman was permitted to ride in the carpool lane because she and her fetus met the two-person minimum requirement).[55] By this reasoning, the fetus is a person incapable of defending him/herself and therefore, the law allows for his/her defense by another if harm is imminent.

Hirsh went on to apply his thesis to the case of Paul Hill after Hill killed John Britton. The defense was rejected by the judge, and Hill refused to offer any alternative defense, ultimately resulting in his conviction and eventual execution by the State of Florida in 2003.

A PERSONAL JUSTIFICATION

Whereas thus far this chapter has focused on the biblical and legal justifications for the use of force to put an end to abortion, the pages that follow will focus on an equally important, though harder to define element of the justification used by the Army of God. Perhaps owing to the emphasis placed on being "called" to the use of violence, several Army of God members recount a deeply personal decision-making process that led to their actions.

Among these accounts, those of John Brockhoeft and Shelley Shannon stand out. Brockhoeft detailed his passage in a series of letters written from prison, self-named "The Brockhoeft Report." According to Brockhoeft, these letters were distributed to about 200 individuals over the course of many years. Beneath the heading of "The Brockhoeft Report" is a descriptive quote written by Joe Bartlett: "The journal for narrow-minded, intolerant absolute abortionists—just like you and me. And if anybody else doesn't like it, that's tough."

The Brockhoeft Report is written in a unique and distinctly folksy style, clearly designed to reach a different demographic than Bray's *A Time to Kill* (Paul Hill had not yet written *Mix My Blood* when these letters came out.) Brockhoeft says that he designed his letters to "provoke an emotional response"[56] The Brockhoeft Report does, however, match some of the sarcastic irreverence that characterizes Bray's work. In the first paragraph of the first report, Brockhoeft apologizes for sending a chain letter, but explains that writing letters to 200 correspondents would be very time consuming. He says "It's hard for me to write short letters, because I'm a little eccentric, a sort of complicated man and I have to explain things. This is especially true in writing to folks who don't know me very well. I'm a convicted abortion chamber bomber. See what I mean? You can't just write a letter and say "I'm a 42 year old divorced bomber and father of five. You have to explain yourself."[57]

And Brockhoeft certainly explains a great deal in the hundreds of pages that follow. Brockhoeft recounts his foray into antiabortion politics following his return from service in Vietnam in 1973. He recalls returning from the war and being shocked by the decision rendered in *Roe v. Wade*. He describes his return as the return from one combat zone into the entrance of another wherein "the U.S. Supreme Court declared war on pre-born American babies."[58] He says, "The truth was so staggering and horrifying my mind refused to accept it at first. When I heard the news in 1973, I tried to deny that it was really happening. I thought to myself, 'There must be something about this I don't understand. They can't mean they are going to allow babies to be killed! Not in this great country!'[59] He recalls being "ashamed before God" for what he saw as the great sin of America and says he sincerely believed that very quickly Americans would repent of their momentary evil and overturn *Roe v. Wade*. He explains his failure to launch a war against the concept right then as part of this belief that Americans wouldn't stand for this injustice for long. He says "If you had taken me aside in 1973 and told me in a hushed tone, 'This is so terrible! We should bomb those places,' I promise I would have recognized your sense of justice immediately and replied, 'You're right! Let's do it! Let's start planning now!' I wouldn't have said, 'Let me think about it.'"[60]

It is important to realize that in the Army of God, the heroes are those that use violence to stop abortion. Brockhoeft later is bashful about telling the story of what he did because he worries that his correspondents will think he is boasting. So his statement is, in effect, a statement of his own worth and bravery, which he says has never wavered in regards to the fight.

Brockhoeft ties his actions in the war against abortion closely to his actions as a soldier in Vietnam. He describes his experience in Vietnam as one for which he gladly volunteered. "My orders to Vietnam didn't just suddenly materialize unexpectedly. I volunteered to go because I saw the South Vietnamese people were being threatened with a communist takeover and I figured if they were willing to fight for freedom, they deserved to be free and deserved help." He goes on to point out "in January of '73, I had just returned from voluntary participation in a bombing campaign . . . in support of the liberty of a people 8000 miles away. So I hope you will believe I would not have turned my back on my own people, American babies, if you had asked for my help in bombing an abortuary in this country, even in '73 and especially since it was not 'mere' liberty but their very lives at stake. I would have gone with you."[61]

Brockhoeft says that he didn't act then because he believed an organized action would have been more effective. He said he was sick with the size of the problem and the knowledge that on his own, he could not save the "1.6 million who were being killed each year."

He says that his focus on 1.6 million babies prevented him from loving a single baby as himself (as the Scriptures called him to do). But one morning, he read an editorial against abortion written by Pat Buchanan, and for Brockhoeft, everything "became crystal clear."[62] Brockhoeft tells of how the figurative scales fell from his eyes—referencing the conversion of Paul in the New Testament book of Acts. (Prior to this moment, the apostle Paul, then named Saul, had been a zealous Pharisee committed to ferreting out Christians and destroying the burgeoning Christian faith. On the road to Damascus, Saul was suddenly confronted by a light and "heard a voice saying to him 'Saul, Saul, why are you persecuting me?'" (Acts 9:4). Saul learned the voice was Jesus and was demanding that he stop persecuting the early church. Saul was blinded during the encounter, a condition that lasted three days, at the end of which scales fell from his eyes and he could once again see. Saul became Paul—one of the most influential figures in Christian history.) The reference to Paul's scales is indicative of the significance Brockhoeft attaches to this moment. Prior to his conversion on the Damascus road, Paul was notorious for his complicity in the murder of Christians. After his conversion, he became a hero of the faith. Brockhoeft's allusion demonstrates a similar reasoning that is present in the works of

Hill and Bray as well. Though they worded it differently, all three men share an understanding that abortion providers are not the only guilty parties. Bray, Hill, and Brockhoeft extend the guilt to anyone who does not stop them, whether they are Christians or not.

Brockhoeft says that it was then he realized that each of the 1.6 million babies were individuals waiting to die. Whereas he had previously viewed them collectively, he now realized that each fetus was a human being. Brockhoeft quotes "the villain Joseph Stalin" as saying "the loss of one life is a tragedy. The loss of a million lives is a statistic."[63] Brockhoeft said that he realized God's command to love thy neighbor demanded he love the unborn babies as much as he loved himself.

He says that one moment it hit him that he did not have to save them all, but could save one and have it mean everything:

> If I saved even one life . . . for that one baby it would mean everything! It would mean all the world! By the time that baby reached 20 years of age, from his or her perspective what I had done would not be little, but big! All the Christmas mornings and all the gifts given and received—they'd all be saved! A total of 210 candles on 20 birthday cakes—they'd all be saved! All the base hits batted out on the little league baseball diamond, all the home runs batted over the fence on the high school diamond, they'd all be saved! Save one baby and you save the world.[64]

He goes on to say:

> In an instant, I saw that this baby, this specific individual, is that neighbor whom I am commanded to love as myself. I had to do unto this helpless baby as I would want others to do unto me if I were helpless and facing death by mutilation . . . tomorrow![65]

Brockhoeft says that he was afraid to begin bombing clinics, but that he countered his fear by putting himself in the minds of the babies he believed he was saving.

> My arms will be torn away from my torso tomorrow! My skull will be crushed until fragments cave inward and cut into my brain! I imagined how terrible the physical pain would be! I thought of my right arm being dismembered and as I thought of it, I bore in mind that my arm would not be taken off cleanly with a sharp surgical instrument while under anesthesia. No, it would be brutally torn out of the shoulder socket and twisted off. It would hurt so bad! But I did not just think of the terrible physical pain. I imagined the mental horror and terror of looking at my right shoulder, and my right arm is gone! And blood gushing out where it had been. So the dread of merely dying in less than 24 hours was only a small part of the fear. It was the torture, agony and terror through which I would be put to death! If I, like the baby, was going to suffer so much and then die tomorrow morning, and I knew I

was being killed unjustly, I would not be afraid to go to the death chamber with gasoline and destroy it tonight. I would be more afraid of not doing it than of going ahead and doing it. So I reasoned that if I loved the baby as myself, I should be too afraid of not doing it. I forced myself to feel these things. I saw it as my Christian duty to feel them.[66]

Brockhoeft later explains that he eventually was even more horrified to realize that all he had been imagining only fulfilled the second of the greatest commandments (Love thy neighbor as thy self). He realized that God watched these babies being aborted and thus felt immense unknowable grief every day. Brockhoeft began then imagining that grief and anguish of God in order to fulfill the first commandment (Love the Lord your God with all your heart and with all your strength and with all your mind. Matt 22:22–35). He explains that from that point on, he "had to share His anguish and be motivated by a desire to keep some of it from Him."[67]

This context led Brockhoeft to conclude that "there is no wrong way to save that child's life. If you save his or her life, that's all I care about; I don't care how you did it. I take my hat off to you. I heartily applaud the fine work of all my friends engaged in these other tactics. They work!"[68]

The Brockhoeft letters were initially edited and distributed by Shelley Shannon (whom John Brockhoeft admires and extols in his letters). Eventually, when Shannon was convicted for maiming George Tiller, she could no longer fulfill this function. In turn, Jayne and Michael Bray wrote Shelley Shannon's biography in 2009, after Scott Roeder killed George Tiller. Shannon also wrote several of her own accounts of her actions and intentions in the years she spent in prison.

In one account, which Shannon titles "Join the Army: How to Destroy a Killing Center if You're Just an Old Grandma Who Can't Even Get a Fire Started in Her Fireplace," Shannon explains how she came to decide to use violence. She says "The biggest hurdle was being willing to even consider that God could indeed require this work of anyone. Christians don't do that kind of thing, do they? But prayer and God cleared that up. Then I realized I needed to stop the killing too."[69]

Shannon says she was filled with ideas—some her own and some from "people who had accomplished Big Rescue." Though Shannon does not say so directly, some of these ideas came from the Army of God manual—a large volume with detailed descriptions of various forms of vandalism, arson, and killing. The manual is acknowledged by all Army of God members, but none admit to authoring it. A copy of it was found buried in Shannon's backyard after she was arrested.

Shannon began corresponding with others rumored to be involved in the use of force. She read Michael Bray's book and had conversations with John Brockhoeft, Curt Beseda, Marjorie Reed, and Don Anderson.[70] According to Bray's account, Shannon made the decision to use force after praying about what Jesus would do about abortion. The Brays quote her as saying,

> What came to my mind was His using the whip in the temple, turning over tables. . . . Every argument raised against the use of force falls before Scripture. . . . It was right, not wrong to use force to save the lives of pre-born babies. In fact, burning down an abortion mill actually saved a lot more lives than did blocking doors.[71]

At this point, Shannon was prepared to use force but was waiting for the opportune time. She said she prayed that God would make very clear when He wanted her to act—and saw His direction when she found herself in need of a five-gallon gas tank and then had one appear in her garage.[72]

Shannon used the gas tank to start a fire at an Ashland clinic and then began a spree of destruction across the state. Shannon kept notes of her thoughts during this period, and when Michael Griffin shot David Gunn, Shannon wrote "He didn't shoot Mother Teresa, he shot a mass murderer such as Saddam Hussein or Hitler. I don't even think it is accurately termed 'murder.'. . . I'm not convinced that God didn't require it of Michael to do this. It is possible. I'm praying God will push more of us 'off the deep end.'"[73] Shannon, shortly thereafter, was apparently pushed herself, as she shot George Tiller and was convicted of attempted murder.

A PRAGMATIC DEFENSE

In contrast to the biblical, legal, and personal arguments in favor of the use of force stands a more pragmatic defense. As with the other three, the pragmatic arguments do not usually occur entirely on their own, but rather in conjunction with one or more of the others. Nonetheless, it is interesting to hear and read the coolly calculated decision-making processes reflected in this line of reasoning, particularly in light of the heated arguments that characterize the other three sides of the discussion.

For example, in an article she wrote to Shelley Shannon, Marjorie Reed (convicted of arson) offered a cost-benefit analysis of the current political climate. She says "If you are going to get a year for just blocking the doors, you might as well do much more drastic measures. . . . It is going to get a whole lot worse. Blood will be shed, not just the babies blood either."[74]

Dan Holman puts it even more succinctly: "Scientists agree: Dead doctors don't murder babies." He goes on to say, "For the sake of argument, let's entertain the thought that Tiller planned to repent on Tuesday; he still intended to kill one child on Monday. For the sake of Monday's child, Mr. Scott Roeder was justified in shooting Roeder at his church on Sunday."[75]

Scott Roeder's own comments reflect a similar weighing of costs. "I was asked how I felt after Tiller was shot. I said relieved. . . . I was relieved that the babies were here in Wichita, no longer dying."[76]

In *The Shelley Shannon Story*, Jayne and Michael Bray articulate Shannon's considerations before she acted:

The practical advantages of the use of force were summarized in five points:

1. It combines protest with successful rescue.
2. It is the most effective method of accomplishing the urgent goal of saving children threatened with imminent death.
3. Forceful and certain rescue expresses the very highest regard for the safety of the child/victim.
4. From the perspective of the threatened child, the most effective and certain means of rescue is best.
5. The covert use of force is particularly advantageous as it permits the shortage in numbers of rescuers to exert a greater number of missions.[77]

In many ways, the pragmatic justification of force rests on the assumption that at least one of the other three forms of justification is also valid. Underlying each of Shannon's five points is a clear reference to a sense of urgency that could not exist if rescue were not a moral duty to begin with. So the pragmatic justification is first dependent on either a biblical or personal decision to place the protection of the unborn before all else. Once this decision is in place, the cost-benefit analysis conducted by Shannon and others begins to make more sense.

Eric Rudolph places his pragmatic decision in its political context:

There are those who would say to me that the system in Washington works. They say that the pro-life forces are making progress, that eventually Roe v. Wade will be overturned, that the culture of life will ultimately win over the majority of Americans and that the horror of abortion will be outlawed. Yet, in the meantime thousands die every day. They say that the mechanism through which this will be achieved is the Republican Party, and under the benevolent leadership of men like George W. Bush the wholesale slaughter of children will be a thing of the past. But with every day that passes, another pile of corpses is added to the pyre. George W. will appoint the necessary justices to the Supreme Court and Roe will be finished, they say. All of this will be achieved through the lawful, legitimate democratic process. And every year a million and a half more die. I ask these peaceful, Christian, law-abiding Pro-Life citizens, is there any point at which all of the legal remedies will not suffice and you would fight to end the massacre of these children? How many decades have to pass, how many millions have to die? Is there any point when the cries of the children will not go unanswered? I think that your inaction after three decades of slaughter is a sufficient answer to all of these questions.[78]

Many Army of God members draw analogies between their actions and those of the heroes of World War II who resisted the Nazis' efforts to exterminate the Jews. The analogy incorporates the biblical, legal, personal, and pragmatic elements into a single example. Hirsh makes this point in his thesis:

> Of course, it is easy to say, on this side of Nuremberg, what "we" would have done, or what another would, could or should have done in the face of tyranny. Looking at these examples of injustice, we can see their lawlessness; we just cannot see our own. A private individual is justified in the use of force against one of these government agents who was attempting to perpetrate some "authorized" harm. How much more compelling that the intervener's actions are if he prevented harms at the hands of another individual (one not in that special relationship). This is the case of Michael Griffin.[79]

Hirsh goes on to condemn those who are not brave enough to stand up for Griffin. "What if someone sought to warn of Nazi terror, or transport slaves to freedom, or attempt to kill Hitler? Knowing what we now know, we would not prosecute but commend. We can see the integrity of their conduct; we just won't acknowledge Michael Griffin's."[80]

The analogy between the Army of God and underground resistance movements during the Holocaust has gained much traction within the Army of God. In the 1990s, members of the group met yearly for the White Rose banquet—where they honored those among them who were suffering for their acts to end abortion. In Germany, the White Rose was an organization created by brother and sister Hans and Sophie Scholl in order to challenge Nazi power. Hirsh quotes,

> Nothing is so unworthy of a civilized nation as allowing itself to be "governed" without opposition by an irresponsible clique that has yielded to base instinct. It is certain that today every honest German is ashamed of his government. Who among us has any conception of the dimensions of shame that will befall us and our children when one day the veil has fallen from our eyes and the most horrible of crimes—crimes that infinitely outdistance every human measure—reach the light of day. If the German people are already so corrupted and spiritually crushed that they do not raise a hand . . . [and] have gone so far . . . toward turning into a spiritless and cowardly mass—then, yes, they deserve their downfall. . . . Do not forget that every people deserves the regime it is willing to endure.[81]

What can be learned about the Army of God from the ideas that define its existence? Three lessons are perhaps most important for the purposes of this book. First, the Army of God does not simply justify their use of force. Rather, and significantly, they defend their *responsibility* to use it. Hill, Bray, Shannon, Rudolph, Brockhoeft, and the others do what they do because they believe that *not* doing so will lead to their condemnation by

God. Second, because they believe that the judgment of God is superior to the judgment of man, a traditional hierarchical structure is not necessary to sustain the willingness to use force. There is no human greater than God— and therefore no human can challenge their responsibility toward the use of force. This leads to the third lesson, which is the inherent challenge this idea poses. Because members of the Army of God believe they have a responsibility to use force, prevention of its use demands an indirect condemnation of the belief. It is this sticky relationship that makes the Army of God so difficult to prosecute as anything other than individuals engaged in unpredictable acts of violence. Indeed, without understanding the ideas that link them, one is hard-pressed to identify any organization at all.

This chapter has provided a loose framework for understanding the categories of justification that link the individuals within the Army. But, as was explained in the introduction to this book, the Army of God is a very individualized organization. Consequently, a full understanding of the organization is dependent on careful consideration of the individuals who compose it and who give feet to the ideas that bind them. It is with this in mind that the next chapter will introduce the individuals that make up the Army of God.

NOTES

1. Said, Edward. 1980. "Islam through Western Eyes." *The Nation,* April 26. www.thenation.com/article/islam-through-western-eyes.

2. Girard, Rene. 1977. *Violence and the Sacred.* London: Johns Hopkins University Press; Schwartz, Regina M. 1997. *The Curse of Cain: The Violent Legacy of Monotheism.* Chicago: University of Chicago Press; Juergensmeyer, Mark. 2000. *Terror in the Mind of God: The Global Rise of Religious Violence.* Berkeley: University of California Press.

3. Tamney, Joseph and Stephen Johnson. 1988. "Explaining Support for the Moral Majority." *Sociological Forum* 3, no. 2: 234–255; Norris, Pippa and Ronald Inglehart. 2004. *Sacred and Secular: Religion and Politics Worldwide.* Cambridge: Cambridge University Press.

4. Phone interview with Donald Spitz, 2010.

5. Bray, Michael. 1994. *A Time to Kill.* Portland, OR: Advocates for Life Publications, 12.

6. Hill, Paul. 2003. *Mix My Blood with the Blood of the Unborn,* 2. http://www.armyofgod.com/PHillBookForward.html.

7. Hill, Paul. 2003. *Mix My Blood with the Blood of the Unborn.* http://www.armyofgod.com/PHillBookForward.html.

8. "Dan Holman." 2010. http://www.armyofgod.com/DanHolmanIndex.html.

9. "Dan Holman." 2010. http://www.armyofgod.com/DanHolmanIndex.html.

10. Bray, Michael. 1994. *A Time to Kill.* Portland, OR: Advocates for Life Publications, 175.

11. Hill, Paul. 2003. *Mix My Blood with the Blood of the Unborn.* http://www.armyofgod.com/PHillBookForward.html.

12. Hill, Paul. 2003. *Mix My Blood with the Blood of the Unborn.* http://www.armyofgod.com/PHillBookForward.html.

13. Phone interview with Donald Spitz, 2010.

14. Bray, Michael. 1994. *A Time to Kill*. Portland, OR: Advocates for Life Publications, 41.

15. Bray, Michael. 1994. *A Time to Kill*. Portland, OR: Advocates for Life Publications, 42.

16. Bray, Michael. 1994. *A Time to Kill*. Portland, OR: Advocates for Life Publications, 42.

17. Bray, Michael. 1994. *A Time to Kill*. Portland, OR: Advocates for Life Publications.

18. Bray, Michael. 1994. *A Time to Kill*. Portland, OR: Advocates for Life Publications, 44–46.

19. Bray, Michael. 1994. *A Time to Kill*. Portland, OR: Advocates for Life Publications, 155.

20. Bray, Michael. 1994. *A Time to Kill*. Portland, OR: Advocates for Life Publications, 155.

21. Phone interview with Donald Spitz, 2010; Levin, Marc and Daphne Pinkerson. 2000. *Soldiers in the Army of God*. 70 minutes. HBO; Interview with Dave Leach, 2006.

22. Bray, Michael. 1994. *A Time to Kill*. Portland, OR: Advocates for Life Publications. 156

23. Bray, Michael. 1994. *A Time to Kill*. Portland, OR: Advocates for Life Publications.

24. Hill, Paul. 2003. *Mix My Blood with the Blood of the Unborn*. http://www.armyof god.com/PHillBookForward.html.

25. Hill, Paul. 2003. *Mix My Blood with the Blood of the Unborn*. http://www. armyofgod.com/PHillBookForward.html.

26. Hill, Paul. 2003. *Mix My Blood with the Blood of the Unborn*. http://www.armyof god.com/PHillBookForward.html.

27. Hill, Paul. 2003. *Mix My Blood with the Blood of the Unborn*. http://www. armyofgod.com/PHillBookForward.html.

28. Bray, Michael. "Thoughts on Tiller, Justifiable Homicide and Persisting Abortionists." http://www.armyofgod.com/MikeBrayThoughtsOnTillerJustifiableHomicide. htm; also see Risen, James and Judy Thomas. 1998. *Wrath of Angels: The American Abortion War*. New York: Basic Books.

29. Bray, Michael. "Thoughts on Tiller, Justifiable Homicide and Persisting Abortionists." http://www.armyofgod.com/MikeBrayThoughtsOnTillerJustifiableHomicide. htm.

30. "Dan Holman." 2010. http://www.armyofgod.com/DanHolmanIndex.html.

31. Bray, Michael. "Who Will You Blame?" http://www.armyofgod.com/MikeBray WhoWillYouBlame.html.

32. "Dan Holman." 2010. http://www.armyofgod.com/DanHolmanIndex.html.

33. Michelson, Lowell and Kristin Neitzel. 2009. Letter from Don Spitz to Reformation Lutheran Church, Wichita, Kansas. www.armyofgod.com/GeorgeTillerBabykiller LetterToChurch.html.

34. Bray, Michael and Jayne Bray. 2009. *Tiller's Unheeded Warning: The Shelley Shannon Story*. http://www.armyofgod.com/POCShelleyShannonBookMikeBray.html.

35. Bray, Michael and Jayne Bray. 2009. *Tiller's Unheeded Warning: The Shelley Shannon Story*. http://www.armyofgod.com/POCShelleyShannonBookMikeBray.html.

36. Bray, Michael. "The Restoration of Fatherhood (Or Some Fresh Ideas for Promise Keepers)." *Army of God*. http://www.armyofgod.com/MikeBrayFathersRights.html.

37. "Dan Holman." 2010. http://www.armyofgod.com/DanHolmanIndex.html.

38. Leach, Dave. 2010. Interview with Scott Roeder. February 5. YouTube. http://www.youtube.com/watch?v=JkIw_fqmC1k.

39. Hirsh, Michael. 1993. "Use of Force in Defense of Another: An Argument for Michael Griffin." Master's thesis, Regent University, Virginia Beach, VA 5.

40. Romans 13 of the New Testament exhorts "Let every soul be subject o the governing authorities. For there is no authority except from God, and the authorities that exist are appointed by God. Therefore whoever resists the authority resists the ordinance of God, and those who resist will bring judgment on themselves."

41. Bray, Michael. 1994. *A Time to Kill*. Portland: Advocates for Life Publications, 158.

42. Bray, Michael. 1994. *A Time to Kill*. Portland: Advocates for Life Publications, 160.

43. See Neal Horsley's Christian Gallery News Source. http://www.christiangallery.com/.

44. Bray, Michael. 1994. *A Time to Kill*. Portland, OR: Advocates for Life Publications, 169.

45. Bray, Michael. 1994. *A Time to Kill*. Portland, OR: Advocates for Life Publications, 171.

46. Hirsh, Michael. 1993. "Use of Force in Defense of Another: An Argument for Michael Griffin." Master's thesis, Regent University, Virginia Beach, VA. vii.

47. Hirsh, Michael. 1993. "Use of Force in Defense of Another: An Argument for Michael Griffin." Master's thesis, Regent University, Virginia Beach, VA. iv.

48. Hirsh defines this term to be "Latin for 'we're going to give you a fair trial and after that a first class hanging.'" Law.com defines it as "n. Latin for 'threshold,' a motion made at the start of a trial requesting that the judge rule that certain evidence may not be introduced in trial. This is most common in criminal trials where evidence is subject to constitutional limitations, such as statements made without the Miranda warnings (reading the suspect his/her rights)." In the case of Michael Griffin, the court ruled that abortion should not be a focus of the trial.

49. Florida Stat. Ann. Sec.782.02 (West 1993), quoted in Hirsh, Michael. 1993. "Use of Force in Defense of Another: An Argument for Michael Griffin." Master's thesis, Regent University, Virginia Beach, VA. 28.

50. Hirsh, Michael. 1993. "Use of Force in Defense of Another: An Argument for Michael Griffin." Master's thesis, Regent University, Virginia Beach, VA. 29.

51. Hirsh, Michael. 1993. "Use of Force in Defense of Another: An Argument for Michael Griffin." Master's thesis, Regent University, Virginia Beach, VA. 29.

52. Florida.Stat.Ann. SEC 776.012 (West 1993).

53. Hirsh, Michael. 1993. "Use of Force in Defense of Another: An Argument for Michael Griffin." Master's thesis, Regent University, Virginia Beach, VA. 30.

54. Hirsh, Michael. 1993. "Use of Force in Defense of Another: An Argument for Michael Griffin." Master's thesis, Regent University, Virginia Beach, VA. 44.

55. Examples are provided by Hirsh on pages 42–44, including *California Welfare Rights Organization v. Brian, 520 p 2d CAL. 1974; Matter of Smith 492 N.Y.S. 2d 331, 334 (Fam. Ct. 1985)*; Adam Z. Horvath. "Carpool—That's an Order." *Newsday*, August 23, 1992, 7.

56. Brockhoeft, John. 1994. "The Brockhoeft Report." *Prayer & Action News* 1: 4.

57. Brockhoeft, John. 1994. "The Brockhoeft Report." *Prayer & Action News* 1: 1.

58. Brockhoeft, John. 1994. "The Brockhoeft Report." *Prayer & Action News* 1: 3.

59. Brockhoeft, John. 1994. "The Brockhoeft Report." *Prayer & Action News* 1: 3.

60. Brockhoeft, John. 1994. "The Brockhoeft Report." *Prayer & Action News* 1.

61. Brockhoeft, John. 1994. "The Brockhoeft Report." *Prayer & Action News* 1: 3.

62. Brockhoeft, John. 1994. "The Brockhoeft Report." *Prayer & Action News* 1: 3.

63. Brockhoeft, John. 1994. "The Brockhoeft Report." *Prayer & Action News* 1: 3.

64. Brockhoeft, John. 1994. "The Brockhoeft Report." *Prayer & Action News* 1: 3.

65. Brockhoeft, John. 1994. "The Brockhoeft Report." *Prayer & Action News* 1.

66. Brockhoeft, John. 1994. "The Brockhoeft Report." *Prayer & Action News* 1.

67. Brockhoeft, John. 1994. "The Brockhoeft Report." *Prayer & Action News* 1.

68. Brockhoeft, John. 1994. "The Brockhoeft Report." *Prayer & Action News* 1: 5.

69. Shannon, Shelley. 2007. "Join the Army (Or How to Destroy a Killing Center if You're Just an Old Grandma Who Can't Even Get the Fire Started in her Fireplace)." http://www.armyofgod.com/ShelleyJoinAOG.html.

70. Bray, Michael and Jayne Bray. 2009. *Tiller's Unheeded Warning: The Shelley Shannon Story*, 14. http://www.armyofgod.com/POCShelleyShannonBookMikeBray.html.

71. Risen, James and Judy Thomas. 1998. *Wrath of Angels: The American Abortion War*. New York: Basic Books, 67, quoted in Bray, Michael and Jayne Bray. 2009. *Tiller's Unheeded Warning: The Shelley Shannon Story*. http://www.armyofgod.com/POCShelleyShannonBookMikeBray.html.

72. Bower, Anne. 1996. "Soldier in the Army of God." *Albion Monitor*, February 19. http://www.albionmonitor.com/abortion/abortionsoldier.html.

73. Bower, Anne. 1996. Soldier in the Army of God. *Albion Monitor*, February 19. http://www.albionmonitor.com/abortion/abortionsoldier.html.

74. Bower, Anne. 1996. Soldier in the Army of God. *Albion Monitor*, February 19. http://www.albionmonitor.com/abortion/abortionsoldier.html.

75. Holman, Dan. "Monday's Child." http://www.armyofgod.com/DanHolmanMondaysChild.html (accessed August, 2010.

76. Interview with Scott Roeder. 2010. YouTube.

77. Bray, Michael and Jayne Bray. 2009. *Tiller's Unheeded Warning: The Shelley Shannon Story*. http://www.armyofgod.com/POCShelleyShannonBookMikeBray.html.

78. Statement of Eric Robert Rudolph. http://www.armyofgod.com/EricRudolphStatement.html.

79. Hirsh, Michael. 1993. "Use of Force in Defense of Another: An Argument for Michael Griffin." Master's thesis, Regent University, Virginia Beach, VA, 97.

80. Hirsh, Michael. 1993. "Use of Force in Defense of Another: An Argument for Michael Griffin." Master's thesis, Regent University, Virginia Beach, VA,

81. Schultz, Arthur R., as quoted in Hirsh, Michael. 1993. "Use of Force in Defense of Another: An Argument for Michael Griffin." Master's thesis, Regent University, Virginia Beach, VA, 98.

4

———❧———

Gods and Generals

Some of the best works on terrorism in the last decade have successfully identified plausible "terrorist profiles" using the data available from contentious network mapping and primary material.[1] Based on the relatively small size of the Army of God and the prolific nature of its members, one could logically conclude then that such a profile would be easy to create for this particular organization. In fact, the contrary is true. The Army of God is an amorphous and incredibly loose network of individuals committed to ending abortion in the United States, but this is where conclusive similarities end. Some members are practicing ministers,[2] others have long histories of involvement in protest politics,[3] some are mothers,[4] and one has run for governor.[5] They hail from all over the United States (and one Hero of the Faith listed on the website lives in Australia), participate in a variety of Christian denominations, and have different levels of education, family background, and political involvement.

Accordingly, this chapter will be laid out as follows: It will begin with an overview of how the Army of God is structured (or perhaps more accurately, *not* structured). It will then continue to offer an overview of the backgrounds of some of the key members of the organization. And it will show the loose connections that exist among the different players in light of the ideology explained in the previous chapter.

The Army of God manual states that the organization is a real army, with God as its general, and the practical implications of this statement are evident in the absence of regular interactions among the members. However, while they may not command their troops or sit atop a hierarchy, the Army of God has several members that prolifically articulate the ideology and methods of the organization. It is perhaps because of the nonhierarchal structure of the organization that the group is as prolific as it is. Each member believes him/herself to answer directly to God, and then frequently conveys the process, method, and outcome of their actions to the wider group.

In *A Time to Kill*, Bray devotes a chapter to redressing the fact that "precious few voices have been raised in proclamation of the truth relative to forceful rescue of the innocent."[6] Though Bray admits he could not list all the "heroes" in one chapter, he does list dozens, some of whom he appears to know, and others he's merely heard of. Most of these individuals also make appearances in the pages of the Army of God website, but others would likely be surprised to be lauded by Bray at all. In addition to the expected "heroes," including Marjorie Reed, Curt Beseda, John Brockhoeft, Don Benny Anderson, and Matthew Moore, Bray also applauds several policemen who refused to prevent protestors from blocking the doors to abortion clinics. He highlights Mayor Larry Bennett for refusing to renew the tax license of a St. Louis abortion clinic, in addition to several judges, journalists, and others. Of these individuals, Bray says, "By the grace of God there remain many good Christian soldiers 'at large' out there. If you suspect them in your neighborhood, don't lock your doors or hide your daughters. These, of course, are not thieves or rapists. They are kind to women and children, rescuing the innocent from death."[7]

The Army of God website designates certain Heroes of the Faith, referring to those who are committed to violent opposition to abortion. The list designates 16 individuals as heroes of the movement, and each name serves as a link to further information about the individual. The Army of God webmaster, Reverend Donald Spitz, explains that the heroes are friends, acquaintances, and "people he's heard to do great things for the babies," and that he puts them on his list based on the recommendation of friends and fellow activists.[8]

The website also provides two different lists of Prisoners of Christ. The first list includes the names of many of the regular contributors to the website, while the second list is preceded by a warning not present on the first list: "Below is a list of prisoners that are supportive of stopping the murder of unborn babies or are in prison/jail for other Christian activities. Be advised, we are not vouching for anyone on this list." The second list is much shorter than the first and includes a brief description of the events leading to the prisoner's incarceration.

Also available on the website are two different "Defensive Action Statements." The two statements were put out after the killings of abortion provider David Gunn (shot by Michael Griffin) and John Britton (shot by Paul Hill). The wording of the documents is similar, with both carefully wording their support of the actions undertaken as conditional upon the truth of the accusations against Griffin and Hill:

Defensive Action Statement I

We, the undersigned, declare the justice of taking all godly action necessary to defend innocent human life including the use of force. We proclaim that whatever force is legitimate to defend the life of a born child is legitimate to defend the life of an unborn child. We assert that if Michael Griffin did in fact kill David Gunn, his use of lethal force was justifiable provided it was carried out for the purpose of defending the lives of unborn children. Therefore, he ought to be acquitted of the charges against him.

Defensive Action Statement II

We the undersigned, declare the justice of taking all godly action necessary, including the use of force, to defend innocent human life (born and unborn). We proclaim that whatever force is legitimate to defend the life of a born child is legitimate to defend the life of an unborn child. We declare and affirm that if in fact Paul Hill did kill or wound abortionist John Britton, and accomplices James Barrett and Mrs. Barrett, his actions are morally justified if they were necessary for the purpose of defending innocent human life. Under these conditions, Paul Hill should be acquitted of all charges against him.

Both action statements were signed by more than two dozen supporters, and several signed both lists. Most signers are affiliated in some way with antiabortion protest activities, with many of them listed as being the director or president of antiabortion activities in their areas. There are a few overlaps, and a small number of individuals from the same city or town, but this is the exception rather than the norm. Even the fact that many of them list themselves as the leader of the antiabortion organization named demonstrates that the Army of God is composed of individuals following their own paths, rather than members of a secret hierarchy following the directions of a human leader.

A third similar document was signed after James Kopp shot abortion provider Barnett Slepian, though the wording was a bit different. This third version was titled "A Declaration of Support for the Defenders of Unborn Children" and stated the following:

We the signers of this declaration, proclaim that we support and stand for righteousness in the defense of the unborn. We WILL NOT turn away and cower in fear of our godless oppressive government and judicial system. We WILL NOT bow to the political correctness of the day, and side with those who slaughter unborn children. We WILL NOT condemn our own brethren. We WILL stand with our brother Jim Kopp. We WILL support him for his love of unborn children. We WILL love unborn children as God loves them—even to sacrifice ourselves. This we affirm before the LORD our Creator, before America, and before those who have made the ultimate sacrifice in defending unborn children—so help us God.[9]

Individuals are invited to send an e-mail expressing their interest in having their name added to the list but are first warned, "if you contemplate ever taking action against babykilling abortionists or their houses of murder, e.g. abortion mills; DO NOT SIGN THIS NOR MAKE YOURSELF OR YOUR PLANS KNOWN IN ANY MANNER WHATSOEVER TO ANYONE AT ANY TIME." The third document was signed by 56 people.

This author asked Donald Spitz, who runs the Army of God website, why there was not a fourth Defensive Action Statement listed extolling Scott Roeder's killing of George Tiller. Spitz explained that he thought fellow antiabortionist Dave Leach had been working on one, but that it was far more wordy and confusing than the previous three, and Spitz had elected not to include it. However, after the interviewer asked whether its absence was indicative of a lesser degree of support for Roeder's act than was present for Griffin's and Hill's, Spitz said he would probably try to find a statement supporting Roeder for publication on his site.[10]

While it would be impossible, and not particularly productive, to convey in this volume the personality, ideology, and actions of every member, supporter, or affiliate of the Army of God, it is useful to highlight some of the most notorious, prolific, and active. Such accounts should not be read as indicative of a particular "type" most likely to participate in or offer support to the Army of God. This book has argued from the beginning that the Army of God is as much a group of individuals as it is an organization. While there are commonalities among members, the differences are more extensive. The individuals highlighted in the pages to follow should be considered as snapshots of individuals linked by a set of ideas, rather than as a prototype for future recruits.

As has been said repeatedly, the members of the Army of God are distinctly diverse, and Bob Lokey demonstrates this more conclusively than any other member. Though Bob Lokey is featured prominently in the most well-known resource available on the Army of God, an HBO documentary,[11] Lokey is unique, even within the Army. The discomfort other Army members feel around Lokey is palatable in the documentary, and Lokey himself appears to prefer to work alone. In an interview with this author, Lokey describes himself as a baby "compared to the other forces" working to end abortion. But baby or not, Lokey sees himself as a powerful force in the antiabortion movement. He told this author that "the more learned will tell you the best way to get your point across is to point and say 'look.' Very soon, I can stand on the midst of rubble and point." When the author asked whether he was speaking literally or figuratively, he emphatically claimed the former. He describes himself as fairly reclusive now, "just waiting for the end." He says, "the effects of what I've done are so far reaching; no one has the ability to grasp it. I just have to sit and watch it work itself out."[12]

Lokey has little or no formal religious training—in fact when he entered prison (convicted of first-degree murder), he had a sixth-grade education. While in prison, court records show that Lokey completed high school, and two years of college. Lokey also attained an associate's degree in art and a

Name	Location	Anti Abortion Heroes of the Faith	Prisoners of Christ (List 1)	Prisoners of Christ (List II)	Defensive Action Statement I	Defensive Action Statement II	A Declaration of Support for the Defenders of Unborn Children	Convictions
Paul Hill	Florida (executed by the state, 2003)	X	X		X			July 29, 1994; first-degree murders (2), FL: Death penalty, lethal injection
Shelley Shannon	Minnesota (prison)	X	X			X		April 11, June 6, August 1, Aug. 18 (2), Sept. 16, Nov. 28 1992; May and Aug. 19 1993; arson (6)*, acid (2), attempted murder: 31 years
James Kopp	Pennsylvania (prison)	X	X					October, 1998, second degree murder, NY: Life in prison
Clay Waagner	Pennsylvania (prison)	X	X					Oct.-Nov. 2001, anthrax hoax: 19 years
Stephen Jordi	Iowa (prison)	X	X					Nov. 2004; attempted firebombing: 5 years plus 5 years probation
Dennis Malvasi		X						Dec. 1985, bombing, attempted bombing, and threatening phone call: 7 years; March 2001, aiding and abetting James Kopp: 29 months
Michael Bray		X			X	X	X	Nov-Dec. 1984, clinic bombings (7): 4 years (with plea bargain)
John Brockhoeft		X			X		X	December 1985, clinic arson: 7 years
John Salvi III	Deceased	X		X				December 1994, first degree murder (2), armed assault with intent to murder (5), MA: Life in prison
Scott Roeder	Kansas (prison)	X	X					May, 2009, first degree murder and 2 counts of aggravated assault, KS: 50 years
Eric Rudolph	Colorado (prison)	X	X					July 1996, Jan. and Feb. 1997, and Jan. 1998, 21 counts, including possession of weapons of mass destruction, detonation, 2 homicides, and injury to over 100 people: Life in prison
Robert F. Weiler Jr.	Virginia (prison)		X					June 2006, possession of pipe bomb, felon with a firearm, attempt to bomb: 5 years
Michael Griffin	Florida (prison)		X					March 1993, first degree murder: Life in prison
David Robert McMenemy	Ohio (prison)		X					September 2006, arson attempt, MI: 5 years + mental health treatment
Peter James Knight	Australia (prison)		X					July 2001, murder, Australia: Life in prison
Paul Ross Evans	Kentucky (prison)		X					April 2007, attempt to use WMD, TX: 40 years
Vincent Whitaker	Kentucky (federal medical center)		X					February 1995, mail threatening communications, threatening the President of the US, WI: 63 months
Linda Gibbons	Ohio (prison)		X					May 2009, disobeying court order to remain outside clinic bubble zone: $500 bail (she refuses)
John Burt	Florida (prison)			X				5 counts of molestation (18 years in prison)
Kent Hovind	South Carolina (prison)			X				Nov. 2003, tax fraud (58 counts), FL: 10 years
William D. Owens-Holst	Iowa (prison)			X				September, 2006, 3rd degree burglary, assault, IA: 5 years probation + $1000 + fine
Joshua Graff	Maryland						X	November 1993, arson, Texas: 3 years imprisonment
Jennifer McCoy	Kansas							1996, conspiracy arson (2), Virginia: 2.5 yrs

Chart 1. Convictions and Connections

certificate in office machine technology, and completed a two-year course in "creative dynamics."[13] Lokey himself claims he also "became a real heavy-duty jailhouse lawyer," and he claims that briefs he wrote were adopted into California law.[14]

However, Lokey also claims to have "taken over the California penal system temporarily" using hypnosis and the power of his mind and in so doing managed to get the state to rewrite the entire penal code, thereby expunging the section that made him guilty. In so doing, Lokey explains, he was able to get himself released from a life sentence. He calls himself an "at large felon" and seems giddy about his freedom (he lives in Alabama) and the fact that "no one can do a damned thing about it."[15]

Lokey became a Christian while in prison. He describes his dramatic conversion as an encounter with a "very powerful force," whom he identified as "God Almighty." He says his Bible was suddenly lit up and animated and when Lokey opened it, he was astonished to find he understood every word inside it perfectly, precisely as God had intended it to be interpreted. He said reading the Bible convinced him that Christianity has "long gone into the wilderness," and this caused him to realize he would have to emerge as a leader with no real hope of fellowship.

Lokey also describes being literally reborn while serving in San Quentin. He describes a moment when he was speaking with his supervisor, when he suddenly could barely breathe. He said he quickly realized he was coming out of the womb and resigned himself to the experience. He says "I couldn't breathe, but I heard a slapping three times and my bottom started burning real bad. I felt myself jerked up by my heels." Shortly after this experience, Lokey learned of the Court's ruling in *Roe v. Wade.* Lokey says he felt the world had gone insane. "The world is butchering babies. . . . Babies need to be protected and I'm not a murderer for that."

Lokey emotionally recounts an experience he says he had on January 22, 1973 (the same day the court case was decided). He says that a voice in the sky called him to paint about what was going on. Lokey did and says that his painting has transformed countless lives. He says that "convicts, cops, and guards look at it and cry. . . . I've had women attack me just for showing it to people."

Lokey has continued to use his interest in visual imagery to impress upon people the seriousness of abortion. Down the road from his small home in Alabama, he proudly sponsors a giant billboard with an aborted fetus on it. While Lokey longs for those involved in the abortion industry to see the error of their ways, he does not think highly of their prospects for salvation, even should they choose to change their path. He conclusively states that "salvation is not available to the woman who commits abortion. I have that directly from the God All Mighty."[16]

When asked by this author to describe the purpose of government, Lokey responded, "The purpose of government is to serve the welfare of the people it governs. When that purpose is perverted, you get what you've got right here." He went on to say that "America is slated for the same horror as Iraq because of the butchered babies."

Lokey views the work of the Army of God as purely righteous and defensive action. Lokey is a vegetarian, because he says he cannot bring himself to hurt animals just so he can eat. He says that the only way he could ever hurt anyone is in self-defense—and killing abortion providers fits perfectly under that category. (After a pause, he also points out that if "someone came to strangle my dog, I'll probably kill them.")

Lokey sees himself as exceptional—both compared to other members of the Army of God and the rest of the world as a whole. He describes himself as able to understand things that are too "complex for the normal human brain" perhaps owing to the "tiny bit" of clairvoyance he perceives himself to have.[17]

STEPHEN JORDI

Where Lokey relies on his unique ability to perfectly interpret God and act accordingly as his reference for behavior and conduct, other members of the Army adopt a more rigorously Scripture-dependent approach. While corresponding from prison with this author, Stephen Jordi wrote an 11-page single-spaced biblical concordance in which he provided the author with more than 1,100 hand-written Scripture references he considered relevant to the antiabortion cause. Each meticulously inscribed column is headed by a title describing the Scripture topics below it. These titles range from "Abortion" to "Neglect of Duty" to "Judging One's Enemy" to "Capital Punishment," and numerous others.

In response to this author's interest in his involvement in the antiabortion movement, Jordi explained that he laboriously pours over Scripture and faithfully studies apologetics in order to "cross examine false religions and prove them wrong to lead them to a saving faith in the only true faith—Christianity, so they can avoid burning in Hell for all eternity. (John 3:16)"[18] He also describes his "recent academic questions into the nature of war and the use of force to defend others (Psalms 82:3–4)." He bitterly describes his arrest as the result of "the exact question that my two brothers and pastor's turned me in for to the horribly corrupt Big Brother thought-police was, and I quote, 'Is it legitimate, though not necessarily legal, to use justifiable force to defend an innocent person in imminent danger?'"

Jordi is referring to his brother Michael's involvement in his arrest in 2003. Michael Jordi, a resident of Bridgeport, Alabama, called the FBI when he became concerned about Jordi's expressed interest in destroying an abortion clinic. Michael Jordi told reporters he believed his brother was mentally unstable.[19] Jordi's brother-in-law describes him as "'overzealous about the Lord' but not a violent person."[20] The call that Michael Jordi made to the FBI resulted in Jordi's arrest for "solicitation to commit a crime of violence; distribution of information relating to making and using explosives and arson; and possession of an unregistered firearm or destructive device."[21]

Stephen Jordi is one of eight children born to Catholic parents in Ham Lake, Minnesota. Jordi describes his home life as "very violent," calls his dad a "practical Atheist God-Hater," and depicts his mother as a "blind Catholic but Biblically illiterate." He says that his mother is pro-life, but "disagrees with actively doing anything to stop [abortion] outside of lip service."[22] In high school, Jordi became a Satanist in order to conclusively reject his Catholic upbringing, with which he associated the abuse he says he suffered at his parents' hands.

Jordi describes becoming a Christian under the tutelage of Dr. Peter S. Ruckman at the Pensacola Bible Institute (Jordi is careful to note that Dr. Ruckman has not responded to Jordi's efforts to contact him while in prison). Jordi says he served as an usher and groundskeeper for Calvary Baptist Church (now called First Baptist) in Hillsboro, Florida, prior to his arrest. He accuses the then-pastor of Calvary Baptist Church of reporting him to the authorities prior to his arrest. He describes his pastor as "pro-life, just not as pro-life as me, apparently." He notes that "none of the members of the congregation approved of my Biblically provable point."

In his letters, Jordi admonishes this author for asking about his use of "violence" to stop abortion. He says, "I do wish to correct your error of terminology with your phrasing. . . . I do not advocate violence! Understand, John the Baptist says in Luke 3:14 'Do violence to no man.' This was addressed to soldiers. He didn't say 'Quit.' Violence is defined as *un*necessary force. This is a common and unwholesome mistake. Murder, unjust killing, is violence. Capital punishment, killing the murderer, is not violence. It is justice. I advocate justice. An Abortionist, against his Hippocratic oath, publicly admits and advertises he murders, tortures kids. Death by dissection while alive or poisoning and burning or impaling the brain through the [illegible script] at the base of the skull are the usual methods. No Anesthetic. They've admitted the child screams, struggles, brain waves skyrocket, heart races and hormones explode. Yes, again, torture. So, I advocate prevention and justice. (Genesis 9:5–6)"[23]

Jordi then goes off on a tangent about Muslims (and Allah the "moon God"), Janet Reno ("non-American paid by foreign IMF agents"), and homosexuality. He returns to the discussion of ending abortion by noting that "I just don't like people who murder babies." He says that he became actively pro-life after watching an interview with "extreme pro-lifers" on television. When asked about the nature of his method, he explains "When I'm not trying to witness to save souls, I show them both sides of the issue. Judgment versus forgiveness etc. I show them all the facts and let them decide. . . . A non-biased approach is the most accurate I believe."

Jordi denies any interaction with other members of the Army of God. He describes hearing their Biblical argument (on the television program) and feeling obligated to either prove or disprove it. He describes the "Army of God-type Christian pro-life fundamentalists" as a "paranoid bunch." But then, accompanied by a smiley face, he reminds the author that "just because you're paranoid doesn't mean they're not after you." He says that most antiabortionists are "antithetical towards answering questions from someone who might be a fed posing as a friend."

And Jordi would certainly know about that after running into trouble in the previous two towns he had lived in with his wife and children (Jordi was issued a trespassing warning at a church in Escambia County after he challenged the pastor's spirituality during a sermon by tossing him a live rattlesnake).[24] In Pensacola, Jordi was arrested and charged with felony child abuse, though the charges were later dropped. Jordi moved to Broward County and joined Calvary Baptist Church, where he met Stewart Welch, a self-avowed antiabortionist. Jordi and Welch found themselves to have much in common on many major issues, including the role of the church, abortion, and homosexuality. According to a court transcript, Jordi confided to Welch that he "didn't have the means to kill abortion doctors, but [he did] have the means to bomb clinics."[25]

Jordi allegedly told Welch that he was planning to wait two years, and then would begin a bombing spree that would begin in Georgia. Jordi expressed admiration for Paul Hill, Eric Rudolph, and Clay Waagner, three well-known "soldiers" in the Army of God. Jordi was present outside the prison when Hill was executed and while there told a reporter that "Conviction warrants action. Paul Hill was given that conviction, but not everyone was." Jordi claimed not to have been given the same conviction by God.[26]

But the killing of Barnett Slepian, a series of anthrax-infused letters sent to federal offices, and other acts of arson, all claimed by associates of the Army of God, led to a heightened need for security. So, when Jordi's brother alerted the FBI to his concerns, Stewart Welch was assigned to bring him in.[27] After Hill's execution, Jordi became more vocal in his questions about the right of the use of force. His pastor at Calvary alerted the Coconut Creek police department but expressed his belief that Jordi would not actually act on his beliefs.

In fact, Jordi had been working with Stewart for some time to acquire the necessary ingredients to make a bomb to blow up a clinic. Court records show that Jordi bought gas cans, gas, starter fluid, and flares, as well as a handgun and silencer.[28] Jordi, however, denies that he was actually going to use the materials to bomb clinics. He speaks in his letter of planning a two- to six- year sabbatical, during which he was planning to "pray, fast and study." Jordi claims he worked alongside Stewart in an effort to learn more about his options to stop abortion—but without firm plans to actually bomb anything.[29]

Whatever his intentions, on November 11, 2003, Jordi was arrested by federal agents and charged with three felonies. After Jordi pleaded guilty to attempted arson, assistant U.S. attorney John Schlesinger requested that the judge follow the Antiterrorism and Effective Death Penalty Act to sentence Jordi as a terrorist and increase the mandatory sentence time by 10 years.

MICHAEL GRIFFIN

On March 10, 1993, Michael Griffin walked up behind Dr. David Gunn and shot him three times in the back, at the Pensacola Women's Clinic, while admonishing him to stop killing babies. Shortly thereafter, Griffin turned himself in to authorities. At the time of the killing, Griffin was a 31-year-old chemical plant employee who had recently become involved in antiabortion politics. The week before he shot David Gunn, Griffin asked members of his church to pray for Dr. Gunn. Police had been called to the clinic to handle an antiabortion protest that had been going on during the morning hours. When they arrived, Griffin walked over, confessed to his act, and handed them his revolver.[30]

Griffin had run into Gunn at a nearby gas station the week before the shooting. Griffin said of the encounter,

> I thought it was Providence. . . . I knew he was getting ready to go kill children that day. I asked the Lord what he wanted me to do. And he told me to tell him that he had one more chance." Griffin relayed the message to Gunn, who reportedly did not respond. Griffin then believed he heard from God again saying that that "he was accused and convicted of murder and that his sentence was Genesis 9:6 'Whosoever sheds man's blood, by man his blood shall be shed.'"[31]

Griffin was charged with first-degree murder and was found guilty, though his lawyers tried to argue that he was insane at the time of the shooting. They said that his involvement in the antiabortion movement had interfered with his ability to recognize right from wrong. The defense was not upheld in court, because Griffin would not consent to be evaluated by psychiatrists.[32] In correspondence with the author, Griffin denies that he is "religious" or was inspired by politics to act.[33] This is in keeping with his renouncement of the antiabortion movement in 1995, wherein Griffin claimed he had been framed in the killing by the pro-life movement.[34]

The Army of God website posts a link to an article allegedly written by Michael Griffin, in which he describes the outrage that inspired him to act. He says

> There are 40 million Americans aged conception to 28 years old. There are 40 million more that are silent (except in their mothers' nightmares). Since

January of 1993, (when I first met John B and I saw for the first time, an abortion in a jar) I had tried endlessly to express how outraged I was at this and the thousands like it that happen every day!! On my 40th birthday, my search was over. Finally after so long, I had something to compare it to, but which still will not come close to the scope of abortion's terror. Abortion will not be stopped with a gun; that only saves a few babies. Abortion will only stop when born again believers of Jesus Christ turn from their wicked ways.[35]

Griffin was the first to kill an abortion provider, but his act served as a catalyst for the many that have followed. Convicted arsonist John Brockhoeft has not followed directly in Griffin's footsteps, but he does reference Griffin's "heroic" acts in his prison letters. John Brockhoeft regularly compared Griffin with World War II hero Dietrich Bonhoeffer. He offers the following syllogism to make his case:

The Brockhoeft Report asserts the following:

1. A. Adolph Hitler's victims were human beings, exactly as we are.
   B. Abortionist David Gunn's victims were exactly as human as were Hitler's.
2. A. Dietrich Bonhoeffer's approach was to use lethal force against the killer.
   B. Griffin's approach was exactly the same and for exactly the same reason.
3. Therefore, Mike Griffin is exactly the Dietrich Bonhoeffer figure for our generation.
4. In order for any pro-lifer not to be able to recognize the three previous assertions requires either:
   A. severe mental illness, or
   B. gross stupidity, or
   C. shameful cowardice, or
   D. some combination of these things.

THE BROCKHOEFT REPORT HEREBY OFFERS $1,000 REWARD* to the first person who can find any pro-life activist who has previously and publicly spoken against Griffin's act and who will now make the following public statement: "I believe that: (1) Bonhoeffer's strategy was just, but (2) Griffin's strategy was unjust."

THE BROCKHOEFT REPORT OFFERS A $50,000 REWARD* to the first person who can find a pro-lifer (such as described above) who will now make the following public statement: "I believe that: (1) Bonhoeffer's strategy was just, but (2) Griffin's strategy was unjust, and (3) the reason for this glaring contradiction is neither because I am stupid nor mentally ill. It is because I am too cowardly, even, to tell the truth."

TBR OFFERS A ONE MILLION DOLLAR REWARD* to the first person who can find a pro-lifer (such as described above) who will now make the following public statement: "I believe that: (1) Bonhoeffer's strategy was just, but (2) Griffin's strategy was unjust, and (3) I am neither a coward nor mentally ill."[36]

Perhaps impressed by Brockhoeft's logic, Shelley Shannon helped distribute Brockhoeft's letters to sympathetic readers before she was convicted of attempted murder.

SHELLEY SHANNON

Griffin's act is identified by many Army of God affiliates to have been a tipping point for their own decision to embark on the use of force. Shelley Shannon recounts her own soul searching that Griffin's act inspired, saying she was forced to conclude that it was possible God had required Griffin to do what he did. She also speaks of praying that God would "push more of us off the deep end."[37] In the end, Shannon was herself pushed when she decided that the choice "was simple, living babies or a dead abortionist."[38]

Before shooting abortion provider George Tiller in both arms, Shannon was no stranger to the use of force in the battle against abortion. Shannon first became involved in Operation Rescue in 1988 and was frequently arrested for her protest activities. In 1991, Shannon claims to have "come to a deeper understanding of just what was happening to innocent babies inside the brick and mortar of the death chambers."[39] She decided to initiate contact with other individuals involved in the use of force and found the Army of God's Prisoners of Christ list, in which the names and address of prisoners were readily accessible. One article posted on the Army of God site describes Shannon's next step as engaging "in a holy war of arson and butyric acid rescues across three states.[40]

Shannon describes her subsequent forays into vandalism as "a very powerful religious experience."[41] She says, "I saw God work when I fumbled. I sensed Him so near, even powerfully in me. I accomplished something so important—though I admit, I feel God accomplished it."[42]

The path that led Shannon to violence was different in many ways from Lokey's, Jordi's, and Griffin's. Shannon grew up in a loving home with both parents and grandparents involved in raising her. Shannon's parents divorced when she was 13, though custody was shared and Shannon continued to regularly see both parents.

Shannon became pregnant her junior year in high school, ironically the same year that *Roe v. Wade* came before the Supreme Court. Shannon gave birth to a daughter, Angela Dawn. While she was pregnant with Angela, Shannon's boyfriend of the time encouraged her to abort the child. Though Shannon described herself as an atheist at the time, she recalls being horrified by the thought.[43] According to the biography of Shannon written by Jayne and Michael Bray, the birth of her daughter was a major turning point in Shannon's life. Shannon watched high school friends encounter rough circumstances and viewed her daughter's birth as God's decision to save her from a similar fate.[44]

Shannon was married in 1974 and in 1975 gave birth to a son. She became a Christian a few years later while attending a Nazarene church in Klamath Falls, Oregon. In 1987, Shannon joined a women's Bible study group at a Wesleyan church, and it was here she became interested in the fight against abortion. The Bible study met weekly, with a different woman leading the study each week. Shannon's turn came on the week they were studying abortion, and Shannon identifies a seed being planted in her mind at that time.[45]

The Shannons eventually moved to Grants Pass, Oregon, and Shelley continued to mull over the abortion issue. During this time, she began reading more about the issue and came across a newsletter called *Americans against Abortion*. One article described the famous film *The Silent Scream*, and Shannon became committed to the cause. She was not impressed by some of the more benign efforts undertaken in light of what she saw as a tragedy of magnificent proportions, and so she joined Operation Rescue and began engaging in illegal—but nonviolent—protest efforts.

Shannon's daughter Angela accompanied her on many of her protests. In February 1988, when Angela was only 14, both Shannon and Angela were arrested for blocking the doors of a clinic in Portland, Oregon. According to the Brays' account, Shannon went on to be arrested more than a dozen times over the course of a three-year period. Shannon's arrests took place in states as diverse as California and North Dakota, and her charges are largely related to criminal trespassing.[46]

The Brays suggest that Shannon was plagued with doubts about the effectiveness of her efforts. She was spending significant amounts of time in jail and away from her own children, but not permanently stopping any abortion providers from doing their work. Around this same time, John Brockhoeft was arrested and imprisoned for burning down two abortion clinics, and Shannon began corresponding with him. This led to the publication of the Brockhoeft Report, as Shannon decided to type and distribute the letters Brockhoeft wrote to her. Shannon also read Michael Bray's book *When Bricks Bleed I'll Cry,*" justifying the use of force to stop abortion, and at some point came across a copy of the elusive "Army of God Manual," which not only justified force, but provided "hypothetical" and eminently practical suggestions for how to undertake it. In the biography they wrote on Shannon, the Brays say she corresponded with Curt Beseda (convicted of burning an abortion facility in Washington State), Michael Bray, Majorie Reed, and Don Anderson.[47]

Shannon herself describes her decision to use force as highly personal and a result of her willingness to "pray about the use of force with an open mind."[48] She says that as she did so, she became more and more aware of "the most Godly Christians" she knew justifying[49] the use of force. She recalls:

> I listened to a Skip Robokoff tape where he first prayed that God would speak through him. He talked about the high places mentioned in the Bible, alters of pagans where children were sacrificed to Satan and much innocent blood was shed. He compared it to abortion facilities. He said those high places had to be torn down in the physical realm as well as by prayer in the heavenlies. Anyway, that's what it seemed to me God was saying, and I had been learning on that very topic at that time and was convinced that the spiritual and the physical were tied together.[50]

Shannon became more firmly convinced that force was necessary to the extent that when a pastor hypothetically asked the question, "What would you do if you knew you only had three days left to live?" Shannon says "I instantly thought of burning down killing centers, as many as possible, as fast as I could."[51]

After her arrest for shooting George Tiller, Shannon provided the government with some insight into her decision to act. She posted a description of everything she told them on the Army of God website, so that anyone she may have implicated could be warned. Shannon describes herself as "humiliated to admit what all I told them" in an effort to reduce her prison time. She said that two people had convinced her that God wanted her to shoot abortionists—though neither was identified on the website, nor did Shannon identify who the two people were. She cryptically warns that although she's pretty sure they don't "have any clues to the identity of these people . . . they do know that one of the first two plans to shoot Allred." Shannon goes on to say, "I can only hope that someone else will somehow notify the person who wants to shoot Allred that the Feds know. Not by phone or email though!"[52]

PAUL HILL

Shannon was not the only person to be influenced by the increasing use of force to stop abortion. Three years after Shelley Shannon shot George Tiller in the arms, Paul Hill killed John Britton and James Barrett. Nine years later, Hill was executed by the State of Florida. Before his death, Hill gave numerous interviews explaining his actions and wrote a book that is available unedited on the Army of God website. In it, Hill says, "I didn't know for certain that my allowing them to kill me would result in fewer children being killed, but it seemed probable this would be the result."[53] According to the Army of God's website, Hill's final words before his execution reflected his belief. "If you believe abortion is a lethal force, you should oppose the force and do what you have to do to stop it. May God help you protect the unborn as you would want to be protected."

Hill grew up in a Presbyterian family, and friends describe him as a popular, strong-willed teenager.[54] When Hill was 17, his father turned him in to the police for assault, an act which his father describes as one intended to turn Hill from the destructive path he was on. According to a fellow student, Hill dramatically converted to Christianity, quit taking drugs, and turned his life around at the age of 17. Hill attended Bellhaven College—a Christian school in Jackson, Mississippi—and then Reformed Theological Seminary, where he graduated with a Master of Divinity. He was ordained as a Presbyterian minister.

Hill's college friends describe him as very structured and persistent in his beliefs—whether about theology, nutrition, or government. John Leonard says, "Everybody liked him, but he went to the extreme on everything. He was a body builder and he was extreme about that. When he got into health food, he became a fanatic. No one could ever change his mind about anything. . . . Once we had an argument because I had gone over the speed limit, because if I disobeyed authority, it was unchristian. . . . Paul didn't come up with his opinions casually."[55]

Leonard's reference to Hill's objection to speeding is interesting in light of the climate in which he attended seminary. The Reformed Theological Seminary of Jackson, Mississippi, was involved in a debate that was dividing the Presbyterian Church at the time. The church was struggling to come to a unified position on the relationship between God's law and the government (whether and in what circumstances one should supersede the other). Hill ultimately joined St. Paul's Presbyterian Church, where the issue had been conclusively decided in favor of God's law over man's.

Hill was married in 1978 to Karen Denise Demuth. The two lived in South Carolina for five years, where Hill served in two different churches. He eventually moved to Lake Worth, Florida, to become the pastor of an Orthodox Presbyterian church. After a series of confrontations with members of the church, Hill left the ministry and the family moved to Pensacola. Hill established an auto-detailing business out of the back of his truck, though much of his time was devoted to protesting outside women's clinics.

When, in 1993, Michael Griffin shot David Gunn, Hill found his calling. Hill called the *Phil Donahue* show and expressed his admiration for what Griffin had done. Virtually overnight, Hill was catapulted to the forefront of the antiabortion movement. Hill was invited to be on *Nightline,* CNN's programs, and *Donahue.* On each show, he argued that a consistent biblical view demanded the forceful prevention of abortion. Hill argued that abortion could have been prevented entirely in America, had only Christians responded as the Bible would urge them to do. He said "I realized that using force to stop abortion is the same means that God has used to stop similar atrocities throughout history. In the book of Esther, for instance, Ahasuerus, the king of Persia passed a law allowing the Persians to kill their Jewish neighbors. But the Jews did not passively submit; their use of defensive force prevented a calamity of immense proportions. . . . In much the same way, when abortion was first legalized in our nation, if the people had resisted this atrocity with the means necessary, it may have similarly saved millions of people from an untimely death. Thus it is not unwise or unspiritual to use the means that God has appointed for keeping His commandments; rather it is presumptuous to neglect these means and expect Him to work apart from them."[56]

Hill regularly stood outside the Pensacola Ladies Center and shouted at women in hopes of convincing them to change their minds as they walked to the clinic. Witnesses say he would call out "Mommy, Mommy, please don't kill me!" as women walked by.

Hill's arguments for Griffin's justification stuck with him as the media moved on to new stories. Hill began to contemplate what would happen if he were to shoot an abortion provider. He concluded that "many important things would be accomplished by my shooting another abortionist in Pensacola. This would put the pro-life rhetoric about defending born and unborn children equally into practice. It would bear witness to the full humanity of the unborn as few things could. It would also open people's eyes to the enormous consequences of abortion—not only for the unborn but for the government that sanctions it, and those required to resist it. This would convict millions of their past neglect, and also spur many to future obedience. It would also help people to decide whether to join the battle on the side of those defending abortionists, on the side of those defending the unborn."[57]

Hill struggled with the idea of killing an abortion provider, because he knew doing so would result in imprisonment—and consequently the loss of his family. Hill speaks of his last day with them before he shot John Britton. The family went to the beach, and Hill said "All my parental instincts were stirred as I played with my children. They enjoyed their father's attention. I took them one by one, into the surf with me. As I carried and supported each child in the water, it was as though I was offering them to God as Abraham offered his son."[58]

Hill describes his decision to kill John Britton as an act of obedience. He defends his choice, saying, "If I had not acted when I did, it would have been a direct and unconscionable sin of disobedience. One of the first things I told my wife after the shooting was 'I didn't have any choice!' That cry came from the depths of my soul. I was certain, and I still am, that God called me to obey His revealed will at that particular time."[59]

On the day of the shooting, Hill prayed that Britton's security would not arrive first. He says he would be justified to kill them as well but hoped he would not have to do so. In the end, Hill shot and killed both Dr. Britton and his security escort. Hill did not try to run after the shooting but laid down his gun and raised his hands. As he was led away by police, he announced to the crowd, "One thing's for sure, no innocent people will be killed in that clinic today!"[60]

Whereas Michael Griffin raised the stakes of antiabortion politics, Hill can be credited with setting the standard for those who followed. Where Griffin eventually recanted his stance, Hill almost eagerly sought martyrdom for himself. When the judge in his case refused to allow Hill to present his views on abortion as his defense, Hill fired his defense team and offered no defense at his trial. When he was sentenced to death he refused to appeal the decision. Further, where Griffin, Jordi, and Lokey can be generously described as eccentric and more than slightly erratic, Hill emerges as a cogent, articulate spokesman for a fanatical cause. His book is significantly more coherent than Brockhoeft's, and his arguments are more artfully crafted.

MICHAEL BRAY

Michael Bray, though more confrontational in rhetorical style than Hill, is another member of the Army that puts his education and obvious intelligence to use for the cause. Bray was convicted in 1985 of conspiracy for his alleged involvement in the bombing of several abortion clinics. Bray spent four years in prison and has spent the time since then articulating the beliefs underlying the Army of God's antiabortion position.

In an essay Bray wrote after Scott Roeder shot George Tiller, Bray lambastes those who would call Roeder—or anyone else using force to stop abortion—terrorists. He speaks specifically of the work of journalist Judy Thomas, whom he accuses of advancing "the propaganda of pro-aborts who charge anti-abortionists with criminal 'conspiracy' and 'leaderless resistance' and what terrorist experts call a 'lone wolf strategy' by which anti-abortionists encourage one another by their praise rather than condemnation of those who terminate abortionists. . . . The fact is that many good citizens on the issue of terminating abortionists are not advocates, but simply pro-choice on the subject."[61]

Bray attributes the beginning of his involvement in abortion politics to his position as an assistant pastor at a Lutheran church in Bowie, Maryland. In 1980, Bray says that the president of Bowie Right to Life approached him about the issue, inspiring Bray to conduct his own research on the topic. Bray incorporated his research into a course he was teaching at the church at that time. Through the course, he met a woman who had had four abortions before converting to Christianity. Bray worked with the woman to found the Bowie Crofton Pregnancy Clinic.[62]

At the same time, Bray began picketing outside local abortion clinics. Though he glosses over the details in his own accounts, Bray was convicted shortly thereafter for his alleged involvement in the destruction of abortion clinics in Washington, D.C., Maryland, Virginia, and Delaware.

Bray emphatically denies involvement in any illegal activity since his release in 1989 but equally emphatically defends his right to speak out about the moral and legal justification for the use of force to stop abortion. Though he has not been arrested again, Bray's defense of his right to express his admiration for those who use force has caused him financial and legal difficulties nonetheless. Of the more consequential examples, in 1995, Planned Parenthood of Columbia/Willamette sued Bray and 12 others in addition to the American Coalition of Life Activists (ACLA). In 1995, the American Coalition of Life Activists published a "wanted" poster listing the names and addresses of doctors who perform abortions. The poster accused the doctors listed of crimes against humanity and promised $5,000 to anyone who provided information that led to the "arrest, conviction and revocation of license to practice medicine.[63] The same year, the ACLA unveiled another poster in front of the St. Louis federal courthouse. This one targeted a single doctor, accusing him of murder and crimes against humanity, listed his home and work addresses, and included his picture.[64] Several months later, the ACLA published a series of files on abortion supporters or practitioners, including doctors, judges, and politicians. The organization called them the "Nuremberg Files" and posted them on a website of the same name. "The website marked the names of those already victimized by the anti-abortion terrorists, striking through the names of those who had been murdered and graying out the names of the wounded."[65]

The doctors initiating the lawsuit claimed that the posters and the website threatened harm and violated the Freedom of Access to Clinic Entrances Act. The jury found in the doctors' favor and awarded them $107 million in damages.[66] However, the ACLA appealed the verdict, and the verdict was reversed by the 9th Circuit Court of Appeals in 2001[67] and then reapplied in 2002.[68] The damages were eventually reduced to a little more than $4 million, of which Bray was expected to pay $800,000. The Bray's claimed they had no means of paying this, and Planned Parenthood moved to force collection of the Brays' assets, including their home in Wilmington, Ohio. According to the lawsuit that Bray eventually filed against Planned Parenthood, in October 2007, A U.S. marshal and an agent from the Bureau of Alcohol, Tobacco and Firearms came to the Bray home to seize some of the Brays' asset and to give them notice to vacate the house within 30 days.[69]

The Brays sued Planned Parenthood for what they called "unlawful and conspiratorial conduct under color of law."[70] In the suit, Bray argues that "the violations of the Plaintiffs' rights and the sanctity of their home . . . occurred for one fundamental reason—the fantasies and 'boogie man' mentality of PPCW and the Defendant Marshals regarding Michael Bray, his family, and others who might agree with Mr. Bray's anti-abortion views."[71] Bray argues, in this lawsuit and elsewhere, that he is no threat to society at large and that, in fact, he is a victim of those who would violate his First Amendment rights.

The lawsuit against Planned Parenthood describes Bray's plight as he sees it:

> Mr. Bray maintains a belief system that is well-rooted in Western Civiliza-tion and Anglo-American jurisprudence. Accordingly, he defends as a moral and ethical proposition the use of force to defend innocent human beings, born and unborn. . . . These are not popular views in a modern society that has accepted the killing of unborn children and it is particularly unpopular among abortionists and other persons devoted to keeping the killing of un-born children legal in the United States of America. Indeed, because of Mr. Bray's calm, intellectual, uncompromising and persistent philosophy on this issue, he is perceived as a gravely dangerous man by PPCW and others in the abortion industry who have called Mr. Bray such things as the "father of violence" in the anti-abortion movement. In spite of Mr. Bray's singular crime for which he paid his debt to society with a prison term in the 1980s, Mr. Bray has never advocated or encouraged anyone to kill or physically at-tack abortionists, nor to inflict damage on facilities where abortionists ply their trade.[72]

Of those affiliated with the Army of God, Bray has unquestionably been the most effective at shifting the nature of the debate away from the practical implications of his argument and instead to the theoretical limits of a per-son's right to free speech. In this way, Bray distinguishes himself from many others in the Army. Whereas for Brockhoeft, Shannon, and certainly Hill, among others, jail time or state "persecution" is worn as a badge of honor, for Bray the story is different. The question observers must ask is why?

In several of the interviews conducted in connection to this research, the author was told that the decision to use force was a personal decision quite separate from the judgment of whether force was justified. Individu-als consistently spoke of needing to be "called" to the use of force, regard-less of their position on its righteousness. Bray elaborates on the difference by comparing it to missions work. He notes that while it would always be right for missionaries to go into dangerous areas to share the Gospel, one cannot demand that they do so.[73]

The comparison to missions is important for several reasons. Christian missionaries are most commonly financially dependent on the support giv-en them by the churches that sponsor their work. Christians that are not called to the mission field are encouraged to support missionaries because they fill a required role in the church (to go and make disciples of all na-tions) that nonmissionaries are either unable or not called to do themselves. Bray's comparison is interesting because it implies a similar arrangement in the use of force to stop abortion. Those who use force are hailed as heroes, doing what others either cannot or were not called to do—and presumably must be supported accordingly.

It should be made clear here that in the case of the Army of God, this author has no reason to believe that support is expressed financially. Rather, support takes the form of communal intellectual, spiritual, and emotional resources, shared over the Internet through practical ideas (how to use butyric acid, etc.) and theological justification (what does the Bible say about force).

The Army of God does not formally assign roles, so much as ask interested parties to consider their calling and apply it to the common cause. Bray's calling is clearly different from Hill's, Shannon's, or Brockhoeft's. Bray is highly educated (he has a BA in English from Colorado Christian University and an MA in New Testament Studies from Denver Seminary). He is fluent in several languages, he has traveled widely, and he appears frequently on television to give interviews about his controversial views. Bray acknowledges that he has been labeled the "Father of Violence" in the antiabortion movement, but this title is really more in reference to his contributions toward defending individuals' rights to speak approvingly of its use than of his propensity toward using it himself.

And of course, it is very likely that there is much about the Army of God that is still not known. Shannon's letters make clear that extensive efforts are made to preserve secrecy within and about the organization, and it is possible that Bray performs roles not discussed in this book. (No members of the Army of God claim authorship of the Army of God manual, but the sarcastic style in which it is written is remarkably similar to many of Bray's own essays.)

DONALD SPITZ

But while authorship of the Army of God manual is still a tightly held secret, Donald Spitz has committed his life to ensuring that little else is. Spitz serves as the "webmaster" for the Army of God, and he documents hundreds of pages of correspondence, essays, books, and observations on the site he oversees.

Reverend Spitz was raised as a Catholic but describes himself as having been a rebellious teenager. He says that he didn't follow the Lord, despite his parents' efforts to teach him the Catholic faith. However, he says that as a Catholic he did learn to recognize abortion as the "worst thing a human being could do,"[74] because it violated God's intended relationship between a mother and her child. Spitz described pregnancy as God's personal creation of a child for a mother to protect until it was ready to be part of the world, and he said that abortion was a violent intrusion on this sacred thing.

After high school, Spitz joined the Navy and was stationed near San Francisco. He recounts being in a hotel on Skid Row after he'd been discharged and reading a Gideon's Bible that he found in the room. He says that at that moment, God began to take root in him. He recalls leaving the hotel room to go for a walk and suddenly being confronted by the presence of the Holy Ghost. The Spirit told him to raise his hands, and he did in the middle of the street. From that moment on, Spitz considered himself a born-again Christian.

Shortly thereafter, Spitz was approached by some street evangelists in Marin County and was invited to live with them in a communal Christian house. Spitz immediately agreed—not even returning to his hotel to collect his things. It was in the presence of these other Christians that Spitz identified his calling as a street preacher.

Spitz moved to New York to continue preaching. He got married there and with his wife established a church in Queens, before feeling called to move to Virginia. Spitz believed he was supposed to start a church in Norfolk and was surprised when it didn't work. He now believes that the church didn't take root because God was calling him to the antiabortion cause. Spitz joined forces with Operation Rescue and then over time came to believe that abortion was so serious a crime that something more than peaceful process was necessary to stop it.

When this author asked Spitz why, if he believed force was morally and spiritually justified, he had not himself chosen to use it, Spitz explained that the point is not to kill abortion doctors. Rather, the point is to save babies. Spitz said that only those who have evaluated all the options, heard God's call, and recognize the sacrifice therein must actually use force to stop abortion. The rest are merely called to support them. When the author asked whether those who use force are considered spiritually superior to those who do not, Spitz emphatically denied it. He said that the only guilt that might be present would be by those who were not called—as they had to wrestle with whether they were actually not called, or whether they simply weren't prepared to heed the call. But Spitz describes the users of force as godly, humble people, appreciative for whatever support they are offered.

The author asked Spitz what forms that support might take. He laughed a little and said that he offered financial support only after they had used violence. He went on to say that he couldn't say that he supported them financially before the act, because doing so would land him in prison alongside them.[75] He said he looks at the website as an opportunity to remind prisoners and those fighting abortion in other ways that they are not alone.

Spitz calls Paul Hill his "best friend" and says that he is also in regular weekly contact both by phone and through letters with Scott Roeder. When asked what they talk about he said they share Scripture and pray together.

The next chapter will show that much effort has been expended on the part of law enforcement agencies and members of the pro-life community to establish organizational connections to the individuals highlighted in this chapter. The next chapter will also show the challenges presented in proving those connections. This chapter has attempted to illuminate the root causes of those complications. Members of the Army of God speak of one another with great fondness and admiration. They describe themselves as being very close—even though they seldom meet. But this closeness is the result of a shared and deeply held idea about a single issue, not the result of structured organizational ties defining the parameters of a relationship. As we will see in the pages to come, the difference is as crucial as it is challenging.

NOTES

1. Sageman, Marc. 2008. *Leaderless Jihad: Terror Networks in the Twenty-First Century.* Philadelphia: University of Pennsylvania Press; Juergensmeyer, Mark. 2000. *Terror in the Mind of God: The Global Rise of Religious Violence.* Berkeley: University of California Press; Stern, Jessica. 2003. *Terror in the Name of God: Why Religious Militants Kill.* New York: Harper Collins.

2. For example, Michael Bray, Donald Spitz, and Paul Hill, among others.

3. For example, Scott Roeder.

4. For example, Shelley Shannon.

5. For example, Neal Horsely.

6. Bray, Michael. 1994. *A Time to Kill.* Portland, OR: Advocates for Life Publications, 129.

7. Bray, Michael. 1994. *A Time to Kill.* Portland, OR: Advocates for Life Publications, 136.

8. Phone interview with Donald Spitz, 2010.

9. "Declaration of Support for James Kopp." In *Declaration of Support for the Defenders of Unborn Children.* www.armyofgod.com/JamesKoppDeclaration.html.

10. Phone interview with Donald Spitz, 2010.

11. Levin, Marc and Daphne Pinkerson. 2000. "Soldiers in the Army of God," 70 minutes, HBO.

12. Interview with Bob Lokey, 2007.

13. *Bob Lokey et al., Plaintiffs-appellants, v. H. L. Richardson, Etc., et al., Defendants-Appellees United States Court of Appeals, Ninth Circuit. - 527 F.2d 949 1975. United States Court of Appeals, Ninth Circuit.*

14. Interview with Bob Lokey, 2007.

15. Interview with Bob Lokey, 2007.

16. Interview with Bob Lokey, 2007.

17. Interview with Bob Lokey, 2007.

18. Written Correspondence from Stephen Jordi, 2006.

19. Murphy, Jarrett. 2003. "FBI: Abortion Bomb Plot Thwarted: Suspect Leapt into Biscayne Bay to Avoid Arrest." *CBS News*, November 13. http://www.cbsnews.com/stories/2003/11/13/national/main583390.shtml.

20. Murphy, Jarrett. 2003. "FBI: Abortion Bomb Plot Thwarted: Suspect Leapt into Biscayne Bay to Avoid Arrest." *CBS News*, November 13. http://www.cbsnews.com/stories/2003/11/13/national/main583390.shtml.

21. Murphy, Jarrett. 2003. "FBI: Abortion Bomb Plot Thwarted: Suspect Leapt into Biscayne Bay to Avoid Arrest." *CBS News*, November 13. http://www.cbsnews.com/stories/2003/11/13/national/main583390.shtml.

22. Written correspondence from Stephen Jordi, 2006.

23. Written correspondence from Stephen Jordi, 2006.

24. Aaronson, Trevor. 2004. "Bombs for Babies: Stephen Jordi Planned to Blow Up Abortion Clinics. Does That Make Him a Terrorist?" *Broward-Palm Beach News Times*, July 15. http://www.browardpalmbeach.com/2004-07-15/news/bombs-for-babies/.

25. *United States of America, Plaintiff-appellant, v. Stephen John Jordi, Defendant-appellee. 2005. United States Court of Appeals, Eleventh Circuit 418 F3d. 1212.*

26. Aaronson, Trevor. 2004. "Bombs for Babies Stephen Jordi Planned to Blow Up Abortion Clinics. Does That Make Him a Terrorist?" *Broward-Palm Beach News Times*, July 15. http://www.browardpalmbeach.com/2004-07-15/news/bombs-for-babies/.

27. Written correspondence from Stephen Jordi, 2006.

28. *United States of America, Plaintiff-appellant, v. Stephen John Jordi, Defendant-appellee. 2005. United States Court of Appeals, Eleventh Circuit 418 F3d. 1212.*

29. Aaronson, Trevor. 2004. "Bombs for Babies Stephen Jordi Planned to Blow Up Abortion Clinics. Does That Make Him a Terrorist?" *Broward-Palm Beach News Times*, July 15. http://www.browardpalmbeach.com/2004-07-15/news/bombs-for-babies/.

30. Booth, William. 1993. "Doctor Killed during Abortion Protest," *Washington Post*, March 11, A01.

31. Risen, James and Judy Thomas. 1998. "Pro-Life Turns Deadly: The Impact of Violence on America's Anti-Abortion Movement." *Newsweek*, January 26, 68–69.

32. Kushner, H. 2003. *Encyclopedia of Terrorism.* Thousand Oaks: Sage.

33. Written Correspondence from Michael Griffin, 2007.

34. Kushner, H. 2003. *Encyclopedia of Terrorism.* Thousand Oaks, CA: Sage.

35. Griffin, Michael. "Michael Griffin Statement." *Army of God.* www.armyofgod.com/MichaelGriffin.html.

36. Brockhoeft, John. 1994. "The Brockhoeft Report." *Prayer & Action News* 1: 4.

37. Shannon, Shelley. "Who Is Shelley Shannon." *Army of God.* www.armyofgod.com/ShelleyWhois.html.

38. Shannon, Shelley. "Who Is Shelley Shannon." *Army of God.* www.armyofgod.com/ShelleyWhois.html.

39. Shannon, Shelley. "Who Is Shelley Shannon." *Army of God.* www.armyofgod.com/ShelleyWhois.html.

40. Shannon, Shelley. "Who Is Shelley Shannon." *Army of God.* www.armyofgod.com/ShelleyWhois.html.

41. Shannon, Shelley. 2007. "Join the Army (Or How to Destroy a Killing Center if You're Just an Old Grandma Who Can't Even Get the Fire Started in her Fireplace)." http://www.armyofgod.com/ShelleyJoinAOG.html.

42. Shannon, Shelley. 2007. "Join the Army (Or How to Destroy a Killing Center if You're Just an Old Grandma Who Can't Even Get the Fire Started in her Fireplace)." http://www.armyofgod.com/ShelleyJoinAOG.html.

43. Bray, Michael and Jayne Bray. 2009. *Tiller's Unheeded Warning: The Shelley Shannon Story.* http://www.armyofgod.com/POCShelleyShannonBookMikeBray.html.

44. Bray, Michael and Jayne Bray. 2009. *Tiller's Unheeded Warning: The Shelley Shannon Story,* 6. http://www.armyofgod.com/POCShelleyShannonBookMikeBray.html.

45. Bray, Michael and Jayne Bray. 2009. *Tiller's Unheeded Warning: The Shelley Shannon Story.* http://www.armyofgod.com/POCShelleyShannonBookMikeBray.html.

46. Bray, Michael and Jayne Bray. 2009. *Tiller's Unheeded Warning: The Shelley Shannon Story,* 11. http://www.armyofgod.com/POCShelleyShannonBookMikeBray.html.

47. Bray, Michael and Jayne Bray. 2009. *Tiller's Unheeded Warning: The Shelley Shannon Story.* http://www.armyofgod.com/POCShelleyShannonBookMikeBray.html.

48. Shannon, Shelley. "Toward the Use of Force." *Army of God.* www.armyofgod.com/ShelleyForce.html.

49. In nearly every account written by members of the Army of God, the authors are careful to avoid saying they advocate force, because of the potential for prosecution. For lack of a better term, this author chooses to use the word justify—though it does not fully convey the obligation most members of the Army of God suggest is appropriate.

50. Shannon, Shelley. "Toward the Use of Force." *Army of God.* www.armyofgod.com/ShelleyForce.html.

51. Shannon, Shelley. "Toward the Use of Force." *Army of God.* www.armyofgod.com/ShelleyForce.html.

52. Shannon, Shelley. "Shelley's Warning." http://www.armyofgod.com/Shelley Warning.html.

53. Hill, Paul. 2003. *Mix My Blood with the Blood of the Unborn.* http://www.armyo fgod.com/PHillBookForward.html.

54. Sawyer, Kathy. 1994. "Turning from 'Weapon of the Spirit' to the Shotgun." *Washington Post*, August 7.

55. Sawyer, Kathy. 1994. "Turning from 'Weapon of the Spirit' to the Shotgun." *Washington Post*, August 7. http://www.washingtonpost.com/wp-srv/national/long term/abortviolence/stories/hill.htm.

56. Hill, Paul. 2003. *Mix My Blood with the Blood of the Unborn.* http://www.armyo fgod.com/PHillBookForward.html.

57. Hill, Paul. 2003. *Mix My Blood with the Blood of the Unborn.* http://www.armyo fgod.com/PHillBookForward.html.

58. Hill, Paul. 2003. *Mix My Blood with the Blood of the Unborn.* http://www.armyo fgod.com/PHillBookForward.html.

59. Hill, Paul. 2003. *Mix My Blood with the Blood of the Unborn.* http://www.armyo fgod.com/PHillBookForward.html.

60. Hill, Paul. 2003. *Mix My Blood with the Blood of the Unborn.* http://www.armyo fgod.com/PHillBookForward.html.

61. Bray, Michael. "Thoughts on Tiller, Justifiable Homicide and Persisting Abortionists." http://www.armyofgod.com/MikeBrayThoughtsOnTillerJustifiableHomicide. htm.

62. Honorable Bob Taft. 2006. Request by Ohio Citizens for Protection from Federal Tyranny Threatening Dispossession of Father, Mother, and Eight at-Home Children, Columbus. www.michaelbray.org/ohioletter.htm.

63. "Planned Parenthood of the Columbia Wilamette Inc. American Coalition of Life Activists." 1995. In *Circuit Judge Kozinski.* http://cyber.law.harvard.edu/ilaw/ Cybercrime/planned-parenthood.html.

64. "Planned Parenthood of the Columbia Wilamette Inc. American Coalition of Life Activists." 1995. In *Circuit Judge Kozinski.* http://cyber.law.harvard.edu/ilaw/ Cybercrime/planned-parenthood.html.

65. "Planned Parenthood of the Columbia Wilamette Inc. American Coalition of Life Activists." 1995. In *Circuit Judge Kozinski.* http://cyber.law.harvard.edu/ilaw/ Cybercrime/planned-parenthood.html.

66. "Planned Parenthood of the Columbia Wilamette Inc. American Coalition of Life Activists." 1995. In *Circuit Judge Kozinski.* http://cyber.law.harvard.edu/ilaw/ Cybercrime/planned-parenthood.html.

67. *Planned Parenthood v. ACLA, 244 F.3d 1007.*

68. *Planned Parenthood v. ACLA, 90 F3d 1058.*

69. *Michael and Jayne Bray vs. Planned Parenthood Columbia Willamette, Inc.* Squires, Sanders and Dempsey L.L.P. 2009. In *Judge John W. Rudduck*: Court of Common Pleas Clinton County, OH. http://michaelbray.org/pplawsuit.htm.

70. *Michael and Jayne Bray vs. Planned Parenthood Columbia Willamette, Inc.* Squires, Sanders and Dempsey L.L.P. 2009. In *Judge John W. Rudduck*: Court of Common Pleas Clinton County, OH. http://michaelbray.org/pplawsuit.htm.

71. *Michael and Jayne Bray vs. Planned Parenthood Columbia Willamette, Inc.* Squires, Sanders and Dempsey L.L.P. 2009. In *Judge John W. Rudduck*: Court of Common Pleas Clinton County, OH.4.16. http://michaelbray.org/pplawsuit.htm.

72. *Michael and Jayne Bray vs. Planned Parenthood Columbia Willamette, Inc.* Squires, Sanders and Dempsey L.L.P. 2009. In *Judge John W. Rudduck*: Court of Common Pleas Clinton County, OH. 4.3. http://michaelbray.org/pplawsuit.htm.

73. Bray, Michael. 1994. *A Time to Kill*. Portland, OR: Advocates for Life Publications.

74. Phone interview with Donald Spitz. 2010.

75. Phone interview with Donald Spitz. 2010.

5

———⊸⊶⊷⊶———

Striking Back

The first chapter of this book endeavored to show that the Army of God has not developed in a vacuum. The ideas, tactics, and structure of the organization are instead an outgrowth of the political, social, and religious environment around them. But where the first chapter emphasized the evolution of antiabortion sentiment through the history of the United States, this chapter will highlight the evolution of the response to the Army of God. Because just as the political, social, and religious environment has dramatically shaped the growth and development of the organization, so also has the organization shaped the political, social, and religious environment. This chapter will seek to identify the greatest challenges facing those who seek to quell the violence of the Army of God.

The introduction to this book argued that one of the most intriguing things about the Army of God is its ability to harness ideas and utilize them to inspire action. It is this same characteristic that makes the actions of the Army of God so difficult to stop. The tactics and methods of the Army of God are always part of a broader campaign of ideas that is nearly impossible to prosecute. The prolific nature of the members of the organization has ensured that in order to condemn an act undertaken by the Army of God, one also becomes enmeshed in the condemnation of an idea. By linking ideas so tightly with action, the Army of God has divided those who, in other circumstances, would stand unequivocally against them.

When one examines the law-enforcement response to the Army of God, party lines are clearly evident. The first chapter of this book discussed the process that led to the Republican Party capturing the pro-life demographic, and the 4 percent gain of support achieved as a result. Whether in fear of losing this critical four percent of support, or for the many other reasons that will be discussed in this chapter, Republican presidents have acted less emphatically in response to attacks undertaken by the Army of God than have their Democratic counterparts. But even this statement is not without its pitfalls. The implication of a less emphatic response is a weaker aversion to the organization. But because ideas are so intricately linked with action in the Army of God, this implication is not necessarily accurate. This chapter will show that the absence of a clear definition of terrorism combines with a tightly knit combination of ideas and action undertaken by the Army of God to result in a small organization capable of wreaking havoc on an enormous industry.

DEFINING TERROR

The early days of the Army of God were plagued by disagreements about how to characterize the group. Pro-choice proponents were quick to characterize the violence as terrorism, but Reagan administration officials were not inclined to agree. In 1984, the year with the highest abortion-clinic bombings to date, FBI director William Webster went on television and informed the public, "Bombing a 'bank or a post office is terrorism. Bombing an abortion clinic is not an act of terrorism . . . because the objective is social in anti-abortion violence, and I don't believe it currently meets our definition' of terrorism."[1]

Webster's distinction is important for several reasons. The United States has been enmeshed in an unsuccessful effort to define the term *terrorism* for some time, and Webster's point highlights the importance of this effort. The use of the term and its supposedly less inflammatory alternatives (gunpersons, for example) has been so hotly debated that words have nearly ceased to be useful. In fact, in many cases, use of the word *terrorism* now reveals much more about the person using it than it does about the organization he/she is endeavoring to describe.

Within the United States, the leaders of the exercise formerly known as the War on Terror: the FBI, the Department of Defense, and the State Department, all operate under different definitions. After 14 years of effort, the United Nations achieved a majority vote in 1987, designating all acts of terrorism as criminal acts, but the United States and Israel voted against the measure.[2] Terrorism expert Walter Laquer identified over 100 different definitions of the word and concluded that the only factor present in all definitions was the consistent involvement of violence.[3]

Beyond this very broad classification exists an exhaustive path of potential pitfalls for the would-be user of the term. Should a definition focus on the actor, action, or intent? The interplay between these three elements is evident in the debate that swarms around attempts at definitions and the results. Those definitions concerned with actors emphasize the nonstate orientation of terrorist organizations, thereby implicitly indicating judgments about legality, legitimacy, and the Westphalian designation of the appropriate wielders of force. In this arena, those who make up the Army of God award themselves legitimacy by identifying the government's abrogation of justice in the case of abortion. Those focusing on actions can find themselves accidentally (or intentionally) capturing states (even democracies) within their definitional net. And those that focus on intent find themselves in the moral morass between cause and consequence.

Not one for nuance of method, Osama bin Laden famously distinguished between different types of terrorism, saying "There are two types of terror: good and bad. What we are practicing is good terror."[4] While bin Laden's definition is not helpful in resolving the conflict about what truly defines terrorism, the sentiment that inspired him to say it most certainly is. Bin Laden has a very firm grasp of the normative system that serves as the foundation for his actions, and as part of that system, what constitutes right and wrong. From his understanding of right and wrong, his definition of terrorism is born. That bin Laden believes his brand of terrorism to be the "good" kind does nothing to undercut the devastation that was experienced by the victims of his attacks. And it likely does little to influence their very different perception of good and bad terror and a right or wrong worldview.

And in reality, most members of the Army of God would characterize their actions in the same vein. They have a firmly established system of right and wrong, and by the standards they use, they have acted rightly, justly, and as God called them to do.

The discussion of absolute truth versus relativism is fodder for a different volume. For this one, it is sufficient to recognize that the definition of a concept and the actuality of a concept are two different things. As such, the emphasis of actor, method, or intent in defining terrorism does not reflect terrorism itself so much as a particular person's understanding of it. William Webster understood terrorism to be about the motivations behind the act—not the act itself, and as a result, did not see the Army of God as a terrorist organization.

The Italian ambassador to Iran, Roberto Toscano, has noted that the problem in defining terrorism is not linguistic imprecision, but political motivation. He laments "the brazen inconsistency of all those who apply the definition of terror to actions carried out against them (and their friends) excluding terror that they and their friends carry out against others."[5] Ultimately, the greatest inhibitor to defining terrorism is the inevitable prerequisite to judge it. In order to define terrorism, scholars, politicians, and pundits are forced to identify what part of terrorism distinguishes it from other forms of political resistance. In so doing, they must make value judgments about actors, methods, and intentions. Definitions reflect as much by what they don't say as by what they do, because definitions of terrorism have come to define not an act, but a condemnation of an act. As a consequence, collisions are inevitable.

And the Army of God has been remarkably successful in using these collisions to their advantage. The organization strongly condemns their counterparts in the pro-life movement for their "betrayal" of the true pro-life vision. One page on the Army of God website is designated exclusively to exposing the "hypocrites" in the pro-life movement who condemn the use of force to prevent abortion:

> The pro-lifers prefer George Tiller to still be killing babies, because they think that is pro-life. There is a place in hell for unfaithful cowards who love the praise of man more than the praise of God. The list of those who betrayed the lives of the unborn is endless. . . . These same people want protection for themselves and their families when threatened with death, even if it means lethal force; yet they deny that same protection to the unborn child in the womb.[6]

In this way, the Army of God tightly ties the pro-life idea with the necessity of force. To condemn the latter, one must also condemn the former. Whether intentionally or not, William Webster's remark reinforces this idea. Because Webster offers motivation the preeminent place in defining terrorism, he is implicitly accepting the Army of God's assertion that violence is defined not by its use, but by its motivation.

The consequences of the difference are important and can be clearly seen in the Reagan administration's response to the violence that characterized the antiabortion movement in the early 1980s. Reagan's position on abortion was well known, and his ability to articulate his position with clarity and humor[7] made his understated reaction to the abortion clinic bombings all the more controversial. Reagan's response is described by antiabortion foes as a "thunderous silence,"[8] and at least one member of the Army of God saw a silver lining in that thunderous cloud. In a 1985 interview with the *Washington Post,* Don Benny Anderson said he "agreed with pro-choice groups that bombers were encouraged by Reagan. . . . [They feel] they have a green light from the president. That's the impression I got."[9]

Sociologist Dallas Blanchard looks not only to Reagan's refusal to publicly condemn the acts as terrorism, but also to his continued support for the pro-life position at the time that the attacks were taking place. Blanchard says:

> President Reagan maintained a two-year silence on the violence despite well-publicized requests that he speak out firmly against it. Moreover, he took public stands against abortion in numerous speeches and in his essay published in the spring of 1983. The wide circulation of this essay in the anti-abortion groups was followed by a drastic increase in the rate of anti-abortion-related violence, and the president's speech before anti-abortion

groups were interpreted by the violent radicals as tacit approval, support by silence. Even though bombers and arsonists may have misinterpreted Reagan's intentions and statements, his failure to speak strongly against violence meant nothing was done to counter the message of approval. The end effect of the bombings, moreover, was to legitimize the public anti-abortion movement as representing "moderates" with essentially democratic goals, rather than inflexible minority positions.[10]

Blanchard's argument highlights the complexity of the challenge the Army of God represents. Blanchard credits even Reagan's position against abortion as (implicit or otherwise) a position in favor of the Army of God. This demonstrates how successfully the Army of God was able to tie their tactics in with their ideology—to the extent that even the most learned of their foes could not distinguish the difference. This is very important. Because ideas are linked so closely to the actions of the organization, the ideas themselves begin to be criticized as dangerous.

And this has significant consequences. When ideas and action are considered to be linked, law enforcement officials have to think carefully about how best to stop the acts, without threatening the right to an idea. The Army of God argues that in their case, the distinction has not been made carefully enough. Several of the members have been instructed by their parole boards to stay away from anyone in the pro-life cause. Members complain that this limits their right to attend church and spend time with their families.

But then again, what is the alternative? If motivation is separated from acts of violence, then terrorism is no more than crime, alternatively named. But as we will see in the pages that follow, when ideas are linked to action, the opportunities for prosecution differ. As a result, the response to the Army of God can be categorized as a series of executive, legislative, and judicial efforts to find a balance between limiting dangerous ideas and prohibiting violent action.

THE REAGAN YEARS

The Reagan administration's response to this conundrum was to treat the antiabortion violence as criminal rather than terrorist acts. When, in 1985, Reagan did condemn the acts, his choice of words was very telling:

During the past few months there has been a series of bombings at abortion clinics throughout the country. I condemn, in the strongest terms, those individuals who perpetrate these and all such violent, anarchist activities. As President of the United States, I will do all in my power to assure that the guilty are brought to justice. Therefore, I will request the Attorney General to see that all Federal agencies with jurisdiction pursue the investigation vigorously.[11]

President Reagan referred to the clinic bombings as "anarchist activities," indicating a total absence of structure in their approach. He identified the perpetrators as individuals, cutting off arguments about the possibility of an antiabortion conspiracy. In so doing, he was effectively denouncing the possibility that the attacks were part of a broader coordinated terrorist campaign.

The pro-choice movement was not nearly so sure. After the first bombing of an Ohio clinic in 1978, local pro-choice activists immediately contacted one of the leading pro-choice advocates of the time, Dr. Bill Baird. Baird quickly made connections between the Ohio case and others that were occurring around the country. In an interview with a reporter for the *Cleveland Plain Dealer,* Baird hypothesized that "a causal connection existed between inflammatory words 'feeding the winds of hatred' and a subsequent 'lawlessness of the anti-abortion side.'" He added that he would call on James A. Hickey, then bishop of the Cleveland Catholic Diocese, "to condemn violence against abortion clinics and their personnel and patients" and would also invite the FBI to explore possible connections between the attack on the Cleveland clinic and those in other states.[12]

Baird was able to convince the Catholic Diocese in Cleveland of the ramifications of inflammatory rhetoric, and the bishop of the diocese published a statement condemning the bombings. But Baird was much less successful in convincing the FBI to ferret out evidence of a greater terrorist network: "After discussing matters with investigators, he received a letter dated April 6, 1978, from the FBI's New York City office stating:

> The facts in this matter indicate a possible violation of Title 18, Section 844i (the use of an incendiary device to damage property affecting interstate commerce) which is investigated by the Bureau of Alcohol, Tobacco, and Firearms (ATF). However . . . the facts as provided . . . showed no evidence of a conspiracy and did not warrant federal investigation but rather should be handled by local authorities. There is no basis for an FBI investigation in this matter under the Federal Bombing Statute.[13]

A year later, Baird's own nonprofit clinic was bombed, and Baird took his case public. On several television interviews, Baird warned of the possibility of a network of antiabortion terrorists and strongly condemned the pro-life camp for not denouncing the use of inflammatory rhetoric more conclusively. Baird sued the FBI for their failure to investigate the conspiracy he believed was at work, but his case was thrown out of court.

THE CLINTON ADMINISTRATION

The incidences of abortion clinic bombing decreased after Reagan came out against them in 1985. While nonviolent protest was still common, the drama of the violence cooled for several years. Violence reared again in the early 1990s with the election of William Jefferson Clinton as president of the United States. Clinton was elected only a year after a pivotal bill was introduced in Congress. The Freedom of Access to Clinic Entrances Act (FACE) was proposed by Democratic Congressman Mel Levine from California. Introduced in 1991, the bill was an attempt to make obstructing access to abortion clinics illegal.[14] Yet, it wasn't until the following year, after antiabortion activists effectively launched the "Summer of Mercy" in Wichita, Kansas, that the bill made it before the House Subcommittee on Crime and Criminal Justice of the Judiciary Committee.

During the Summer of Mercy campaign, thousands of pro-life activists flooded Wichita, Kansas, in an effort to close down the few abortion clinics in the town of 300,000. In an effort to forestall potential violence, Wichita police asked the city's clinics to close for the week of scheduled protest. The coordinators of the protest—Randall Terry and Keith Tucci of Operation Rescue—were ecstatic when the clinic directors agreed, and they widely publicized their success in making Wichita "abortion free." However, Terry and Tucci were so enamored of their success that they decided to extend their siege beyond the original scheduled date. Wichita police and clinic workers were less than pleased, and an intense clash ensued.[15]

On the first day of the second week, hundreds of Operation Rescue volunteers blocked the entrance to George Tiller's Wichita clinic. Police dressed in riot gear cleared enough of a path to get Tiller and the clinic workers through the blockade, but in response Operation Rescue called for more volunteers. Later the same day, Operation Rescue teams lay down on the street outside the clinic, forcing police to pick up their dead weight in order to move them. The mayor of Wichita told police they were not responsible for helping women to get into the clinic, and police largely gave up trying to fight through the enormous crowds of protestors. A series of court battles ensued, which launched the debate back onto the national stage, and the Justice Department eventually became involved when they argued that states had the right to determine how to handle access to abortion clinics. The Summer of Mercy eventually ended more than six weeks after it began.

The Summer of Mercy resulted in a national battle to define the rights of protestors and patients to access abortion clinics. FACE was introduced to set specific limits regarding what protestors could or could not do in front of abortion clinics. While many decisions about specific distances and boundaries would be left to the states, FACE added the penalties that could be assessed against an individual when that individual committed a crime having to do with an abortion protest.

Democratic Rep. Charles Schumer from New York would not only chair the FACE hearings, but would also become a leading cosponsor of FACE along with Republican Rep. Connie Morella from Maryland and Democratic Rep. Louise Slaughter, also from New York. The presence of FACE in the Senate touched off a national debate. Nonetheless, legislation concerning clinic blockades would remain dormant until the murder of Dr. David Gunn in 1993.

At the time that Michael Griffin shot Dr. David Gunn, President Clinton was in office and had already established himself as a strong proponent of abortion rights. Five months later, Rachelle Shannon shot Dr. George Tiller multiple times while he was driving away from his Wichita clinic, injuring both of his arms. The Clinton administration quickly expressed staunch condemnation and committed to making the creation and enforcement of legislation against antiabortion violence a priority.

Attorney General Janet Reno subsequently met with members of the Senate and Labor Human Resources Committee to outline S. 636, a piece of legislation that eventually became the FACE bill that made it through the House and Senate. The bill outlined specific protest acts, including the use or threat of force, physical intimidation or obstruction, or interference with anyone planning to obtain abortion services. A companion version was introduced in the House.[16]

On May 26, 1994, the Democratic Congress passed the Freedom of Access to Clinic Entrances Act (FACE), making it a federal offense to obstruct access to abortion clinics. The bill was signed into law by President Clinton shortly thereafter. President Clinton explained his support for FACE:

> We simply cannot—we must not—continue to allow the attacks, the incidents of arson, the campaigns of intimidation upon law-abiding citizens that (have) given rise to this law . . . No person seeking medical care, no physician providing that care should have to endure harassments or threats or obstruction or intimidation or even murder from vigilantes who take the law into their own hands because they think they know what the law ought to be.[17]

The opposition to the bill was largely from Republicans (only 4 of the 30 votes against the bill were from Democrats). Some of the senators, like Republican Sen. Mitch McConnell, who rhetorically condemned antiabortion violence and the murders of abortion providers, also voted for the FACE act. Others who also rhetorically condemned antiabortion violence and sought prosecution of the perpetrators, like Republican Sen. John McCain, did not vote for FACE.[18]

FACE was a by and large a response to the aggressive antiabortion movement that was developing fatal consequences. Both the murder of David Gunn and the wounding of George Tiller were committed by individuals hailed as heroic by the Army of God. FACE made the use or threat of force, as well as any kind of physical obstruction to those accessing abortion clinics, a federal crime. FACE act also allowed federal officials to bring civil lawsuits against perpetrators. Criminal penalties depended on several prerequisites, such as criminal background, specific conduct in violation of the act, and repetitive violations. Maximum sentences ranged from $10,000 fines for first-time nonviolent offenders to 10 years imprisonment for violent offenders.[19] FACE would become the catalyst for several lawsuits from both sides of the abortion movements, including the case of *Willamette Planned Parenthood v. the ACLA*, which began a few years later.

The passing of the FACE legislation cemented into law what—on different sides of the debate—both William Webster and Dallas Blanchard had argued: motivation is at least as important as consequence. But where Webster saw crimes against abortion providers as not meeting the qualifications of terrorism, FACE paved the way for future legislation to establish that it did.

Indeed, Clinton came to identify these abortion-related crimes as terrorism less than two months after FACE was enacted. When Paul Hill shot and killed abortion provider Dr. John Britton and his volunteer escort James Barrett outside of the provider's Pensacola clinic, President Clinton quickly condemned the shootings as "senseless," stating: "I am strongly committed to ending this form of domestic terrorism that threatens the fabric of our country. I encourage a quick and thorough investigation into this tragic incident as the local officials work closely with the resources of the Federal law-enforcement community."[20]

President Clinton threw his full support behind then-Attorney General Janet Reno, and she came to play a significant role in the administration's formation of a response. Within a day of Hill's murder, Reno dispatched U.S. marshals to several abortion clinics in an effort to prevent further violence. She had ordered an investigation of Dr. Gunn's murder a year earlier and was now "disturbed" that little progress was made, allowing the killings to continue.[21] As a result, she worked toward establishing an interagency antiabortion violence task force that would aid the investigations. The investigation began pursuing links to the Army of God, using the signatories of the Defensive Action statements as a logical starting point.

Attorney General Reno and the Clinton administration exerted extensive pressure on known affiliates of the Army of God. Suddenly Baird's earlier claims of conspiracy were interpreted as prescient rather than paranoid, and the ideas promulgated by the shadowy organization were given far greater weight.[22]

In 1994, a federal grand jury was convened to look into claims of a conspiracy. Several members of the Army of God were subpoenaed to attend, including Michael Bray and Donald Spitz. The grand jury was disbanded in 1996 without having been able to find evidence of a conspiracy. Army of God affiliates say this is because there never was one to be found.[23] Army of God supporter Dave Leach challenged the claims of conspiracy as being a direct threat to free speech. Leach said, "There's no conspiracy here. Conspiracy is where you secretly talk with others about how you're going to commit a crime. Unless we're going to redefine it to mean when people talk about what's right and wrong and say it publicly and put it on TV shows and Internet blogs, there's nothing going on here."[24]

Leach's comments highlight the challenge inherent in trying to prosecute an action based on a particular set of ideas. The grand jury spent two
years looking for organizational ties where primarily ideological ties existed. Although FACE awarded pro-choice proponents a powerful weapon
in their prosecutorial armory, it did not afford law enforcement a means of
prosecuting the presence of ideas independent of an act. As a result, FACE
could only reach as far as greater penalties after violence occurred.

FBI, Bureau of Alcohol, Tobacco and Firearms (BATF), and U.S. Marshals Service (USMS) investigations and security measures increased and
expanded as shootings against clinic personnel, death threats, and "hit list"
websites continued. In addition, the 1995 Oklahoma City bombing motivated Reno to "revise guidelines on domestic terrorism investigations,
granting federal law enforcement officers greater authority to open cases,
recruit informants, . . . use other aggressive investigative techniques, [and
loosen] rules out of concern that the FBI would be overly cautious in responding to what they identified as a major new threat."[25]

In fact, the entire way that law enforcement looked at terrorism was
changing. Whereas in the past, the expectation was that terrorist organizations were tightly controlled hierarchies led by charismatic individuals,
the Army of God challenged law enforcement officials to realize that ideas
could be as deadly as organization. A Justice Department report revealed
the changing profile of terrorists whom they described as "individuals who
are inspired by, but not affiliated with, terrorist groups, thus making them
harder to identify and stop."[26]

Just how hard these individuals would be to stop was proven by Eric
Rudolph in July 1996. When Rudolph bombed the Atlanta Centennial Park
where the Olympic Games were being held, a woman was killed and hundreds of people were wounded. President Clinton insisted that the Olympics continue: "An act of vicious terror like this is clearly directed at the
spirit of our own democracy. We must not let these attacks stop us from
going forward. We cannot let terror win. That is not the American way."[27]

Clinton's response demonstrates two important themes. First, he again
defined the act as one of terrorism. At the early stages of the investigation,
the bomber's intentions were not known, so this use of the word referred
to the act itself rather than its motivation. But Clinton's remarks are interesting for another reason as well. By noting that terror "is not the American way," Clinton entered the fray in the war of ideas. His juxtaposition of
the violence of terror with the freedom of American ideals is one that is
common in antiterrorism rhetoric, but it is particularly significant here.
Whereas previous responses to antiabortion violence had largely ignored
the motivation in favor of decrying the act, Clinton began to set a standard
here to define both the motivation, and the act, as un-American.

Clinton maintained this position when less than a year later, Rudolph
bombed an Atlanta abortion clinic, injuring several people when a second

bomb detonated. President Clinton condemned the bombing as "a vile and malevolent act" of terrorism: "Nobody has a right to use violence in America to advance their own convictions over the rights of others. We will get to the bottom of this. We will punish those responsible to the fullest extent that the law provides."[28] A month later, Rudolph bombed a gay nightclub in Atlanta. The incident caused several injuries but no fatalities. President Clinton addressed the bombing as a hate crime. While the concept of "hate crimes" would emerge in greater force several years later in American history, Clinton's wording is indicative of the changing nature of terrorism prevention—the emphasis continued to shift to the intention or idea of the crime as much as the action itself.

The Army of God's use of force continued despite the implementation of FACE and ongoing federal investigations. In January 1998, Rudolph bombed a Birmingham abortion clinic. President Clinton quickly condemned the incident, calling it "an unforgivable act that strikes at the heart of the constitutional freedoms and individual liberties all Americans hold dear." He later added, "We will continue to enforce that law to its fullest extent—and to protect our nation's family planning clinics."[29] Although the administration emphasized the promises of prosecution under FACE,[30] the Army of God consistently remained one step ahead of the administration and federal agents. About eight months later, Army of God member James Kopp shot and killed Dr. Barnett Slepian inside his Amherst, New York, home.

"No matter where we stand on the issue of abortion, all Americans must stand together in condemning this tragic and brutal act," President Clinton immediately responded.[31] Reno described the incident as an "outrage": "We will do whatever it takes to track down and prosecute whoever is responsible for this murder."[32] She encouraged the public that federal investigators, who were convinced that the antiabortion motivation was obvious, were actively searching for the perpetrator.[33] New York governor George Pataki later stated, "The killer should face the death penalty. It's beyond a tragedy—it's really an act of terrorism and, in my mind, a cold-blooded assassination."[34]

Governor Pataki's comment clearly evidences the evolving emphasis placed on motivation behind violence. And although President Clinton refers to the motivation of the crime, however obliquely, in his statement, he asks citizens to essentially ignore any sympathy they may have for the motivation while formatting their opinion of the act. The changing nature of threat can be seen to be slowly impacting those assessing it. In other words, as the motivation for an act increases in influence, ideology behind the condemnation of the act necessarily decreases.

Within four days of Slepian's assassination, Reno met with several pro-choice leaders, including the Slepian's clinic director, Marilyn Buckham. "The buck stops here. Tell me what you need," encouraged Reno.[35] Her primary objective was to keep Slepian's clinic open, a request personally made by the provider's widow. Buckham asked for strong security for both clinic and the providers that volunteered to cover Slepian's spot. Reno not only immediately dispatched U.S. marshals to the clinic and to the specified providers, but she also dispatched BATF agents to protect a gathering crowd for a memorial of Slepian.[36] Within 10 days of the shooting, she officially established and forcefully activated the interagency task force, known as the National Task Force on Violence against Health Care Providers. The Task Force's purpose was "to assist local and regional law enforcement agencies investigate and prosecute attacks on clinics and people offering abortion services."[37]

The following year, the White House proposed a budget for fiscal year 2000 that included $4.5 million towards physical security for abortion clinics.[38] The proposal would enhance Reno's Task Force as it trained local and state law enforcements with terrorism awareness and procedures. Four years after the assassination of Dr. Slepian by James Kopp, Democratic senator Harry Reid pushed his congressional colleagues to hamper future efforts of the Army of God by recognizing the group as greater than the sum of its parts:

> While Kopp alone might have pulled the trigger and fired the shot that killed Dr. Slepian, we have learned that he was part of an organized network of violent extremists, including a group that calls itself the Army of God. (Imagine that a group would invoke the Lord's name and believe that God sanctions their lawless violence. And this group of murderers professes a respect for life!) Those who resort to violence are violating not only our laws but our American principles and values. We in the Senate must identify them as terrorists. The American people must recognize them as terrorists. And law enforcement officials must treat them as terrorists—for that is what they are.[39]

THE GEORGE W. BUSH ADMINISTRATION

The counterterrorism changes that were hinted at under the Clinton administration were cemented under the second Bush administration. The World Trade Center attacks of September 11, 2001, confirmed that terrorist organizations had largely shifted away from hierarchical organizational structures into the much harder to trace cell-strategy model. The ambiguity of both international and national law regarding the classification of terrorist attacks as crimes of war or federal crimes forced a much deeper examination of both the causes and consequences of terrorism. Finally, the heightened security state that ensued as a result of the attacks led law enforcement officers to react immediately and decisively in the face of potential threats.

Army of God affiliate Clayton Waagner was more than ready to take advantage of the changed environment. Capitalizing on the panic that ensued when anthrax-laced letters were mailed to the offices of congressional leaders and news organizations, Waagner decided the time was ripe to send threat letters to hundreds of abortion clinics, movements, and organizations. Between October and November, Waagner sent out hundreds of envelopes containing a harmless white powder that exhibited similar biological qualities to anthrax.

In December 2003, Waagner was convicted by a federal jury on 51 charges, covering, among other things, violations of the FACE act, mailing threatening letters and making threats. Although the prosecution urged the judge to sentence Waagner as a terrorist, the judge interpreted terrorism to be limited to attacks against the federal government—a criteria that Waagner did not meet.[40] Waagner himself was evidently quite anxious to be identified as a terrorist. He "told the jury he was 'tickled' that some of the recipients of his letters were still traumatized, adding, 'It's been clearly demonstrated that I am the antiabortion extremist, a terrorist to the abortion industry. There's no question there that I terrorized these people any way I could'"[41]

Bush administration attorney general John Ashcroft was unequivocal in his condemnation of antiabortion-related violence. Ashcroft sought to prosecute Barnett Slepian's killer, James Kopp, to the fullest extent of the law: "Kopp committed a heinous crime that deserves severe punishment. We need to send a strong message that no matter what our differences are violence is not the solution."[42] In 2001, Ashcroft dispatched U.S. marshals to protect Dr. George Tiller, as was receiving threats and would be the target of a massive protest at his Wichita clinic. Ashcroft stated that his views on abortion would not "deter" him from "aggressive enforcement" of FACE and the prevention of antiabortion violence.[43]

Army of God members voiced their disappointment in Ashcroft, in whom—as a vocal born-again Christian—they had anticipated having a strong ally.[44] Michael Bray discounted Ashcroft's condemnation of the violent antiabortion movement as the act of a politician seeking votes, rather than an individual standing for what he actually believed.[45]

Whatever Ashcroft's position, the number of prosecutions under FACE decreased during the tenure of the Bush administration.[46] The National Abortion Federation (NAF) reported 17 "extreme" cases of antiabortion violence between 2000 and 2008, excluding the anthrax hoax.[47] Eleven individuals were prosecuted for violence committed against abortion clinics within those eight years. The civil component within FACE, which permits the attorney general to seek compensatory damages for crimes proven to be motivated by antiabortion activism, was not used by Bush's Department of Justice during this time.[48] In addition, in contrast to Clinton's Department of Justice, which filed 17 civil suits under FACE within five years, Bush's Department of Justice filed 1 civil suit within eight years.[49]

Further, *Congressional Quarterly* reports that a draft planning document listing the terrorist organizations the Department of Homeland Security believed likely to act between 2005 and 2011 included "adversaries such as al Qaeda and other foreign entities affiliated with the Islamic Jihad movement, as well as domestic radical Islamist groups. It also lists left-wing domestic groups, such as the Animal Liberation Front (ALF) and the Earth Liberation Front (ELF), as terrorist threats, but it does not mention anti-government groups, white supremacists and other radical right-wing movements, which have staged numerous terrorist attacks that have killed scores of Americans."[50] The document made no reference to the Army of God. However, in 2009 in the early days of the Obama administration, Scott Roeder would encourage the correction of the oversight.

Four months after President Obama's inauguration, Army of God affiliate Scott Roeder shot and killed Dr. George Tiller inside the abortion provider's Lutheran church.[51] President Obama quickly made a public statement condemning the murder: "I am shocked and outraged by the murder of Dr. George Tiller as he attended church services this morning. However profound our differences as Americans over difficult issues such as abortion, they cannot be resolved by heinous acts of violence."[52] Attorney General Eric Holder also made a statement:

> I have directed the United States Marshals Service to offer protection to other appropriate people and facilities around the nation. The Department of Justice will work to bring the perpetrator of this crime to justice. As a precautionary measure, we will also take appropriate steps to help prevent any related acts of violence from occurring.[53]

Fifteen years after FACE was passed by Congress, Democratic senators Amy Klobuchar, Jeanne Shaheen, and Barbara Boxer proposed a bill in the Senate condemning Scott Roeder's killing of Dr. Tiller as the use of violence for political ends.[54] Members of Congress came to an impasse over the language of the bill, which stated "acts of violence should never be used to prevent women from receiving *reproductive health care* [emphasis added]." Pro-life senators argued that the wording glorifies abortion. The bill's sponsors contended there was nothing controversial about reproductive health. The U.S. House unanimously passed a less controversial version on June 9, which condemned the murder of Tiller but also a half-dozen other murders that occurred in places of worship. This version did not mention Tiller's profession, the reason he was murdered, or the terms "abortion" or "reproductive rights."[55]

Roeder was tried and convicted of first degree murder by the State of Kansas in February 2010. At the time of this writing, federal prosecutors were still deciding on whether they would seek additional charges against Roeder under the FACE act. Previous acts by Army of God members have been tried at both the state and federal level. Paul Hill was first convicted by the federal government to two life sentences in federal prison, and then months later he was tried, convicted, and sentenced to death by Florida courts. James Kopp was sentenced to life in prison by the State of New York and to life in prison without the possibility of parole by a federal court.

STATE RESPONSES

While FACE did much to increase the uniformity of prosecution and sentencing guidelines across the country, state laws still carry enormous weight in the determination of what constitutes criminality in cases against abortion providers. Buffer zones are particularly influential and are entirely regulated by individual states. Whereas FACE prohibits damage to property, threats of force, or physical obstruction as means of preventing women's access to abortion facilities, state laws regarding buffer zones more specifically address what actions can be undertaken and designate in what areas.

For example, the state of Maine specifically regulates noise outside of clinics. The intentional use of substances that release an "unpleasant odor" inside or around the clinics is also prohibited.[56] Other states, including California, New York, and Washington, have created state versions of FACE. Much as the federal version of the law opened more prosecutorial options to law enforcement, state versions of FACE offer greater opportunities for states to act against antiabortion-inspired activities.

In some states, buffer zones aid in this effort. Buffer zones are divided into two categories. A floating buffer zone applies to those or that which is in transit. It protects personnel and patients exiting and entering clinics. A fixed buffer zone only applies to the territory surrounding the clinic area. The reach of these zones differ from state to state. Colorado limits protestors for up to 100 feet within any health-care facility. Within this space, protestors may not come within 8 feet of approaching or departing patients. In Montana, the zone extends to 36 feet. Chicago, Illinois, has a bi-provision buffer zone, which limits protestors to 50 feet of the clinic and 8 feet from incoming and outgoing patients. In addition, protestors can be fined up to $500 for attempting to talk to patients as they enter or exit the clinic.[57] Oakland, California, has a bi-provision buffer zone, which limits protestors to 100 feet of the clinic and 8 feet from incoming and outgoing patients.[58] Massachusetts passed a bi-provision buffer zone limiting protestors to 18 feet of the clinic and 6 feet from both patients and clinic personnel. This act was struck down by a district judge, who stated that the nonreciprocity of the floating buffer zone created a discrepancy; however, an appellate court restored the laws several months later.[59] Pittsburgh, Pennsylvania, had a bi-provision buffer zone, which limited protestors to 15 feet of the clinic and protected both clinic personnel and patients with an 8-foot floating zone. In 2009, an Appellate court struck down the provision, saying that while either the floating or fixed buffer zone was legal on its own, in combination, the zones violated protestors' right to free speech.

The state laws governing access to clinics are created in an attempt to fill holes left by the FACE act. Given that FACE was initially enacted to address gaps in conceptual understandings of criminality, terrorism, and ideas, it is not surprising that challenges to both FACE and state regulations pivot on the same contentious issues. Pro-life protestors argue that buffer zones, whether fixed or floating, limit their right to free speech and assembly. However, pro-choice advocates contend that the aggressive protest techniques violate their rights to privacy.

The Army of God's response to these laws has been mixed. In some cases, members take pride in being arrested for standing up to an "evil" system, but others threaten that the more laws that are passed prohibiting their ability to protest without violence, the more they will be driven to protest using more effective—if more violent—methods.[60]

THE JUDICIAL RESPONSE

The response to antiabortion violence has not been limited to the legislative and executive branches of the American government system. In fact, the acts undertaken by the Army of God have affected the types of cases presented to and the decisions rendered from both federal and local judicial benches. While there have been hundreds of cases brought before the judiciary on issues relating to abortion and the right to protest, there are a few that stand out as particularly influential.

In June 1986, the National Organization for Women (NOW) foundation coordinated with the Delaware Women's Health Organization and the Pensacola Ladies Center to file a suit against Joseph Scheidler. The NOW contingent claimed that Scheidler was part of a criminal conspiracy to close abortion clinics and claimed that in so doing, Scheidler had violated antitrust laws.[61] In January 1989, NOW added charges of extortion and violation of federal racketeering laws.

The case was dismissed by the first trial judge to review it, on the grounds that racketeering laws require evidence of an economic interest in the commitment of the crime, which Scheidler did not have. However, NOW appealed the dismissal before the U.S. Supreme Court, and the Clinton administration filed a brief supporting NOW's claims of violation of racketeering charges—whether or not economic gain was the motive. The Supreme Court agreed with the brief, and this allowed NOW to revive their original suit at the district level. In 1997, NOW was granted the authority to represent "whose rights to the services of women's health centers in the

United States at which abortions are performed have been or will be interfered with by defendants' unlawful activities."[62]

In 2003, by an 8–1 decision, the U.S. Supreme Court agreed that pro-life activists could not be charged in violation of the Racketeer Influenced and Corrupt Organization act (RICO), a law enabling organizations to sue for violations of the Hobbs Act, a law that prosecutes those involved in "organized crime," particularly extortion through force, violence, or fear, on interstate commerce.[63] The Court ruled that rights potentially violated by clinic protestors—women's right to seek medical services, clinic doctors' rights to perform their jobs, and clinics' rights to provide medical services and otherwise conduct their business—were not "property" that could be "obtained" within the meaning of the Hobbs Act. On that basis, the court overturned a jury verdict against clinic protestors, in which jurors had found that the protestors used improper means to obtain "property" belonging to the plaintiffs (clinics, and patients or prospective patients), and had therefore committed extortion. The Court upheld this decision in 2006. The case bounced around the courts for another nine years, before the Supreme Court ruled that Scheidler and PLAN could not be found guilty of racketeering because of their efforts to stop abortion.[64]

At the same time that the Scheidler case was working its way through the system, other cases were brought that would address the tension between the right to free speech and the protection of individuals from undue intimidation. *Madsen et. al. v. Women's Health Center* was argued before the Supreme Court on April 28, 1994, and a decision was rendered by the Court on June 30 of the same year. While the case could simplistically be described as one about the proper size of buffer zones, in reality it is significant for the decision the Court made and its recognition of the motivation of acts beyond the actual acts themselves.

The case came to the Supreme Court after having wound its way through Florida's court system. In the original case, antiabortion protestors were accused of interfering with women's ability to enter Florida abortion clinics, and thereby "having deleterious physical effects on patients and discouraging some potential patients from entering the clinic."[65] The Florida court issued an injunction prohibiting demonstrators from entering a 36-foot buffer zone around the perimeter of the clinic, as well as around private property to the north and west of the clinic in question. The decision restricted excessive noisemaking and the display of images anywhere that potential patients might see. The antiabortion protestors appealed the decision, contending that the restrictions were deleterious to their right to free speech, and this argument was recognized by the Florida Supreme Court—which said that the "the restrictions were narrowly tailored to serve a significant government interest."[66]

Justice Renquist delivered the Supreme Court's judgment revising the Florida Supreme Court's decision. Renquist argued that the restrictions imposed by the original verdict were appropriate given the nature of the protest. He said that the decision rendered was not "directed at the content of petitioners' anti-abortion message."[67] He said "The combination of the governmental interests identified by the Florida Supreme court—protecting a pregnant woman's freedom to seek lawful medical or counseling services, ensuring public safety and order, promoting the free flow of traffic on public streets and sidewalks, protecting citizens' property rights, and assuring residential privacy—is quite sufficient to justify an appropriately tailored injunction."[68]

This case would become a precedent for other court decisions regarding security and rights of patients, clinic personnel, and protestors, including *Schenck v. Pro-choice Network of Western New York*.[69] This case was brought before the U.S. Supreme Court two years after *Madsen.* The facts of the two cases were very similar: New York abortion doctors and clinics filed a District Court complaint against protestors who were consistently blockading their clinics. Police had been unsuccessful at helping women to get through the blockades, and the District Court issued a restraining order and then an injunction against the protestors, prohibiting them from gathering within 15 feet of the clinic or any person trying to get inside the clinic.

In 1997, by an 8–1 decision, the U.S. Supreme Court upheld fixed buffer zones around abortion clinics while striking down floating buffer zones, ruling the latter as excessive.[70] The Court ruled that the facts presented for prosecution were insufficient in determining whether the claimed governmental interests were hindered by a mere zone created between individuals. The legalized fixed buffer zone constituted a provision that allowed two sidewalk counselors to approach patients within the fixed buffer zone, but they had to yield back outside the zone upon the patient's request.[71] The decision creates a sort of balance between the rights of protestors and the rights of women seeking health services. Protestors are allowed to express their views by picketing, singing, counseling, and the like as long as they do not physically hinder access to abortion clinics. The decision clarified rather than redefined the rights of both sides of the movements.

Planned Parenthood of the Columbia Willamette v. American Coalition of Life Activists was born after the 1995 White Rose banquet. At the event, Michael Bray, among others, ceremoniously unveiled a poster listing the names of a dozen doctors who performed abortions. In addition to the names, the doctors were declared guilty of crimes against humanity. At the banquet the following year, Bray and the American Coalition for Life Activists went a step further and revealed the "Nuremberg Files," a compilation of names, home addresses, pictures, and other information about a long list of abortion providers. Neal Horsely posted the list online and kept track of the doctors that were killed or injured. The posters offered rewards for the prevention of future abortions committed by these doctors but did not explicitly threaten any of them directly.

Nonetheless, a group of doctors sued the ACLA for violating the FACE act. The jury found in favor of the doctors and levied a $107 million verdict against the 12 defendants. In 2002, the 9th Circuit Court affirmed the 1999 District Court's decision that "wanted posters" created and distributed by ACLA, displaying abortion providers' information and promising rewards for antiabortion violence, violated the FACE act: "In conjunction with the 'guilty' posters, being listed on a Nuremberg Files scorecard for abortion providers impliedly threatened physicians with being next on a hit list. To this extent only, the Files are also a true threat. However, the Nuremberg Files are protected speech."[72] This case established a precedent for how the definition of threat would be interpreted under FACE. In this case, a threat was understood to be "a statement which, in the entire context and under all the circumstances, a reasonable person would foresee would be interpreted by those to whom the statement is communicated as a serious expression of intent to inflict bodily harm upon that person. So defined, a threatening statement that violates FACE is unprotected under the First Amendment." This case became the precedent in which a court ordered the closing of an Internet website.[73]

But judicial decisions are dependent on law enforcement agencies to protect the laws they define. The very same tensions that dominate the seminal judicial cases examined here are present in the options available to law enforcement agencies. In the following section, we will examine the work and limitations of the federal agencies most closely involved in antiabortion violence.

LAW ENFORCEMENT RESPONSE

Since the 1994 grand jury failed to find conclusive evidence of a conspiracy, federal investigators have had to be satisfied with other explanations for the relationship among antiabortion activists. The term "lone wolf" is frequently used, though many lament the inaccuracy of its description.[74]

Loners, such as Eric Rudolph, have become symbolic for both violent antiabortion campaigns and law enforcement. Though Rudolph sent letters from "The Army of God" and claimed to be part of a group committed to stopping abortion, law enforcement agencies have been unable to substantiate his claims. He is lauded as a hero on the Army of God website, but there is no evidence to suggest that he worked with any other members as he planned and executed his attacks. Not surprisingly, investigators say that individuals who are inspired by, but not otherwise connected to, known terrorist groups are "harder to identity and stop," and thus are "the most dangerous domestic terrorists."[75]

Investigators attempt to find similarities in profiles, and many accounts describe certain common characteristics. The problem is that few of them have any signs of aggressive histories or alarming interests or activities. The only clear commonality is the ideology that unites them—in theory if not in practice. But this takes the discussion once again into the propriety of prosecuting for belief, rather than action. Former head of the FBI's domestic counterterrorism Robert M. Blitzer said, "for us, it is a real challenge to stay ahead of them."[76]

When letters from the Army of God were found in association with Rudolph's bombings, investigators tried to determine the group's level of influence and involvement in the attacks. But just as the grand jury in 1994 failed to find evidence of a broader conspiracy, investigators eventually concluded that Rudolph worked alone. "Federal investigators suspect that the 'Army of God' exists not as an actual organization in this case but was invoked by Rudolph to represent the ideas and possibly the people who inspired him."[77]

Nonetheless, counterterrorism has been one of the fastest-growing sectors within federal law enforcement since newspapers began reporting antiabortion violence throughout the nation, particularly in 1994. A new interagency command center, joint response teams with local officials in most major cities, hundreds of new FBI agents, and a higher budget for counterterrorism have all been added or created since the heightened violence from "right-wing militia extremists."[78]

This may be in large part a reflection of the realization that discussions of whether or not the Army of God is a "real" organization largely miss the point and the scope of the threat. The Army of God has successfully used for three decades techniques that have only recently been recognized as deadly at the international level. Just as international agencies have struggled to define, much less capture, al Qaeda affiliates, the FBI, the ATF, and other federal agencies have struggled in their conceptualization of the Army of God.

Contending against an organization that is linked only by a series of ideas is in many ways an anathema to the America that so many presidents have extolled in speeches condemning terrorism. Because there is no membership roster for the Army of God, parole boards are forced to demand that parolees simply avoid interaction with other individuals from the pro-life movement—a restriction that Army of God members lambaste as an infringement on their rights to practice religion (many churches have a majority of pro-life members), to freely assemble (how can they exercise their right to protest abortion without encountering other antiabortion activists), or to freely speak (they believe they are being prohibited from sharing truth). Given the circumstances, even a perfectly implemented prohibition of this type of "organization" very closely borders the violations most law enforcement agencies labor to avoid.

Many pro-choice organizations and congressional leaders criticize the Department of Justice and the FBI for their failure to respond to attacks on both abortion clinics and personnel. Kim Gandy, executive vice president of NOW, articulated her frustration: "We believe there is a nationwide conspiracy. . . . The Justice Department and the F.B.I. do not have a handle on it yet. They don't know the extent of the problem."[79]

However, FBI officials claim the problem is not apathy toward religious or political violence, but rather a reluctance stemming from "the memory of the scandal surrounding its improper and sometimes illegal efforts to disrupt the civil rights and anti-war movements of the 1960s and 1970s while supposedly investigating national security threats."[80] In the midst of the investigation of Paul Hill—and his relationship to other members of the Army of God—FBI agents sought "clear directions before [they] again made a major commitment to combating domestic terrorism."[81] Yet, even once then-FBI director Louis Freeh publicly announced his support for a more aggressive investigation, the *New York Times* reports "the investigation was an uncomfortable step for many of the bureau's senior managers . . . . Some of these officials [felt] that the line between the anti-abortion movement's violent elements and its militant but nonetheless nonviolent groups can easily be blurred. Given that, these managers [said], they cannot be certain that with the benefit of hindsight, a future Administration opposed to abortion will not accuse them of crossing the line from investigation of a criminal conspiracy to surveillance of legitimate political activity."[82]

Some of the frustration stemmed from the numerous examples of violations of FACE and the appearance of a coordinated effort. A month before Paul Hill was arrested for his multiple killings in 1994, he was investigated but not arrested by the FBI for allegedly violating FACE: "Prosecutors weighed the clinic's rights against Paul Hill's right of free speech and decided an arrest wasn't warranted," stated FBI spokesman George Wisnovsky at the time.[83] The FBI recovered and identified Shelley Shannon's daughter Angie Shannon's fingerprints, on multiple death threats to abortion providers. They investigated Angie's boyfriend, who told them he had mailed the letters for her.[84] Further, after Dr. Slepian was killed in home in 1998, the FBI warned Dr. Tiller that he was on the top of the violent antiabortion campaign's "hit list."[85] And yet, investigators could not produce evidence suggesting that any of the events were organizationally related. The grand jury sought evidence, subpoenaed members, and in the end concluded that the individuals were linked by an idea, not an organization. As a result, there was little law enforcement could do, and Army of God members, affiliates, and supporters continue to meet without fear of repercussions.

For example, in 2009, the FBI investigated some of Scott Roeder's prison visitors, most of whom had known connections to the Army of God.
Two regular Army of God visitors, Spitz and Bray, said they had yet to be
contacted by law enforcement officials regarding the visit. Both men believed they knew the reason for the delay. Spitz stated, "If they do come
calling, I won't talk to them."[86] Bray later added: "I always tell the FBI when
they come around, if you want me to help you find something on such-
and-such, I'll do that, but if you want to find someone who's trying to save
babies, I've got nothing to say to you. So they don't ever bother coming
around anymore."[87]

BUREAU OF ALCOHOL, TOBACCO AND FIREARMS

The BATF has legal jurisdiction in cases involving explosives.[88] Since
the antiabortion violence began and increased during Reagan's presidency, BATF played a vital role by directing almost half of their field agents
to the clinic incidents. When the Washington, D.C., mayor at the time
complained about the FBI's lack of response to the antiabortion violence,
White House spokesman Larry Speakes stressed that BATF was the primary investigating agency. He explained that besides BATF having legal
jurisdiction over the incidents, there were also "legal problems with brand-
ing the abortion clinic bombings as 'terrorist' attacks that would bring in
the FBI."[89] In any case, the FBI then and continues to aid BATF in their
investigations, providing help on "fingerprints and psychological profiles
of likely suspects."[90]

With or without FBI assistance, the BATF has been involved in nearly all
the investigations regarding antiabortion violence.[91] In response to heightened antiabortion violence in 1995, the BATF arrested 49 people in 77 of
the bombing and arson cases.[92] After Rudolph's serial bombing, the BATF,
along with the FBI, showcased credited letters from the Army of God, asking the public to call in if they recognized the handwriting of the letters.[93]
After Roeder shot Dr. Tiller, his ex-wife found both BATF and FBI agents
searching her home.[94]

U.S. MARSHAL SERVICE

Although the agency is primarily concerned with judicial security, including court personnel and the public, it is also assists in the investigation of
violent crimes, including the apprehension of wanted criminals. The USMS
is consistently dispatched by the Department of Justice (DOJ) to abortion clinics and personnel affected by violence. Both the Clinton and Bush
administrations used the marshals for clinic protection and abortion rallies.

Recently, U.S. marshals took part in the raid on Michael Bray's home in conjunction with the findings against him in the case brought by the Willamette Women's Clinic. Bray has now filed a lawsuit against both the agency and Planned Parenthood for "exceeding the scope of a court order" and taking household items from his Wilmington home, which, he says, is "contrary to the Writ of Execution."[95] The court order authorized the U.S. Marshal Service to "seize specified personal property in the Bray home to help pay the money damages awarded to Planned Parenthood" from a prior lawsuit.[96]

NATIONAL TASK FORCE ON VIOLENCE AGAINST HEALTH CARE PROVIDERS

Although the Task Force is not a separate agency, it combines the agents, efforts, and intelligence of the FBI, BATF, and USMS, and lawyers from the DOJ's criminal and civil divisions.[97] Established by Attorney General Janet Reno in 1998, the Task Force oversees and coordinates antiabortion violence investigations and assists in the prosecution of antiabortion crimes. The Task Force keeps a database of attacks against clinics and offers clinics advice for how to make their facilities safe from attacks. The Task Force's most recent investigation was the murder of Dr. Tiller.

BROTHER TO BROTHER

But what many law enforcement and pro-choice agencies say is that law enforcement will never be enough. They look to nonviolent participants in the pro-life cause to stand up and speak out against the use of force. And in many cases, the activists have been more than willing to oblige—with a twist. The vast majority of activists within the pro-life movement condemn the use of force, but their statements reflect the tension between the idea and the act, which we have highlighted throughout this book. Consider Joseph Scheidler's comment about the use of force: "We understand why it occurs. Still, I reject it. I don't think it is helpful, or that it will work to change anything. We prefer persuasion."[98] Jerry Falwell is more adamant: "The bombings are criminal and terroristic and very damaging to the cause of the unborn."[99]

Others reject any accusations of complicity: "There is not this collective soul-searching on the part of our movement because we have been responsible and we have been nonviolent," said the Rev. Patrick Mahoney, director of the Christian Defense Coalition. There are "extremists in every movement . . . . I think that extremists opposed to abortion got frustrated, felt they were losing the battle and felt it was incumbent upon themselves to resort to violence." [100]

Others, including Rev. Flip Benham, see the problem coming from the other side of the debate. He says "those in the abortion-providing industry" are "committing most of the violence in an attempt to discredit the anti-abortion movement. He said he would soon bring evidence to Washington that would undermine the government's statistics."[101]

But as bombings evolved into targeted killings, the condemnation from pro-life leaders intensified. In 1994, the president of the Southern Baptist Convention's Ethics & Religious Liberty Commission convened a group of Southern Baptist ethicists and theologians and wrote a comprehensive statement now known as the Nashville Declaration of Conscience,[102] in which the ministers condemned the use of force in no uncertain terms.[103] The 11-page document offers a detailed rejection of the Army of God's justification for force and concludes with the following points:

> Our conclusion is that the killing of abortion doctors is not a morally justifiable or permissible Christian response to abortion. We utterly reject such conduct as inconsistent with Scripture and call on all Christian people to join us in this stance. We believe that Christians are, nevertheless, morally obligated to oppose legalized abortion on demand and to reduce the number of abortions through other, morally legitimate, channels. We must do so more actively and faithfully than ever before. Pro-life Christians must act quickly and vigorously to prevent a small but vocal band of militant activists from destroying the credibility, effectiveness, and witness of the mainstream Christian pro-life movement. We pray earnestly that God will bless the efforts of all who employ morally legitimate means in order to save the lives of the most vulnerable among us, the unborn children. We are persuaded that this reflects the mind of Christ."[104]

Other groups have gone further and endeavored to assist law enforcement efforts by offering rewards for the capture of perpetrators. In 1998, before Rudolph was arrested for the bombing of a Birmingham clinic, Feminists for Life offered a $50,000 reward toward an arrest of those responsible.[105] Then, in 2001, Priests for Life offered a $50,000 reward for information that would lead to arrests of those responsible for violence against abortion clinics.[106]

The Center for Bio-Ethical Reform and Pro-Lifers against Clinic Violence have purposed themselves in condemning violent means with the movement. Several representatives within the Catholic Church have publicly condemned violent means within the movement, using Scripture and Catholic doctrines to compare such actions to being "equally detestable to war and abortion" itself.[107]

The Army of God does not respond favorably to Christians who question their methods. One page of the website is dedicated to exposing the traitors who would question their techniques. They title the page "George

Tiller Baby Killer List of Judas Pro-Life Organizations" and fill it with the statements of pro-life organizations that have condemned Scott Roeder's killing of George Tiller.[108]

> The pro-lifers prefer George Tiller to still be killing babies, because they think that is pro-life. There is a place in hell for unfaithful cowards who love the praise of man more than the praise of God. The list of those who betrayed the lives of the unborn is endless. . . . These same people want protection for themselves and their families when threatened with death, even if it means lethal force; yet they deny that same protection to the unborn child in the womb.[109]

Eric Rudolph expresses a similar sentiment in a statement he posted on the Army of God website offering his reasons for the attacks. In his statement, he addresses his lesser known enemies: "But then there are those who call themselves 'Pro-Life', and who claim that abortion is murder; they also claim that those who would use force to prevent it are just as morally reprehensible as the abortionists. For these people I have nothing to say other than you are liars, hypocrites, and cowards."[110]

SUMMARY

What then, can be concluded about the effort to strike back at the Army of God and the use of force to stop abortion? Three themes have emerged in this chapter. First, although significant evolutions in policy have occurred—particularly through the Freedom of Access to Clinic Entrances act—these evolutions have still left important gaps in the space between the right to free speech and the right to protection from intimidation. The courts have addressed these issues on a case-by-case basis, but an institutional standard is still lacking. Secondly, in the absence of an institutional standard, prosecution of violence against abortion providers is subject to political parties, ideologies, and interests. State laws vary widely in the access allowed to protestors, and the enforcement of violations varies as well. Prosecution according to FACE varies according to presidential administrations and, as a result, there is no clear standard for what constitutes terrorism, conspiracy, or independent actors. Finally, the effort to stop antiabortion violence is plagued by the same tension between ideas and organization that has been evident through the rest of the book. The preservation of the freedom to practice religion, to speak, and to assemble is threatened by any alternative focus on the ideas that form the ambiguous structure of the organization. As a result, law enforcement agencies are left with few ways to anticipate and prevent future attacks.

NOTES

1. Scott, Joni. 1999. "From Hate Rhetoric to Hate Crime: A Link Acknowledged Too Late—Anti-Abortionists Alleged Crimes Not Investigated." *The Humanist*, January/February. http://findarticles.com/p/articles/mi_m1374/is_1_59/ai_53536191/.

2. Prabha, Kshitij. 2000. "Defining Terrorism." *Strategic Analysis* 24, no. 1: 125–135.

3. Pauker, Benjamin. 2007. "The Fog of Words." *World Policy Journal* 24, no. 1: 103–107.

4. Quoted in Toscano, Roberto. 2007. "A War against What?" *World Policy Journal* 24, no. 1: 40–43, 40.

5. Toscano, Roberto. 2007. "More on Defining Terror." *World Policy Journal* 24, no. 3: 111–112, 111.

6. "'Pro-Life' Organizations Condemn Scott Roeder." http://www.armyofgod.com/GeorgeTillerBabykillerJudasOrg.html.

7. In an interview with the *New York Times* in 1980, Reagan pointed out, "I've noticed that everybody that is for abortion has already been born."

8. Joffe, Carole. 2000. "There's More at Stake Than Roe vs. Wade: From Clinic Access to Anti-Abortion Terrorism, the Next President—Whoever He Is—Will Have a Profound Effect on a Woman's Right to Choose." *Salon.* http://www.salon.com/health/feature/2000/10/31/abortion.

9. *Washington Post*, January 4, 1985, 27A. Quoted in Blanchard, Dallas A. and Terry J. Prewitt. 1993. *Religious Violence and Abortion*. Edited by the Gideon Project. Gainesville: University Press of Florida, 270.

10. Blanchard, Dallas A. and Terry J. Prewitt. 1993. *Religious Violence and Abortion*. Edited by the Gideon Project. Gainesville: University Press of Florida, 270.

11. Magnuson, Ed, Patricia Delaney and B. Russell Leavitt. 1985. "Explosions over Abortion." *Time*, January 14. http://www.time.com/time/magazine/article/0,9171,962698,00.html.

12. Scott, Joni. 1999. "From Hate Rhetoric to Hate Crime: A Link Acknowledged Too Late—Anti-Abortionists Alleged Crimes Not Investigated." *The Humanist*, January/February. http://findarticles.com/p/articles/mi_m1374/is_1_59/ai_53536191/.

13. Scott, Joni. 1999. "From Hate Rhetoric to Hate Crime: A Link Acknowledged Too Late—Anti-Abortionists Alleged Crimes Not Investigated." *The Humanist*, January/February. http://findarticles.com/p/articles/mi_m1374/is_1_59/ai_53536191/.

14. Campbell, Regina. 1996. "FACE'ing the Facts: Does the Freedom of Access to Clinic Entrances Act Violate Freedom of Speech?" *University of Cincinnati Law Review* 64: 947; Risen, James and Judy Thomas. 1998. *Wrath of Angels: The American Abortion War*. New York: Basic Books; Tepper, Arianne K. 1997. "Comment: In Your F.A.C.E.: Federal Enforcement of the Freedom of Access to Clinic Entrances Act." *Pace Law Review* 17, no. 2: 489–551.

15. Risen, James and Judy Thomas. 1998. *Wrath of Angels: The American Abortion War*. New York: Basic Books.

16. H.R. 796.

17. Eviatar, Daphne. 2009. "DOJ Abortion Violence Suits Cratered under Bush." *Washington Independent*, June 12. http://washingtonindependent.com/46673/doj-abortion-violence-suits-cratered-under-bush.

18. Clymer, Adam. 1993. "Senate Passes Abortion-Clinic Crime Bill." *New York Times*, November 17. http://www.nytimes.com/1993/11/17/us/senate-passes-abortion-clinic-crime-bill.html.

19. For full text version of the law, see http://www.justice.gov/crt/crim/248fin.php.

20. Smothers, Ronald. 1994. "Death of a Doctor: The Overview—Abortion Doctor and Bodyguard Slain in Florida; Protester Is Arrested in Pensacola's 2nd Clinic Killing." *New York Times,* June 30. http://www.nytimes.com/1994/07/30/us/death-doctor-over view-abortion-doctor-bodyguard-slainin-florida-protester.html.

21. Risen, James and Judy Thomas. 1998. *Wrath of Angels: The American Abortion War.* New York: Basic Books, 366.

22. Risen, James and Judy Thomas. 1998. *Wrath of Angels: The American Abortion War.* New York: Basic Books, 366.

23. Thomas, Judy. 2010. "Federal Charges Possible for Scott Roeder." *Wichita Eagle,* February 8. http://www.kansas.com/2010/02/07/1170334/federal-charges-possible-for-roeder.html.

24. Thomas, Judy. 2010. "Federal Charges Possible for Scott Roeder." *Wichita Eagle,* February 8. http://www.kansas.com/2010/02/07/1170334/federal-charges-possible-for-roeder.html.

25. Suro, Roberto. 1998. "A Most Dangerous Profile: The Loner." *Washington Post,* July 22, A01.

26. Suro, Roberto. 1998. "A Most Dangerous Profile: The Loner." *Washington Post,* July 22, A01.

27. "Bomb Rocks Atlanta Olympics." 1996. *BBC,* July 27. http://news.bbc.co.uk/onthisday/hi/dates/stories/july/27/newsid_3920000/3920865.stm.

28. "Blasts Probed at Atlanta Family Planning Clinic: 2nd Explosion Injures Six." 1997. *CNN,* January 16. http://cgi.cnn.com/US/9701/16/atlanta.blast.update/.

29. Baker, Donald P. 1998. "Blast at Alabama Abortion Clinic Kills a Policeman, Injures Nurse." *Washington Post,* January 30, A01.

30. Baker, Donald P. 1998. "Blast at Alabama Abortion Clinic Kills a Policeman, Injures Nurse." *Washington Post,* January 30, A01.

31. Fletcher, Michael A. 1998. "Sniper Kills Abortion Doctor Near Buffalo." *Washington Post,* October 25. http://www.washingtonpost.com/wp-srv/national/longterm/abortviolence/stories/sniper.htm.

32. Fletcher, Michael A. 1998. "Sniper Kills Abortion Doctor Near Buffalo." *Washington Post,* October 25. http://www.washingtonpost.com/wp-srv/national/longterm/abortviolence/stories/sniper.htm.

33. Fletcher, Michael A. 1998. "Sniper Kills Abortion Doctor Near Buffalo." *Washington Post,* October 25. http://www.nytimes.com/1998/10/25/nyregion/abortion-doctor-in-buffalo-slain-sniper-attack-fits-violent-pattern.html.

34. Yardley, Jim and David Rohde. 1998. "Abortion Doctor in Buffalo Slain; Sniper Attack Fits Violent Pattern." *New York Times,* October 25. http://www.nytimes.com/1998/10/25/nyregion/abortion-doctor-in-buffalo-slain-sniper-attack-fits-violent-pattern.html.

35. Joffe, Carole. 2000. "There's More at Stake Than Roe vs. Wade: From Clinic Access to Anti-Abortion Terrorism, the Next President—Whoever He Is—Will Have a Profound Effect on a Woman's Right to Choose." *Salon.* http://www.salon.com/health/feature/2000/10/31/abortion.

36. Joffe, Carole. 2000. "There's More at Stake Than Roe vs. Wade: From Clinic Access to Anti-Abortion Terrorism, the Next President—Whoever He Is—Will Have a Profound Effect on a Woman's Right to Choose." *Salon.* http://www.salon.com/health/feature/2000/10/31/abortion.

37. Joffe, Carole. 2000. "There's More at Stake Than Roe vs. Wade: From Clinic Access to Anti-Abortion Terrorism, the Next President—Whoever He Is—Will Have a

Profound Effect on a Woman's Right to Choose." *Salon.* http://www.salon.com/health/feature/2000/10/31/abortion.

38. Joffe, Carole. 2000. "There's More at Stake Than Roe vs. Wade: From Clinic Access to Anti-Abortion Terrorism, the Next President—Whoever He Is—Will Have a Profound Effect on a Woman's Right to Choose." *Salon.* http://www.salon.com/health/feature/2000/10/31/abortion.

39. Reid, Harry. 2002. "Remembering Barnett Slepian and Condemning Anti-Abortion Violence." In *United States Senate*, ed. CSPAN, June 13.

40. "Antiabortion Advocate Convicted of Sending Anthrax Hoax Letters to Abortion Clinics Sentenced to 19 Years in Prison." 2005. *Medical News Today*, July 11. http://www.medicalnewstoday.com/articles/27290.php.

41. "Antiabortion Advocate Convicted of Sending Anthrax Hoax Letters to Abortion Clinics Sentenced to 19 Years in Prison." 2005. *Medical News Today*, July 11. http://www.medicalnewstoday.com/articles/27290.php.

42. Kopp, James. *Man of Peace.* http://www.christiangallery.com/koppdidit.htm.

43. Kopp, James. *Man of Peace.* http://www.christiangallery.com/koppdidit.htm.

44. Johnston, David. 2001. "Ashcroft Orders U.S. Marshals to Protect an Abortion Doctor." *New York Times*, July 13. http://www.nytimes.com/2001/07/13/us/ashcroft-orders-us-marshals-to-protect-an-abortion-doctor.html.

45. Johnston, David. 2001. "Ashcroft Orders U.S. Marshals to Protect an Abortion Doctor." *New York Times*, July 13. http://www.nytimes.com/2001/07/13/us/ashcroft-orders-us-marshals-to-protect-an-abortion-doctor.html.

46. Eviatar, Daphne. 2009. "DOJ Abortion Violence Suits Cratered under Bush." *Washington Independent*, June 12. http://washingtonindependent.com/46673/doj-abortion-violence-suits-cratered-under-bush.

47. Eviatar, Daphne. 2009. "DOJ Abortion Violence Suits Cratered under Bush." *Washington Independent*, June 12. http://washingtonindependent.com/46673/doj-abortion-violence-suits-cratered-under-bush.

48. Eviatar, Daphne. 2009. "DOJ Abortion Violence Suits Cratered under Bush." *Washington Independent*, June 12. http://washingtonindependent.com/46673/doj-abortion-violence-suits-cratered-under-bush.

49. Eviatar, Daphne. 2009. "DOJ Abortion Violence Suits Cratered under Bush." *Washington Independent*, June 12. http://washingtonindependent.com/46673/doj-abortion-violence-suits-cratered-under-bush.

50. Rood, Justin. 2005. "Animal Rights Groups and Ecology Militants Make DHS Terrorist List, Right-Wing Vigilantes Omitted." *Congressional Quarterly*, March 25. http://www.cq.com/corp/show.do?page=crawford/20050325_homeland.

51. See chapter 2.

52. Obama, Barack. 2009. "Statement from the President on the Murder of Dr. George Tiller." Washington, DC: The White House.

53. "Abortion Doctor Shot Dead in Wichita, Kan: George Tiller, Who Performed Late-Term Abortions, Killed at Church; Suspect in Custody." 2009. *ABC*, May 31. http://abcnews.go.com/US/story?id=7719860.

54. Birkey, Andy. 2009. "Klobuchar Bill Condemning Tiller Murder Faces GOP Opposition." *Minnesota Independent*, June 22. http://minnesotaindependent.com/37518/klobuchar-bill-condemning-tiller-murder-faces-gop-opposition.

55. Birkey, Andy. 2009. "Klobuchar Bill Condemning Tiller Murder Faces GOP Opposition." *Minnesota Independent*, June 22. http://minnesotaindependent.com/37518/klobuchar-bill-condemning-tiller-murder-faces-gop-opposition.

56. Guttmacher Institute. 2010. "Protecting Access to Clinics." *State Policies in Brief*, August 1. http://www.guttmacher.org/statecenter/spibs/spib_PAC.pdf.

57. Ertelt, Steven. 2009. "Chicago Mayor Daley to Sign Bubble Zone Law Limiting Pro-Life Abortion Actions." *Life News*, October 9. http://www.lifenews.com/2009/10/09/state-4496/.

58. Abcarian, Robin. 2009. "Federal Judge Upholds 'Bubble Ordinance' for Abortion Protesters." *Los Angeles Times*, August 5. http://articles.latimes.com/2009/aug/05/local/me-abortion5.

59. Gottlieb, Scott. 2000. "Buffer Zone Law for Abortion Clinics Declared Unconstitutional." *British Medical Journal* 321 (December). http://www.bmj.com/content/321/7273/1368.6.full; Pope, Justin. 2001. "Massachusetts Abortion Buffer Zone Law Upheld." *Associated Press*, August 13.

60. Shannon, Shelley. "Who Is Shelley Shannon." *Army of God*. www.armyofgod.com/ShelleyWhois.html; see also Booth, William. 1993. "Doctor Killed during Abortion Protest." *Washington Post*, March 11, A01.

61. *Now v. Scheidler* Timeline. http://www.nowfoundation.org/issues/reproductive/scheidler-timeline.html.

62. *Now v. Scheidler* Timeline. http://www.nowfoundation.org/issues/reproductive/scheidler-timeline.html.

63. Health Clinics are considered businesses and protected under this definition of interstate commerce. As a result, the penalties in these cases are more severe than in standard cases.

64. *Scheidler v. National Organization for Women (04–1244)* and *Operation Rescue v. National Organization for Women.* 2005. U.S. Supreme Court.

65. *Madsen et. al. v. Women's Health Center, Inc.* 1994. U.S. Supreme Court.

66. *Madsen et. al. v. Women's Health Center, Inc.* 1994. U.S. Supreme Court.

67. *Madsen et. al. v. Women's Health Center, Inc.* 1994. U.S. Supreme Court.

68. *Madsen et. al. v. Women's Health Center, Inc.* 1994. U.S. Supreme Court.

69. Hudson, David L. Jr. 2006. "Abortion Protests and Buffer Zones." *First Amendment Center*, February 4. http://www.scribd.com/doc/34735576/Abortion-Clinic-Buffer-Zones.

70. *Scheidler v. National Organization for Women (04–1244)* and *Operation Rescue v. National Organization for Women.* 2005. U.S. Supreme Court.

71. *Scheidler v. National Organization for Women (04–1244)* and *Operation Rescue v. National Organization for Women.* 2005. U.S. Supreme Court.

72. Planned Parenthood of the Columbia Wilamette Inc. American Coalition of Life Activists. 1995. In *Circuit Judge Kozinski*. http://cyber.law.harvard.edu/ilaw/Cybercrime/planned-parenthood.html.

73. Cohen-Almagor. 2010. "In Internet's Way." In *Ethics and Evil in the Public Sphere: Media, Universal Values and Global Development*, ed. Mark Fackler and Robert Fortner, NY Hampton Press.

74. Robb, Amanda. 2010. "Not a Lone Wolf: Scott Roeder Is Now Serving a Life Term for Murdering Abortion Doctor George Tiller. But Did He Really Act Alone? *MS*, Spring. http://www.msmagazine.com/spring2010/lonewolf.asp.

75. Suro, Roberto. 1998. "A Most Dangerous Profile: The Loner." *Washington Post*, July 22, A01.

76. Suro, Roberto. 1998. "A Most Dangerous Profile: The Loner." *Washington Post*, July 22, A01.

77. Suro, Roberto. 1998. "A Most Dangerous Profile: The Loner." *Washington Post*, July 22, A01.

78. Suro, Roberto. 1998. "A Most Dangerous Profile: The Loner." *Washington Post*, July 22, A01.

79. Johnston, David. 1994. "F.B.I. Undertakes Conspiracy Inquiry in Clinic Violence." *New York Times*, August 4. http://www.nytimes.com/1994/08/04/us/fbi-undertakes-conspiracy-inquiry-in-clinic-violence.html.

80. Johnston, David. 1994. "F.B.I. Undertakes Conspiracy Inquiry in Clinic Violence." *New York Times*, August 4. http://www.nytimes.com/1994/08/04/us/fbi-undertakes-conspiracy-inquiry-in-clinic-violence.html.

81. Johnston, David. 1994. "F.B.I. Undertakes Conspiracy Inquiry in Clinic Violence." *New York Times*, August 4. http://www.nytimes.com/1994/08/04/us/fbi-undertakes-conspiracy-inquiry-in-clinic-violence.html.

82. Johnston, David. 1994. "F.B.I. Undertakes Conspiracy Inquiry in Clinic Violence." *New York Times*, August 4. http://www.nytimes.com/1994/08/04/us/fbi-undertakes-conspiracy-inquiry-in-clinic-violence.html.

83. "FBI Investigated Suspect before Clinic Killings." 1994. *Los Angeles Times*, August 1. http://articles.latimes.com/1994-08-01/news/mn-22419_1_abortion-clinics.

84. *UNITED STATES v. SHANNON, UNITED STATES of America, Plaintiff-Appellee, v. Angela Dawn SHANNON, Defendant-Appellant.* 1998. U.S. Court of Appeals, 9th Circuit.

85. Pilkington, Ed. 2009. "For Years Anti-Abortionists Tried to Stop Doctor Tiller. Finally a Bullet Did." *The Guardian*, June 1. http://www.guardian.co.uk/world/2009/jun/01/us-doctor-tiller-killing-abortions.

86. Thomas, Judy. 2009. "FBI's Investigation of Tiller Killing Looks at Roeder's Jail Visitors. *Kansas City Star*, August 9. http://www.kansascity.com/637/story/1373179.html.

87. Thomas, Judy. 2009. "FBI's Investigation of Tiller Killing Looks at Roeder's Jail Visitors. *Kansas City Star*, August 9. http://www.kansascity.com/637/story/1373179.html.

88. Magnuson, Ed, Patricia Delaney and B. Russell Leavitt. 1985. "Explosions over Abortion." *Time*, Monday, January 14. http://www.time.com/time/magazine/article/0,9171,962698,00.html.

89. "Reagan Assails Bombing of Abortion Clinics." 1985. *United Press International,* January 3. http://articles.latimes.com/1985-01-03/news/mn-11134_1_abortion-clinics.

90. Magnuson, Ed, Patricia Delaney and B. Russell Leavitt. 1985. "Explosions over Abortion." *Time*, Monday, January 14. http://www.time.com/time/magazine/article/0,9171,962698-2,00.html.

91. Magnuson, Ed, Patricia Delaney and B. Russell Leavitt. 1985. "Explosions over Abortion." *Time*, Monday, January 14. http://www.time.com/time/magazine/article/0,9171,962698,00.html; "Reagan Assails Bombing of Abortion Clinics." 1985. *United Press International.*

92. Goodstein, Laurie and Pierre Thomas. 1995. "Clinic Killings Follow Years of Anti-Abortion Violence." *Washington Post*, January 17, A01.

93. "Feds Seek Public Input on 'Army of God' Letters." 2009. *CNN*, June 9.

94. "Abortion Doctor Shot Dead in Wichita, Kan: George Tiller, Who Performed Late-Term Abortions, Killed at Church; Suspect in Custody." 2009. *ABC.*

95. Huffenberger, Gary. 2009. "Bray Sues Planned Parenthood, U.S. Marshals." *Wilimington News Journal*, October 14. http://www.wnewsj.com/main.asp?FromHome=1&TypeID=1&ArticleID=180179&SectionID=49&SubSectionID=156.

96. Huffenberger, Gary. 2009. "Bray Sues Planned Parenthood, U.S. Marshals." *Wilimington News Journal*, October 14. http://www.wnewsj.com/main.asp?FromHome=1&TypeID=1&ArticleID=180179&SectionID=49&SubSectionID=156.

97. Goodstein, Laurie and Pierre Thomas. 1995. "Clinic Killings Follow Years of Anti-Abortion Violence." *Washington Post*, January 17, A01.

98. Magnuson, Ed, Patricia Delaney and B. Russell Leavitt. 1985. "Explosions over Abortion." *Time*, Monday, January 14. http://www.time.com/time/magazine/article/0,9171,962698,00.html.

99. Magnuson, Ed, Patricia Delaney and B. Russell Leavitt. 1985. "Explosions over Abortion." *Time*, Monday, January 14. http://www.time.com/time/magazine/article/0,9171,962698,00.html.

100. Goodstein, Laurie and Pierre Thomas. 1995. "Clinic Killings Follow Years of Anti-Abortion Violence." *Washington Post*, A01.

101. Goodstein, Laurie and Pierre Thomas. 1995. "Clinic Killings Follow Years of Anti-Abortion Violence." *Washington Post*, A01.

102. A full version of the *Nashville Declaration of Conscience* is available in the appendix of this book.

103. *The Nashville Declaration of Conscience: The Struggle against Abortion: Why the Use of Lethal Force is Not Morally Justifiable*. 1994. Nashville, TN: Ethics and Religious Liberty Commission. http://erlc.com/article/nashville-declaration-of-conscience/. Full text available in the appendix to this volume.

104. *The Nashville Declaration of Conscience: The Struggle Against Abortion: Why the Use of Lethal Force is Not Morally Justifiable*. 1994. Nashville, TN: Ethics and Religious Liberty Commission. http://erlc.com/article/nashville-declaration-of-conscience/.

105. Toalston, Art. 1998. "Fatal Abortion Clinic Bombing Condemned by Pro-Life Leaders." *Baptist Press*, January 30. http://www.bpnews.net/bpnews.asp?Id=1965.

106. http://www.priestsforlife.org/pressreleases/01–04–01pressrewardfund.htm.

107. U.S. Conference of Catholic Bishops. (n.d.). *Catechism of the Catholic Church.*

108. A full list of each of these statements is available at the Army of God website http://www.armyofgod.com/GeorgeTillerBabykillerJudasOrg.html.

109. "George Tiller's Reformation Lutheran Church Has George Tiller's Blood on Their Hands." http://www.armyofgod.com/GeorgeTillerBabykillerJudasOrg.html.

110. Eric Rudolph Statement. http://www.armyofgod.com/EricRudolphStatement.html.

Conclusion

In one of the final scenes in *The Sound of Music*, the Von Trapp family tries to escape from Austria and finds themselves hiding in the same convent that had once categorized Fraulein Maria as so difficult to define. As the Von Trapps speed away, with the Nazis supposedly hot on their trail, the scene turns back to the nunnery, where two sisters sheepishly reveal they stole critical components of the Nazi's car engines so they would be unable to catch the Von Trapp family. The nun that had been so hard on Maria in the beginning of the film justified her thievery by saying that God would approve her work on behalf of a greater good.

Interestingly, this fictional scene generated a robust debate on the Internet forum "Catholic Answers." After watching this scene from *The Sound of Music* with her eight-year-old daughter, one mother asked whether the action of the sisters was a sin. Dozens of responses were posted—ranging from resounding affirmatives to firm condemnations. Some argued that stealing—regardless of the motivation—was a sin. Thus, whether the car parts were removed from cars owned by Nazis or cars owned by monks, the theft remained wrong in the eyes of God. More moderately, others agreed that it was a sin, but suggested that in the "Great Lawbook," God would give the sisters a pass because He would have known their real intentions. Others still argued that theft, in this case, was actually a moral duty, because to act otherwise would have allowed the evil of the Nazis to triumph. In other words, an individual must protect the Law of God over the laws of man, regardless of the cost.

As we have seen in this book, it is the same manner of thinking that characterizes the ideology of the Army of God and the debate that surrounds them. Killing an abortion doctor, according to the Army's ideology, is not a sin, but a virtue. The Law of God demands respect for life. Morality demands that murder (abortion) be met with death. To deny this responsibility is to deny the sovereignty of God. This understanding establishes a powerful ideology that fulfills many functions for the Army of God.

The actions of the Army are difficult to predict, and the nature of the organization challenging to define because the individuals who compose it are not predictable criminals. As we have seen in this book, the Army of God is composed of housewives and pastors, young teenagers and elderly adults. They have no identifiable demographic characteristics, save the ideology that at once unites them, inspires them, and defines them.

The ideology of the Army of God is quite specific. As we saw in chapter 1, the organization's beliefs about abortion are the product of a long and controversial political history. The contentious nature of the abortion issue influences not only political activism, but also the scholars who would seek to understand it. There is no consensus about the history of abortion in America: some accounts suggest it was a ubiquitous and amoral practice, while others suggest it was so abhorrent as to be nearly unspeakable.

Whatever its historical place, in the 20th and 21st centuries abortion has become representative of a host of other issues on both sides of the contemporary social debate. For those who support its legality, it is a reflection of women's rights, the freedom of choice, and a right to privacy. For those who advocate against it, it is representative of the loss of Christian values in America. Accordingly, both sides face challenges in distinguishing between a narrow position on abortion and its place in the broader political context. When the availability of abortion becomes the canary in the coal mine of morality or freedom in America, individuals are poised to react at the slightest chirp of change.

For most opponents of abortion, its practice is murder. The Army of God is distinguished from their nonviolent counterparts by their perceived responsibility in the face of these murders. Members of the Army have constructed an ideology that makes action against abortion a moral imperative. As we saw in chapter 2 of this book, the methods used by the Army of God have changed over time, generally reflecting an increasing intensity of protest. Nonviolent responses to abortion largely peaked in the late 1980s, in part because of law-enforcement efforts to limit protestors' access to clinics and those needing to access them. But at the same time, violent protest increased dramatically, first with the killing of Dr. David Gunn in 1993, then the shooting of George Tiller later that year, followed by the killings of Dr. John Britton, Dr. Barnett Slepian, and Dr. Tiller in 1994, 1998, and 2009 respectively. The Army of God manual mirrors this evolving intensity by distinguishing between the minimally and truly courageous.

Even as the Army of God is demographically diverse, the ideology is remarkably monolithic. The theology of the members is distinct from this characteristic, as members hail from congregations ranging from Episcopalian to Charismatic Renewal. But if ideology is understood to be a set of linked ideas that inform the *action* of an individual (rather than the study of deism), the Army of God has a distinctly cogent and unified set of beliefs.

First, members of the Army of God believe that God calls His followers to act toward the preservation of His laws. In chapter 3, we saw how Paul Hill identified sins of omission in which every commandment is accompanied by a concomitant inverse commandment. For example, thou shall not kill is joined by thou shall prevent others from killing. Thus a good Christian not only follows the commandments of God, but ensures that others do as well.

Second, it is clear that members of the Army of God believe abortion is murder. Pregnant women carry fully human children, blessed by God with life. The decision to have an abortion is a decision to destroy a life. The killing of an unborn child is in no way less abhorrent than the killing of three-year-old.

These first two beliefs are linked to form the third and most distinctive element of the Army of God's ideology. If good Christians are called to prevent others from committing murder, and if abortion is murder, then good Christians are called by God to prevent abortion by any means necessary.

In chapter 3, we saw that members of the Army of God justify the use of force from different perspectives, but all share the linked set of ideas outlined in the previous three paragraphs. When it becomes clear that nonviolent protest will not stop abortion, an individual has a responsibility to escalate the protest to a level that will stop the practice.

But as was demonstrated in chapter 4 of this book, although the ideology is shared by all members of the Army of God, the resulting organization is manifestly individualistic. This characteristic also relates to the ideological nature of the organization. Although individuals are firmly similar in their ideas, they are not beholden to anyone other than God in their implementation. No member answers to any other member for his/her actions, and the currency of interaction within the organization is praise, admiration, and occasionally, recommended tactics.

It is this characteristic that has made the organizational ties so difficult to track and the conspiracy of the Army so challenging to prosecute. While this book has spoken liberally of "members" of the Army of God, the reality is not nearly so evident. Membership is determined by little more than sympathy to and/or admiration for a cause, and rarely does any physical evidence prove these sentiments. Law enforcement officers can look for tangible manifestations of ideas but are significantly constrained from having to do so. The alternative, however, is more dangerous still, as the ability to prosecute based on nothing more than an idea is a direct challenge to the foundations of American democracy.

When a member of the Army of God kills an abortion provider, there is inevitably a national uproar lamenting the paralysis of a system that cannot stop this dangerous organization. But the nature of the organization is such that the characterization of an individual as a member is dependent on one of two extremes. As we saw in chapter 5, either the state or federal government must decide that belief can be illegal—and prosecute any individuals who have expressed sympathy for the Army of God and their violent tactics; or state and federal governments must wait for individuals to commit an illegal act before they can identify them as a threat.

It is this characteristic of the Army of God that makes them such an important organization in the present day and age. Seen as a single, unique organization, the Army of God is a fairly limited threat. Certainly abortion providers have cause for concern, but the broader community suffers no danger from this specialized organization. But when recognized as an example of the evolving nature of terrorist organizations, the Army of God becomes both informative and unnerving.

Perhaps the most significant lesson to be learned from the Army of God is that in modern terrorist organizations, ideology has the capacity to play multiple roles at once in the facilitation of successful operations. We can see from the Army of God that ideology serves as a lens through which the world is viewed, a link through which disparate individuals are connected, and a litmus test by which the willing are tested. It is useful to look at each function in turn.

IDEOLOGY AS A LENS

Ideology has been characterized as "the most elusive concept in the whole of social science,"[1] and thus it is not surprising that it fills so many roles in organizations today. The word was originally coined to refer to the science of ideas—and the study of the way ideas were related to the senses. In this way, ideology is understood to comprehensively encompass emotion, thought, and action into a single lens through which individuals view the world around them.

This lens focuses on what is good or just and makes basic assumptions about the nature of man, the world, and man's role in the world.[2] Ideologies are typically held by groups of individuals and are shared through symbols, slogans, and metaphors. When an ideology is in place, new events, thoughts, and ideas can be tucked into the existing ideology, which forms the analytical frame by which these new ideas will be judged.

Ideology is cemented and affirmed through the extensive use of metaphor. As Fine and Sandstrom explain, "Metaphor, then, is a handy tool for the ideologist in presenting pictures of 'how things are' and 'how they might ought to be'—pictures that both resonate with people's lived experience and offer them an appealing sense of how they can and should live.

Through metaphorical images, the ideologist mobilizes images that enable people to experience the 'moral.'"[3]

Understood as a lens, ideology offers individuals a method for processing new experiences while simultaneously giving meaning to past experiences. It is the set or system of ideas that unite what would otherwise be insensible, disparate, or meaningless. In the case of the Army of God, individuals feel deep grief and despair over the existence of abortion in America. The ideology of the organization situates this grief in a broader political perspective. Individuals are encouraged to realize that though their values have been pushed to the periphery of the political arena, they are faithfully representing the unchanging nature of God. They are conditioned to realize that though the world is changing around them, the changes can be explained by the dominance of Satan in the world, and the increasingly rebellious nature of secular humanists. The ideology allows members of the Army of God to understand the angry reaction to their use of force to be a further sign of the ills of a sinful society.

The repetitious use of pictures of aborted babies is a graphic reminder of the evil against which the organization fights. Atrocious in their own right, the pictures represent a newly secular society ripped from its place as a faithful servant of God. The Army of God website is filled with graphic images of flames (to remind the viewer of the eternity of hell that awaits the unrepentant) and blood (to evoke the violence of abortion and the life it destroys).

In fact, at the very bottom of the Army of God website, Hebrews 12:4 is quoted: "Ye have not yet resisted unto blood, striving against sin." In Christianity, blood plays a central role in redemption. Jesus alone could redeem the sin of God's people because He alone, among humans, was sinless. And in the Army of God, blood not only represents the aborted children, but also deliberately calls forth the central message of Jesus's blood that was shed for all sin. Moreover, because man was made in the image of God, abortion is explained to be a grievous crime against God—as it results in the death of his image.

Thus the image of blood—and the connotations it invokes—represents an ideology that is far larger than abortion. Abortion is painted to be one ill among many in a society that has declared war against the image of God and has rejected the sacrificial blood He shed on their behalf. In this way, the ideology of the Army of God offers members a lens that focuses a myriad of events, changes, and circumstances into a single vision with a clear consequential action.

Ideology, when seen from this perspective, becomes an answer to a list of lingering questions about society. It is a salve to grievance, an explanation for injustice, and a solution to a vexing problem. While for the Army of God, this answer is a violent effort to end abortion, for other terrorist organizations it can be something else entirely. The influence of ideology as a lens is not the prescription of a specific vision, but rather the diagnosis of a better way to view the world.

Scholars debate whether terrorism is better explained as a reaction to grievance or ideology, but the Army of God is a reminder that the two ideas are not exclusive. Ideology addresses grievance and offers emotional compensation to its victims. Moreover, ideology *explains* grievance and gives control to the aggrieved to address the wrong.

IDEOLOGY AS A LINK

We saw in chapter 5 of this book that despite years of effort, no government agency has been able to conclusively prove the existence of a conspiratorial network linking members of the Army of God. And yet, we saw throughout this book that many of the members know each other, and all use suspiciously similar methods to forcibly stop abortion. The appendix to this volume includes the preface to the Army of God manual—a manuscript that encourages and facilitates the use of specific types of force to permanently close down abortion clinics. There are records of individuals closely affiliated with the Army of God working with imprisoned members to publish detailed accounts of their work, and members themselves recount interactions in which the encouragement of one spurred the action of another.

But the Army of God has successfully evaded conspiracy convictions because they have established a different type of network. Whereas conspiracy charges depend on proof of mutual planning a specific illegal act, the Army of God does not, as a group, plan anything. Instead, their network is almost entirely ideological. The frames and metaphors discussed earlier in this chapter are consistently reinforced through articles and web publications open to any and everyone. Individuals "join" the Army of God through a realization of ideological compatibility. Thus the network that links them is measured by ideological resonance, rather than physical ties.

Donald Spitz acknowledged that he hailed some of the Prisoners of Christ as heroes on the Army of God webpage based on second-hand information about their acts and the motivations behind them. He identified a degree of ideological compatibility and consequently "inducted" them into the Army of God.

The process works in reverse as well. Numerous members recount seeing graphic pictures of aborted babies and making a personal commitment to end abortion in the United States. Shelley Shannon has an article posted on the Army of God website titled "Join the Army." In it she explains that her personal time with God was what led her to use violence against abortion providers. She explains that individuals horrified by abortion should seek God's will for themselves. She goes on to say, "Let me tell you my story while I pray that the Holy Ghost will use some of the information in it like He did with other testimonies to help me."

Shannon's article is available to anyone who can type a URL, and she has not written it to anyone in particular. And yet it is clear from her statement that she expects her testimony to influence the decisions of future "soldiers" of God. Such soldiers will be drawn by the powerful frame Shannon has depicted, in which God brings honor and peace to those who act against abortion. They will respond to the comprehensive explanation for a sinful world and be inspired to lend their hands and feet to overcome it. As a result of this compelling ideology, they may come to interact with other members of the Army of God, but such interaction will be the consequence of belief, not the catalyst for it.

Chapter 5 demonstrated the challenge this type of network provides to law enforcement. When networks are linked by belief rather than interaction, and plans are made through encouragement rather than directives, prosecution must rest only on the acts of individuals. In other words, a self-proclaimed soldier in the Army of God cannot be prosecuted until he/she has committed an illegal act, even if the same individual has professed a willingness to kill.

The Army of God is an example of the immense challenges stemming from religious terrorism. Individuals are compelled to act based on a set of ideas; however, democracies are founded on the freedom to express ideals. Therefore, the elimination of ideologically inspired terrorism also threatens to splinter the base of democracy.

As the Internet becomes more and more ubiquitous, the tension between the freedom of speech and the need to restrain it will intensify. FACE attempted to give greater weight to crimes based on their ideological motivation, but the legislation did not justify charges for ideological inspiration. In other words, though individuals who commit crimes based on certain ideologies can be penalized more heavily, those who promulgate the ideology without committing a crime will not be prosecuted at all. As a result, organizations that successfully compartmentalize their duties will continue to thrive even as members are arrested for specific crimes. As long as the ideology continues to be compellingly promoted, the potential for recruitment will not diminish.

The Army of God's Defensive Action statements were accompanied by a disclaimer advising anyone plotting to forcibly stop abortion not to sign the petition, lest they tip off law enforcement to their intentions. In light of the present limitations on prosecution for ideological inspiration, this disclaimer is significant. The Army of God strategically divides their labor between those who offer inspiration and those who undertake acts to stop abortion. In so doing, they limit exposure to those who are not legally guilty of a crime. Repeatedly in conversations with this author, Army of

God members emphasized the importance of recognizing God's calling for their service. Some individuals were called to use force, others only to advocate the right to its use.

As long as members continue to carefully navigate this line between inspiration and action, law enforcement efforts will continue to run into dead ends. Terrorism is an act, while belief is a condition. Ideological inspiration is the thread that links the two. The source of ideological inspiration cannot be threatened, and thus the pool of potential soldiers is hypothetically unlimited.

IDEOLOGY AS A LITMUS TEST

The third significant component of ideology in the present-day terrorist threat is its function as a litmus test. Perhaps the greatest influence on the shift from hierarchical to cell-structured terrorist organizations has been the increased need for secrecy. As technology has rapidly increased the reach and capability of law enforcement efforts, terrorist organizations must develop more and more discreet and untraceable systems. As the most effective way to maintain secrecy is to limit interactions between members of an organization, the cell structure model has emerged.

But it is generally recognized that the level of secrecy maintained by a group is inversely proportionate to the level of effectiveness of that group. Thus, while cells are difficult to trace, they are also difficult to control. The task facing terrorist organizations has been to develop a model wherein both secrecy and effectiveness are maintained.

It is here that the Army of God offers another useful example. This organization has straddled the fence between secrecy and effectiveness by making organizational affiliation dependent on proof of ideological support. In other words, because Army of God members are linked by their ideological affiliation, action is dependent upon belief in the idea—not connections to or directions from other members.

Interested individuals can read the openly available resources and understand the clear parameters of the Army of God's ideology. But to "belong" to the group, ideological affiliation must be established, and this establishment is proven by action. Just as Louis Beam promised that his leaderless resistance model would weed out the less committed, the emphasis on ideology in the Army of God serves as an effective litmus test for courage and determination in the fight against abortion.

Confessions made by members of the organization indicate that at a minimum, members are sometimes aware of the plans of other members. But never are those plans directed by anyone other than the individual(s) involved. Michael Bray did not order Shelley Shannon to shoot George Tiller, any more than John Burt demanded Michael Griffin kill David Gunn. In both cases, however, there are clear examples of encouragement and inspiration offered to the would-be shooters. Nonetheless, neither Shannon nor Griffin could effectively implicate Bray or Burt in their plotting, given the ambiguous nature of their influence.

As was explained in chapter 4, there are no membership rosters in the Army of God, and yet there are lists of supporters and heroes in the movement. To be on these lists, one either has to openly declare the right to the use of force, or use it in pursuit of the organization's goals. In organizing (if this term can be used appropriately here) the structure in this way, the Army of God has ensured that the capture of one member will rarely lead to the successful prosecution of another. And yet, there are still distinct social and ideological benefits to membership—and therefore, violent action.

When God is understood to demand the use of force, an ideology has been constructed that simultaneously protects secrecy and maintains efficiency. A hierarchy is established between the individual and God, wherein the individual takes orders from a deity. It is easy to hear from God, but very hard to prosecute Him. Thus the individual, who is acting on God's behalf (as understood by a carefully constructed and openly promulgated ideology), can prove his/her worth without endangering the organization as a whole.

MOVING FORWARD

Great strides have been made in deradicalization studies in recent years. Several countries have begun successfully using deradicalization programs within prisons to slowly counter radical ideologies.[4] While it is hard to measure the success of these programs, it is difficult to fault the reasoning behind them: if ideology is playing such a significant role in the radicalization process, deradicalization must be dependent on an equally compelling, if less dangerous ideology.

The question, then, is who can best counter the ideology of the Army of God? To answer this, one must first consider why the ideology is appealing in the first place. This book has argued that the ideology of the Army of God represents more than a position on abortion. It is a comprehensive explanation for and solution to the problem of secularization in American society. It diagnoses the expulsion of Christian values from the core of society to the political periphery, and it provides individuals with a concrete method for contesting that expulsion. If this is correct, then the best option for countering the radical ideology of the Army of God will come from other Christian organizations.

There have been limited efforts on this front to date. The appendix to this volume includes a response by the Southern Baptist Theological Seminary to the use of force to stop abortion. In it, members of the seminary constructed a detailed and Christian refutation of the use of force to stop abortion. Several members of the Army of God mention this response in their writing, and at least one has written a refutation to the refutation. While the Southern Baptists points were conclusively rejected by the Army of God, the response started a dialogue.

This is in contrast to many other antiabortion groups that condemn the use of force but do not engage the Army of God in theological discussions about its justification. Instead, many organizations use the same rhetoric as the Army, condemning abortion as murder and abortion providers as murderers, but then they are dismayed when violence against clinics or providers is revealed. Army of God members speak derisively of these groups as hypocrites and cowards, highlighting the apparent contradiction between their inflammatory rhetoric and their watered-down actions. Army of God members view themselves as courageous alternatives to these organizations who know what is right but lack the gumption to undertake it.

Why don't more antiabortion organizations engage in dialogue about the use of force? Such a question falls outside the purview of this book, and so the author offers only a few hypothetical explanations. Many pro-choice organizations condemn the antiabortion movement in sweeping assumptions about the modernity (or lack thereof) of the movement. There are times when little care is taken to distinguish between the violent fringe and the antiabortion movement as a whole. Instead, the entire movement is painted as antiwomen, antimodern, and antichoice.

In this environment, the antiabortion movements most likely to succeed are those that can operate close to the political center. The more savvy organizations realize this and are thus limited in the manner in which they can react to antiabortion violence. In the wake of terrorism, it is difficult to coherently explain the distinction between supporting a principle and condemning a method.

But the challenge extends further than this. Many pro-life groups find themselves in a strange position when the Army of God strikes. Nonviolent pro-life movements use nearly identical rhetoric when describing abortion. Doctors are murderers, fetuses are children, abortion is a massacre. When the Army of God acts violently, pro-life groups must not only condemn the use of force, but justify its condemnation. In other words, they have to explain to their followers, why, if abortion *is* murder, stopping it at any cost is wrong.

When this author spoke with a leading member of the Christian right about this issue, the individual emphatically defended his efforts to save the unborn. He interpreted a question about why he didn't use force to actually mean the author was questioning his commitment to the cause. He grew angry and said he didn't use force because his efforts were better extended elsewhere. He understood the question to be a challenge to the sincerity of his concern for aborted babies. This may have been an isolated reaction, but it is informative nonetheless.

Deradicalization efforts are working in places like Singapore and Saudi Arabia because the individuals conducting the programs share many of the core beliefs of those they are counseling. The difference between the counselor and the radical is that the counselor has come to firm conclusions about why force is not the answer. More importantly, the counselor understands where the rejection of force fits within his own religious ideology. When pro-life groups use inflammatory rhetoric about abortion, they are hard-pressed to justify their unwillingness to use force. As a result, with a few notable exceptions, they are ill-equipped to counsel radicals toward deradicalization.

The Army of God has been remarkably successful at defining the ideological higher ground in the rhetorical debate about abortion. While it is unlikely that their group will grow significantly in size, neither will it diminish in intensity until other pro-life organizations can analytically defend their position not to use force from a theological perspective.

This effort can be aided by the pro-choice movement as well. Though the Army of God represents a minority of pro-life organizations, it is common to see the entire movement painted as radical, ignorant, enemies of women's rights. When the pro-life position is categorized in this way, the movement's exclusion from the political core becomes more evident. Several members of the Army of God explain their decision to use force as a response to the decrease of nonviolent options for protest. Just as radicalization has been demonstrated to flourish when opportunities for involvement diminish, the permeability of the political sphere to pro-life positions will continue to influence the actions of the Army of God.

What then, is the future for the Army of God? In *The Sound of Music*, when the nuns are struggling to identify the problem of Maria, they seek a word that describes her and melodically choose "a flibberti gibbet, a willo' the wisp, and a clown." Each of these, in one way or another, has also been used to characterize this elusive organization.

There is no such thing as a flibberti gibbet, and the same claim is often made about the Army of God. But as we have shown in this book, though it is not a traditional organization as defined by physical networks and ordered actions, it exists nonetheless. The individuals believe deeply in the cause they advance and are not dependent on one another to advance it. As terrorism continues to evolve, it is likely that more "organizations" of this sort will emerge, and scholars or policy makers would do well find a word, or a series of words to adequately describe and address it.

A willo' the wisp evokes images of wind, shadows, and elusive floating objects. All appropriately describe the Army of God because at its core, the Army of God is an idea. The idea is present in the minds of its members and made flesh by their violent actions. Law enforcement has endeavored to stop the Army but has continuously run up against its own inability to prosecute an idea. Efforts to end antiabortion violence cannot stop at the prosecution of individual offenses. For this reason, it is possible that law enforcement officers are not the best equipped to stop it at all. Ideas must ultimately be confronted with other—better—ideas. The Army of God must be confronted by individuals who understand their belief in God, their passion for the unborn, and their guilt for their inability to stop it. These individuals must work within the context of the organization's comprehensive ideology to challenge the idea of moral justification of force.

Finally, the Army of God has been ridiculed as a clown. Certainly some individuals within it are more memorable than others, but most harbor serious and deeply held beliefs about a very contentious issue. The organization is not a silly group that will honk their noses at a few children and then willingly leave the stage. The Army of God has demonstrated they have staying power. They have existed, in some form or another, for almost 30 years. Will they ever achieve their objectives? Unlikely. But will they keep trying? Undoubtedly. They are small, but when they choose to be, they are deadly. It is imperative, then, that they are taken seriously. In fact, their determination, their ability to evolve, and their ideologically based structure are no laughing matter. They are emblematic of new forms of terrorism and need to be considered accordingly.

This book could not and did not solve the problem of the Army of God. Instead, the purpose was to identify an organization that is important for its own sake as well as for what it can teach us about other terrorist organizations. The Army of God is not easy to define, to categorize, or to catch. But like the nun's wave upon the sand, it will keep coming back until someone figures out how to pin it down.

NOTES

1. McLellan, David. 1986. *Ideology*. Minneapolis: University of Minnesota Press.

2. Fine, Gary Alan and Kent Sandstrom. 1993. "Ideology in Action: A Pragmatic Approach to a Contested Concept." *Sociological Theory* 11, no. 1: 21–38.

3. Fine, Gary Alan and Kent Sandstrom. 1993. "Ideology in Action: A Pragmatic Approach to a Contested Concept." *Sociological Theory* 11, no. 1: 27.

4. Bergin, Anthony, Sulastri Bte Osman, Carl Ungerer and Nur Azlin Mohamed Yasin. 2009. "Countering Internet Radicalization in Southeast Asia." *Australian Strategic Policy Institute*, March: 22.

Appendix 1

———◆———

Army of God Third Edition

EDITOR'S PREFACE TO THE THIRD EDITION

The third edition of this manual, like the second, is a result of the over-whelming response and demand for the previous edition, each published less than a year before the other. In fact, many copies have appeared circulation in samizdat for several months prior to this Third Edition.

A book of this kind is never finished. Virtually everyone who reads it will have an idea for a new Termite tactic, or for a refinement of one presented in the book. Thank God! For that is proof enough that the babies are not being forgotten, and that untold numbers of thoughtful individuals are even now planning battle strategy in this war against the child killers. Only a tiny minority of these warriors have even seen this book, but have been moved by the Holy Spirit to take up the cause of the babies, knowing that there is a limit to how long our land can be allowed to run red with the blood of God's children crying out to heaven for vengeance.

God Himself, Jesus of Nazareth, described Himself, "I am the way and the truth and the LIFE". there exists within the Pro-life, Anti death community, every shade of attitude and commitment to active involvement in this war not against flesh and blood but against principalities and powers, and rulers of the darkness of this world, and against spiritual wickedness in high places. (Ephesians 6:12) Picketing, prayer, sidewalk counseling, prayer, rescue, prayer, covert activity, prayer, . . . all fruits of that true and lively faith our Lord requires of those who would call Him "Lord". He is Life, and

---

Reprinted with permission.

that Life is the Light of mankind. We who are Pro-Life recognize that those countless souls who, for the sake of their commitment to Jesus Christ, gave up their very lives over a period of nearly two thousand years did not do so because they enjoyed ridicule, imprisonment, suffering, and even death. They knew that they could not be silent, could not refuse—let alone neglect—to live their faith. And then, as now, when a Christian lives his or her faith, a collision with society and its value-less system is inevitable.

Lord Jesus Christ, Son of God, have mercy on me, a sinner.

Genesis 9:6 Whoso sheddeth man's blood, by man shall his blood be shed: for in the image of God made He man.

Numbers 35:33 So ye shall not pollute the land wherein.

Appendix 2

⸺⊗⊗⊗⸺

The Nashville Declaration of Conscience

THE STRUGGLE AGAINST ABORTION: WHY THE USE OF LETHAL FORCE IS NOT MORALLY JUSTIFIABLE

"The LORD examines the righteous, but the wicked and those who love violence his soul hates" (Psalm 11:5 NIV).

September 1994

1. Preamble

1.1 Acts of lethal violence recently have been used in an attempt to stop abortion doctors from performing abortions. Such violence has been perpetrated, in some cases, by those who seek to justify their acts on the basis of Christian moral principles. Dozens of violent incidents of other sorts have also occurred in and near abortion clinics over the past fifteen years.

1.2 The aftermath of these violent acts has made it clear that the views of the perpetrators are not merely idiosyncratic, but instead reflect the perspective of a small number of Americans, some of them Christians, who are strongly opposed to abortion.

1.3 Representatives of a wide range of "pro-choice," "pro-abortion," and "pro-life" positions have offered public statements condemning such use

_____

Reprinted with permission.

of deadly force and the moral justification of such acts. It has been a rare instance of agreement. We join in condemning these killings.

1.4 However, the divergent reasons that pro-choice and pro-life groups have offered for their moral rejection of such acts as the Pensacola shootings, and of the moral claims that undergird such acts, bear witness to the continuing and seemingly unbridgeable gulf between these polarized parties to the abortion conflict.

1.5 We who offer this statement speak from a Christian pro-life perspective. Even though we share the moral condemnation of the killings that pro-choice groups and leaders have expressed, we have yet to read a statement from such persons that reflects our point of view concerning why such killings are not morally justifiable.

1.6 In particular, some claim that unborn life is not fully human life, and thus that it is wrong to use lethal force in an attempt to prevent abortion. We strongly disagree with the claim that an unborn child is not fully human life, deserving of full protection. We will reject the killing of abortion doctors on other grounds.

1.7 At the same time, we find the response thus far from the pro-life community deserves more elaboration and depth. We are glad to see that all responsible pro-life groups and leaders have condemned such killings, as do we. But mere denunciation, however passionate it may be, is not enough. We believe that the point of view of persons advocating violence against abortion doctors requires serious moral reflection and engagement, more serious than has thus far publicly occurred. A number of profound questions of Christian morality and Christian citizenship are at stake.

1.8 As pro-life Christians, we are concerned about the possibility that some of our fellow pro-life Christian friends and colleagues will drift into an embrace of violence directed against abortion providers. Lack of serious engagement with the views of persons who advocate the use of violence will only increase the risk that this drift will occur. We are equally concerned that such violence will lead pro-life Christians to withdraw from morally legitimate forms of action to prevent abortion.

1.9 This statement, therefore, is intended as a moral analysis and rejection of the killing of abortion doctors, offered from a Christian pro-life perspective. It is at the same time intended as an urgent plea for intensified Christian involvement in all morally permissible forms of anti-abortion activities. We offer this statement in the name of Jesus Christ, our Savior and Lord, to any who will listen, and especially to our fellow laborers in the protection of the unborn.

2. Murder in Christian Perspective

2.1 Murder, the culpable killing of a human being, is an extraordinarily grave offense against civil law as well as against the moral law of God (Ex. 20:13) on which all morally legitimate civil law is ultimately based.

2.2 The Bible teaches that each human life is sacred, for every human being is made in the image of God (Gen. 1:26–27). For this reason, each human life bears divinely granted and immeasurable value. Human beings are not free to take the lives of others, for those lives belong to God, their Creator. This is the meaning of the divine prohibition of murder in the Ten Commandments. "Thou shalt not kill" means that God prohibits the unjustified taking, and mandates the protection, of human life.

2.3 In the Sermon on the Mount (Matt. 5:21f.), Jesus affirmed the prohibition against murder. Indeed, He warned of God's judgment even on intense expressions of anger and contempt for others, while calling His hearers to seek reconciliation with any persons from whom they might be estranged, even their enemies (Matt. 5:43–44). Jesus also proclaimed God's special favor upon those who make peace (Matt. 5:9). While wholeheartedly committed to the spread of the Kingdom of God (Matt. 6:10, 6:33), Jesus personally rejected the use of violence to accomplish even this holy aim.

2.4 The Apostle Paul frequently reaffirmed the centrality of peacemaking and reconciliation, even describing God's saving act in Jesus Christ as an act of divine peacemaking between those who had once been enemies— an act that not only reconciled God to humanity but also reconciled estranged human beings to each other (Eph. 2:11–22).

2.5 Paul also argued that the governing authorities of this world have been established by God. Their mandate in a world deeply marred by sin is to serve God by deterring wrongdoing and bringing punishment on wrongdoers, thus protecting the innocent (Rom. 13:1–7). In this work, Paul writes, the authorities "do not bear the sword in vain" (Rom. 13:4). Most Christians have understood this to be a divine authorization of the use of force by governing authorities, even deadly force at times, when such force is finally required to accomplish government's divinely mandated purposes. Through the centuries, strict criteria have been developed for the just employment of such force.

2.6 In Christian theology a historic split has existed between those who believe that the witness of Scripture prohibits any taking of human life under any circumstance by any person or institution, and those who believe that under the conditions of sin the taking of human life is in a very small number of tragic circumstances morally justifiable and thus morally permissible.

2.7 Those taking the former position could ground a rejection of the killing of abortion doctors in their uniform and absolute rejection of any killing of any human being under any circumstances by any person or institution. This point of view would be coherent and consistent, and no further argument would need to be made.

2.8 While respectful of this position, we believe that the overall witness of Scripture, including Romans 13, leads to the latter conclusion—that there are indeed a small number of tragic and exceptional circumstances in a fallen world in which the taking of human life can be morally justifiable.

2.9 However, from our perspective the Bible establishes a profound presumption in favor of preserving life rather than ending it. God wills that human beings should make peace with each other, should be reconciled, and should treat every life with the respect its divine origin and ownership demands. There is at the very least a *prima facie* moral obligation to refrain from killing. This means that an extraordinarily stringent burden of proof is imposed upon any who would seek to justify the taking of a human life.

2.10 To the extent that United States civil law reflects the divine moral law, it likewise is structured both to deter and to punish severely the unjustifiable taking of a human life. Civil law does generally recognize that under certain unusual circumstances normally involving defense of self or third persons against deadly force, the taking of another human life by a private citizen might be justified. A stringent burden of proof in every case rests on those who would justify any taking of life.

2.11 United States civil law is also structured to recognize the broader mandate of government to use force and the threat of force, judiciously and carefully, to deter and punish evil and to protect the innocent from wrongdoing. The government protects its citizenry from domestic wrongdoers through the law enforcement and criminal justice systems, and from foreign wrongdoers through the armed forces. Private citizens rightly are barred from authorizing themselves to perform these functions.

2.12 Those advocating acts of lethal force against abortion doctors claim that such acts qualify as morally justifiable homicide, despite the current status of civil law in the United States.

2.13 This assertion requires Christian consideration of the moral and legal status of the act of elective abortion, as well as the moral obligations of Christians living in a democratic society that by statute permits elective abortion under most circumstances.

3. The Moral and Legal Status of the Act of Elective Abortion

3.1 Since 1973, the United States Supreme Court has interpreted the United States Constitution in such a way as to create a right of a woman to choose to secure the services of a physician who is paid to "terminate her pregnancy"—that is, deliberately to end the existence of that life which is developing within her body. This state of affairs is justly called "abortion on demand" in that abortion is permitted on the basis of no criteria other than a pregnant woman's demand for an abortion. The abortion workers who have been killed or injured have been relying on this decisional law to justify their conduct legally.

3.2 The moral status of the act of elective abortion is arguably the most bitterly contested moral and, consequently, legal, social, cultural, religious, and political question of our time. This is not the place in which to offer a rehearsal of the arguments that pertain to this question. We will instead simply state our position in the following way.

3.3 As indicated above (2.2), we believe that each human life bears a divinely granted sacredness. We believe that its sacredness begins at conception, when biological life begins. We believe that gestational life—life in the womb from conception to birth—must be understood as human life in its earliest stages rather than as pre-human, nonhuman, potential, or any other less-than-fully-sacred kind of human life. We know that, if allowed to continue developing without hindrance through a normal pregnancy, a gestating human life becomes a newborn baby. Thus, we are compelled to consider elective abortion the killing of a human being.

3.4 We have already argued that, given the sacredness of human life, the burden of proof is on any who would morally justify its deliberate extinguishing. The terrible flaw at the heart of federal abortion law is that abortions are currently permitted *while requiring a woman to meet only a minimal burden of proof which may be imposed by state laws.* In terms of gestational life, the federal government has wrongfully abdicated its responsibility to protect the innocent and to establish and enforce stringent criteria for the justifiable taking of human life.

3.5 We recognize that for a woman (or, for a couple) an unwanted pregnancy may well be a crisis pregnancy. We acknowledge that women seek abortions for a wide range of reasons. Tragically, these range from the most serious and justifiable (i.e., a threat to the physical life of the mother) to the least serious and justifiable (i.e., gender preference, interruption of vacation plans, and so on). The effect of current abortion law is that any reason for an abortion, or no particular reason, is as good as any other. The great majority of abortions in the United States are performed for what can best be described as reasons of convenience.

3.6 We recall the biblical principle that it is morally forbidden for a private citizen to end a human life except in the act of self-defense. Only in cases when gestational life poses a serious threat to the physical life of the mother, in our view, does elective abortion clearly meet this self-defense criterion. A significant number of pro-life Christians are willing to grant the possibility that abortion in the cases of rape, incest, and/or radical fetal deformity also ought to be included among those exceptions to the general prohibition of abortion that should be recognized by law. We disagree. But we recognize that rewritten abortion laws framed along those lines would still disallow all but a very small percentage of abortions in this country.

3.7 Instead, our nation continues to operate under a law that requires no significant burden of proof for abortion. This represents a fundamental assault on the sanctity of human life. Human beings are not at liberty to lower the threshold for the taking of human life, but that is precisely what abortion laws have done. Lowering that threshold is one of humanity's greatest temptations, one to which human beings have succumbed all too frequently, especially in our own century of world war and genocide.

3.8 But we need not look elsewhere for examples. Our own violence-wracked nation bears witness each day to the devastating consequences of disrespect for the sacredness of human life. Truly the blood of the murdered cries out from the ground (Gen. 4:10; Lev. 18:28). We believe that abortion on demand is the leading, but not the only, example of a broader national moral and social crisis of disrespect for human life.

3.9 From our perspective, then, the overwhelming majority of abortions represent a morally unjustifiable form of killing. It is a unique form of killing, involving several parties. An abortion is undertaken by a physician who performs abortions, at the request of an unborn child's mother. Often, a woman is pressured by the child's father to have an abortion. Pressure may also come from family members, friends, and others. Her decision is then permitted by the civil law of the United States. Each participant in this act of unjustifiable killing, including the government of the United States (and ultimately "we the people," who are the sovereign of this government and have elected its officials), bears a share of the responsibility.

3.10 For twenty-one years, since the 1973 *Roe v. Wade* and *Doe v. Bolton* Supreme Court decisions, abortion on demand has been the controlling interpretation of the Constitution in the United States. In that time over thirty million abortions have been performed in this country. We believe that this state of affairs can only be called a moral outrage.

3.11 We share the intense frustration of tens of millions of this nation's citizens who grieve each of the lives lost, the futures never realized, the human beings who unjustly have been prevented from ever "seeing the light of day" (Job 3:16). We also grieve for the many mothers and fathers who spend much of their lives profoundly regretting their choice to have an abortion, mourning the children they never had the chance to love and enjoy.

4. Legitimate Forms of Christian Response

4.1 Most Christians who believe, as we do, that the overwhelming majority of abortions are morally unjustifiable acts of killing, rightly feel the need to offer significant moral response. Indeed, millions of American Christians even today are engaged in activities that constitute such a response; most of these activities, in our view, are fully and morally justifiable and quite constructive. They are aimed at saving lives, and are directed at each of the participants in the abortion decision.

4.2 For example, many Christians are involved in supporting abstinence- and valuesbased sex education programs in schools, civic institutions, and churches. The Southern Baptist Convention's "True Love Waits" program is an effective example. Such programs are rooted in the biblical moral norm that sexual intimacy is designed by God to be reserved for marriage (1 Cor. 6:9–20; 7:9; etc.). It is obvious, but important to point out nonetheless, that the demand for abortion would decrease radically if God's intentions for sexuality were heeded. Abortions happen because unwanted pregnancies happen; unwanted pregnancies happen, most of the time, because of sexual activity outside of marriage. It is important to note again that it takes both a man and a woman to engage in such sexual activity, and both are responsible for the consequences.

4.3 Christians are also involved in helping pregnant women "choose life," that they and their children "may live" (Deut. 30:19). Christians have led the way in establishing crisis pregnancy centers and maternity homes. In such places pregnant women are cared for and prepared either to raise their children themselves or to give their children to others who can do so via adoption. This is a noble form of Christian ministry to women and their children. We give thanks to God for those women who avail themselves of these ministries and thus save their children's lives.

4.4 Pro-life Christians, especially those in the health care professions, are also on the front lines in the struggle over abortion as an aspect of medical practice. Such health care professionals bear witness to their convictions by refusing to "regularize" abortion as an aspect of medical care. They remind fellow health care providers of the "first, do no harm" provision of the Hippocratic Oath. This kind of witness—a witness of winsome moral suasion and example, rather than invective and violence—is an important and appropriate part of the struggle against abortion. It is one of the reasons why very few physicians are willing to perform elective abortions.

4.5 Abortion on demand became law in our democratic society by the decision of persons who attained their office by legitimate processes, and remains lawful through the same processes. Christians, anguished at this state of affairs, are rightfully involved in the wide-ranging kinds of political engagement afforded us within the democratic process.

4.6 Such involvement includes voting, lobbying, campaigning for pro-life candidates, drafting legislation, writing letters to government officials, getting involved in political party platform drafting, running for office, initiating boycotts, and so on. We believe that there is no doubt whatsoever that such activity is our right as citizens and our obligation as Christians.

4.7 Some pro-life Christians are involved in lawful public witness in the vicinity of abortion clinics, such as the handing out of printed materials and the organizing of prayer vigils. We believe that public witness of this type is morally justifiable.

4.8 Some Christians have engaged in various forms of nonviolent, public, civil disobedience in the vicinity of abortion clinics as an aspect of their protest against legal abortion on demand. This kind of activity has been a matter of considerable debate in pro-life circles and concern in the broader society.

4.9 From a biblical perspective, Christians clearly are required to submit to and obey the governing authorities of the lands in which they live. This responsibility flows from the divinely authorized nature of these governing authorities (see 2.5).

4.10 Scripture does recognize, however, that governments sometimes violate their Godgiven purposes, even to the extent of enacting laws and policies that are in direct and specific conflict with the divine moral law. History bears frequent tragic witness to the same reality. The Bible teaches that Christians are morally permitted, and sometimes even obligated, to violate a civil law that is in direct, specific conflict with the law of God (cf. Ex. 1:16–2:10; Dan. 6; Acts 4:1–31, 5:12–42).

4.11 The burden of proof for justifying civil disobedience rests with those considering it. Besides being intended as a challenge to a morally illegitimate law or policy, such nonviolent civil disobedience should follow the failure of a range of other, less radical forms of action; should have some likelihood of effectiveness; and should have positive consequences that are likely to outweigh negative consequences.

4.12 Christians living in a democratic society who make the grave judgment to engage in public, nonviolent, civil disobedience must willingly submit to the consequences of their actions. Thus, Christians involved in civil disobedience related to abortion should expect to be prosecuted. To break a morally illegitimate law, and to submit willingly to the consequences of doing so, is in fact an attempt to change civil law via moral witness—and thus, to affirm all morally legitimate civil law.

4.13 We believe that laws concerning access to abortion clinics and protests around abortion clinics function as a fence around the immoral law that permits legalized abortion on demand. Because the abortion law is a permission for private citizens to have and to perform abortions, rather than a mandate requiring behavior of one type or another, it is impossible to perform direct civil disobedience in the matter of legalized abortion on demand. This means that nonviolent civil disobedience, if it occurs, can only be directed at subsidiary laws.

4.14 We have outlined several lawful ways in which Christians can offer constructive moral response to the morally illegitimate law permitting abortion on demand. These can by no means be described as having been exhausted. There is much more to be done. This raises the question of whether nonviolent civil disobedience is justified.

4.15 On balance, we believe that acts of *nonviolent* civil disobedience related to abortion, though not morally *obligatory* for Christians, may be seen as morally *permissible*. This is ultimately a matter of individual conscience before God.

4.16 Legalized abortion on demand has become deeply entrenched in our society. What many Christians once hoped would be a temporary aberration has become an institutionalized reality. We must acknowledge that this has occurred because significant portions of our society have wanted it to occur. The tragic and abhorrent legal reality reflects an equally tragic and abhorrent social, cultural, and moral reality.

4.17 Pro-life Christians should work to change these social, cultural, and moral realities in which legalized abortion on demand is rooted. It is a heart-by-heart, home-by-home, city-by-city, state-by-state struggle. We must greatly intensify our efforts in the morally justifiable anti-abortion activities described above. It is our moral obligation.

5. Why Lethal Force is Not Morally Justified

5.1 The killing of abortion doctors by private citizens raises the important question of whether such an action is a morally legitimate Christian response to legalized abortion on demand. We strongly contend that killing abortion doctors is not a moral option for Christians, and respond to the various arguments as follows:

5.2 First, we reject the argument some have made that such killings are valid as an act of defending the innocent from harm. We reply that according to both civil law and divine moral law private citizens are permitted to use lethal force against another human being only if this occurs as an unintended effect of the act of defending oneself or another against an assailant's unjust attack. Private citizens are not allowed to *intend* to kill another human being and are not allowed to engage in *premeditated* acts of deadly force in order to accomplish what they intend. In other words, a private citizen can intend to stop, but not to kill, an assailant regardless of the final result. Attacks on abortion doctors fail this test.

5.3 Furthermore, an act of homicide is unjustifiable if the attacker's victim could have been adequately defended in any way other than causing the attacker's death. We believe that the many pro-life measures outlined in section 4 do offer a range of constructive (even if not fully adequate) forms of defense of the lives of the unborn, and thus, the killing of abortion doctors is unjustifiable.

5.4 We believe, further, that the killing of an abortion doctor in actuality does not constitute a meaningful defense of unborn life. This is the case because an abortion doctor is only one of the participants in the act of elective abortion, and not the most important one. It is the woman seeking an abortion who drives the process. The killing of an abortion doctor does nothing in itself to diminish a woman's demand for an abortion. If abortion is legal, and she perceives no alternatives to abortion, she will find another abortion provider. As long as abortion is legal, if we wish to save the lives of unborn children we must influence the actions of women who are considering abortion. The best and most Christ-like way to do so is lovingly to provide her with viable alternatives to abortion. This does not absolve others, especially the baby's father, who may be exerting enormous pressure on the child's mother.

5.5 Second, we reject the argument that the killing of an abortion doctor is justifiable as a form of capital punishment. We reply that the moral legitimacy of capital punishment in contemporary American society is a point of dispute among pro-life Christians. More germane to the argument is the fact that whatever right there may be to execute a criminal is reserved exclusively to governing authorities, and is never the prerogative of a private citizen. A peaceful and orderly society can have no place for self-appointed executioners.

5.6 Third, we reject the argument that killing an abortion doctor is an act of violent civil disobedience made necessary by the gravity of the moral evil of abortion on demand. It is our conviction that no act of lethal force can be properly ascribed to the rubric of civil disobedience. Moreover, the contradiction between the use of lethal force and civil disobedience is especially glaring in a democracy, in which so many alternative forms of activism for social and legal change are permitted. We contend that such an act is better described as an act of revolution rather than an act of civil disobedience intended to accomplish reform.

5.7 Fourth, we reject the argument that a government that allows legalized abortion on demand has of necessity lost its legitimacy, and that in such a circumstance private citizens are free to resist it "by any means necessary."

5.8 To this we reply that we accept the legitimacy of the government of the United States, despite its failure to protect the lives of the unborn and its sanction of access to abortion on demand. It is the people of the United States who have, in fair and free elections, selected the leaders of our government, and it is these duly elected leaders who have appointed judges to the Supreme Court and other federal courts. The actions and inactions of persons in all three branches of the federal government over more than twenty years are responsible for legalized abortion on demand. In turn, their decisions have reflected the pressures brought to bear on them by citizens of the United States, functioning through the democratic process.

5.9 From this we conclude that it is the people of the United States, acting through legitimate governmental institutions, who are responsible and ultimately accountable for immoral laws permitting and protecting the taking of unborn human lives. We do not believe that laws permitting abortion on demand remove the legitimacy of our government. Rather, the authority of our legitimate government has been perverted to allow and protect abortion on demand.

5.10 To us, legalized abortion on demand is the single gravest failure of American democracy in our generation. But we recognize it as a failure of a legitimate democracy rather than as the imposition or decree of an illegitimate regime. For this reason, we reject what can only be described as *the logic of revolution* that some have articulated. Instead, among our other pro-life efforts, we pledge intensified commitment to change the law through the democratic processes of the United States of America.

5.11 Fifth, we reject the claim that private individuals have a right to circumvent the processes of democratic government by using deadly force where the law sanctions abortion on demand. We realize that what is legal and what is moral are not always identical. Where they diverge, Christians bear a dual responsibility, first to act in accordance with the moral law, and second to respect and obey the legitimate authority of government. So long as a government retains legitimacy, and so long as opportunities for reform remain, individuals and groups must work within the democratic process and must resist the temptation to take the law into their own hands.

5.12 We believe that a government may lose its legitimacy as it sets itself against divine law and loses the popular support of its people. Should such circumstances arise, and should that government preclude all opportunities for reform, then Christians, for sake of conscience, may be forced to consider more drastic measures. We deny that our nation is nearing or has reached such a crisis. Our goal must be reform, not revolution.

5.13 We understand that no government can allow laws against the taking of human life to become a matter of private interpretation without placing its own existence and legitimacy in jeopardy. A private citizen who makes the decision to use lethal force against human life contrary to established law is not merely breaking the law against murder, he or she is also assaulting and undermining the authority of the government itself. Thus, any private decision to break the law against murder—even where there is an intention to do good—is an act of rebellion that threatens the existing governing authority, contrary to the will of God (Rom. 13:2). It is not simply an act of civil disobedience. It is certainly not an act of legal reform.

5.14 The distinction between nonviolent civil disobedience and the private use of lethal force can be illustrated from American history. Many Christians felt compelled during the 1850s to violate the fugitive slave laws by participating in the Underground Railroad, which illegally assisted slaves in escaping to freedom. That was nonviolent civil disobedience. On the other hand, John Brown and his supporters fomented slave insurrection and rebellion against the state by lethal force. That was the advocacy and exercise of lethal force by private citizens and is beyond the prerogative of individuals, Christian or non-Christian.

5.15 We wish to call attention to the fundamental difference between nonviolent and violent forms of action for social and legal change. We believe that the witness both of Scripture and of history affirms that a social movement's crossing over from nonviolence to violence is a most perilous, and almost always unjustifiable, step. One consequence of such a transition is that resistance to certain *deeds*, such as abortion, is often transformed into attacks on certain *persons,* such as those who perform abortions.

5.16 When the distinction between the wrong and the wrongdoer is obliterated, social change or resistance movements tend to focus on doing away with the wrongdoer rather than taking concrete steps against the wrong. The morally worthy original goal of the movement is replaced by one that is new and unworthy. Any possibility of reconciliation with the wrongdoer, of conversion of that wrongdoer, and of peacemaking, possibilities at the heart of the life and ministry of Jesus, is eviscerated. Instead, efforts focus on how to kill rather than how to make change occur. The people who are the intended recipients of this violence respond in kind. The devastating cycle of violence is intensified.

5.17 Once the bloodshed escalates, social movements embracing violence tend to slide rapidly along the continuum from violent resistance limited to specified targets toward unlimited violence directed at an ever wider range of persons (are judges and politicians going to be the next targeted?). Even at the first stage, innocent bystanders often are injured. One reason God wisely prohibits murder is precisely because of the incendiary effect of bloodshed on the minds and hearts of sinful human beings.

6. Conclusion

6.1 Our conclusion is that the killing of abortion doctors is not a morally justifiable or permissible Christian response to abortion. We utterly reject such conduct as inconsistent with Scripture and call on all Christian people to join us in this stance.

6.2 We believe that Christians are, nevertheless, morally obligated to oppose legalized abortion on demand and to reduce the number of abortions through other, morally legitimate, channels. We must do so more actively and faithfully than ever before.

6.3 Pro-life Christians must act quickly and vigorously to prevent a small but vocal band of militant activists from destroying the credibility, effectiveness, and witness of the mainstream Christian pro-life movement. We pray earnestly that God will bless the efforts of all who employ morally legitimate means in order to save the lives of the most vulnerable among us, the unborn children. We are persuaded that this reflects the mind of Christ.

THE DRAFTING COMMITTEE:

Mark T. Coppenger, Ph.D. Richard D. Land, D.Phil.
Vice President for Convention Affairs Executive Director-Treasurer
Executive Committee Christian Life Commission of
The Southern Baptist Convention The Southern Baptist Convention
Nashville, Tennessee Nashville, Tennessee
David P. Gushee, Ph.D.* C. Ben Mitchell, Ph.D. (Cand.)
Assistant Professor of Christian Ethics Consultant on Biomedical and Life Issues
Southern Baptist Theological Seminary The Christian Life Commission
Louisville, Kentucky Nashville, Tennessee

Daniel R. Heimbach, Ph.D. R. Albert Mohler, Jr., Ph.D.

Associate Professor of Christian Ethics President

Southeastern Baptist Theological Seminary Southern Baptist Theological Seminary

Wake Forest, North Carolina Louisville, Kentucky

*At the Christian Life Commission's request, Dr. Gushee constructed a first draft, which was then revised by the entire draft committee during a Christian Life Commission consultation meeting in Nashville, September 17–18, 1994. Selected Christian Life Commission staff also participated in the consultation.

Bibliography

Aaronson, T. (2004). "Bombs for Babies: Stephen Jordi Planned to Blow Up Abortion Clinics. Does That Make Him a Terrorist?" *Broward-Palm Beach News Times,* July 15. http://www.browardpalmbeach.com/2004-07-15/news/bombs-for-babies.

"Abortion Opposition Stressed in Kidnapping Trial in Illinois." (1983). *New York Times,* January 26. http://www.nytimes.com/1983/01/26/us/abortion-opposition-stressed-in-kidnapping-trial-in-illinois.html.

Arendt, H. (2006). *Eichmann in Jerusalem: A Report on the Banality of Evil.* New York: Penguin Classics.

Arquilla, J. and D. Ronfeldt (1996). *The Advent of Netwar.* Santa Monica, CA, RAND.

Baker, D. P. (1998). "Blast at Alabama Abortion Clinic Kills a Policeman, Injures Nurse." *Washington Post.* January 30: A01.

Beam, L. (1992). "Leaderless Resistance." *The Seditionist* 12. http://www.christiangallery.com/ExplodingArmyofGodMyth.htm.

Bergin, Anthony, Sulastri Bte Osman, Carl Ungerer and Nur Azlin Mohamed Yasin. (2009). "Countering Internet Radicalization in Southeast Asia." *Australian Strategic Policy Institute.* March: 22.

Birkey, A. (2009). "Family, Army of God Defend Man Who Drove Car into Abortion Clinic." *The Minnesota Independent,* May 21. http://www.tcdailyplanet.net/article/2009/05/20/family-army-god-defend-man-who-drove-car-abortion-clinic.html?mini=eventcalendar/2009/06/all.

Blanchard, D. A. (1994). *The Anti-Abortion Movement and the Rise of the Religious Right.* New York, Twayne Publishers.

Blanchard, D. A. and T. J. Prewitt (1993). *Religious Violence and Abortion.* Edited by the Gideon Project. Gainesville, University Press of Florida.

Bob Lokey et al., Plaintiffs-appellants, v. H. L. Richardson, Etc., et al., Defendants-appellees. 527 F.2d 949 U.S. Court of Appeals, Ninth Circuit (1975).

Booth, W. (1993). "Doctor Killed during Abortion Protest." *Washington Post.* March 11: A01.

Bowen, D. and T. R. Gurr (1968). "Deprivation, Mobility and Orientation toward Protest of the Urban Poor." *American Behavioral Scientist.* March–April: 20–24.

Bower, A. (1996). "Soldier in The Army of God." *Albion Monitor.* February 19. http://www.albionmonitor.com/abortion/abortionsoldier.html.

Bray, M. "The Restoration of Fatherhood (Or Some Fresh Ideas for Promise Keepers)." http://www.armyofgod.com/MikeBrayFathersRights.html.

Bray, M. (1994). *A Time to Kill.* Portland,OR: Advocates for Life Publications.

Bray, M. (2006). "Request by Ohio Citizens for Protection from Federal Tyranny Threatening Dispossession of Father, Mother, and Eight at-Home Children." H. B. Taft. Columbus. www.michaelbray.org/ohioletter.htm.

Bray, M. (2009). "Thoughts on Tiller, Justifiable Homicide, and Persisting Abortionists." http://www.armyofgod.com/MikeBrayThoughtsOnTillerJustifiableHomicide.html.

Bray, M. and J. Bray. (2009). *Tiller's Unheeded Warning: The Shelley Shannon Story.* http://www.armyofgod.com/POCShelleyShannonBookMikeBray.html.

Brockhoeft, J. (1994). "The Brockhoeft Report." *Prayer & Action News* 1. http://www.armyofgod.com/BrockSelect.html.

Cohen-Almagor (2010). "In Internet's Way." In *Ethics and Evil in the Public Sphere: Media, Universal Values and Global Development,* ed. M. Fackler and R. Fortner, 93–115.NY: Hampton Press.

Craig, B. H. and D. M. O'Brien. (1993). *Abortion and American Politics.* Chatham, MA, Chatham House Publishers.

Daly, C. (1996). "Salvi Convicted of Murder in Shootings." *Washington Post,* March 19, A01.

Domingo, R. (1999). "Media Zeroes in on White Rose Banquet." *Life Advocate* 13 (5). http://www.lifeadvocate.org/3_99/nation3.htm.

Freedman, L. (2008). *A Choice of Enemies: America Confronts the Middle East.* New York, Public Affairs.

Ginsburg, F. (1989). *Contested Lives: The Abortion Debate in an American Community.* Berkeley, University of California Press.

Girard, R. (1977). *Violence and the Sacred.* London, Johns Hopkins University Press.

Goodstein, L. and P. Thomas (1995). "Clinic Killings Follow Years of Anti-Abortion Violence." *The Washington Post,* January 17, A01.

Griffin, M. (2007). Correspondence with Jennifer Jefferis.

Guttmacher Institute. (2010). "Protecting Access to Clinics." *State Policies in Brief.* August 1. http://www.guttmacher.org/statecenter/spibs/spib_PAC.pdf.

Hill, P. (2003). "Mix My Blood with the Blood of the Unborn." http://www.armyofgod.com/PHillBookForward.html.

Hirsh (1993). *Use of Force in Defense of Another: An Argument for Michael Griffin. School of Public Policy.* Virginia Beach, VA, Regent University.

Hoffman, B. (1999). "Terrorism: Trends and Prospects." In *Countering the New Terrorism,* ed. I. O. Lesser, B. Hoffman, J. Arquilla, D. Ronfeldt and M. Zanini, 7–38. Santa Monica, CA: RAND.

Horne, T. (2003). "Man Questioned in Museum Fire: Ex-Convict Who Had Set Fire to an Office of Planned Parenthood Denies Being Involved." *The Indianapolis Star,* November 26. http://www.docstoc.com/docs/46593682/Man-questioned-in-museum-fire.

Horsley, N. (2003). "Exploding the Myth of the Army of God." *Christian Gallery News Service,* November 14. http://www.christiangallery.com/ExplodingArmyofGodMyth.htm.

Jefferis, J. (2006). Interview with Dave Leach.

Jefferis, J. (2006). Interview with Pat Robertson.

Jefferis, J. (2007). Interview with Bob Lokey.

Jefferis, J. (2010). Phone interview with Donald Spitz.

Jefferis, J. (2010). *Religion and Political Violence: Sacred Protest in the Modern World.* New York, Routledge.

Joffe, C. (2000). "There's More at Stake Than Roe vs. Wade: From Clinic Access to Anti-Abortion Terrorism, the Next President—Whoever He Is—Will Have a Profound Effect on a Woman's Right to Choose." *Salon.* http://www.salon.com/health/feature/2000/10/31/abortion.

Johnston, D. (1994). "F.B.I. Undertakes Conspiracy Inquiry in Clinic Violence." *New York Times,* July 13. http://www.nytimes.com/2001/07/13/us/ashcroft-orders-us-marshals-to-protect-an-abortion-doctor.html.

Jordi, S. (2006). Written Correspondence with Jennifer Jefferis.

Juergensmeyer, M. (2000). *Terror in the Mind of God: The Global Rise of Religious Violence.* Berkeley, University of California Press.

Kirby, A. (2007). "The London Bombers as 'Self Starters': A Case Study in Indigenous Radicalization and the Emergence of Autonomous Cliques." *Studies in Conflict and Terrorism* 30: 415–428.

Krebs, V. (2002). "Uncloaking Terrorist Networks." *First Monday* 7: 4.

Kushner, H. (2003). *Encyclopedia of Terrorism.* Thousand Oaks, CA, Sage.

Lesser, I. O., B. Hoffman, John Arquilla, David Ronfeldt and Michele Zanini. (1999). *Countering the New Terrorism.* Santa Monica, CA, RAND.

Levin, M. and D. Pinkerson. (2000). *Soldiers in the Army of God.* HBO, 70 minutes.

Luker (1984). *Abortion and the Politics of Motherhood.* Berkeley, University of California Press.

Madsen et al. v. Women's Health Center, Inc., U.S. Supreme Court (1994).

Magnuson, E., P. Delaney, and B. R. Leavitt. (1985). "Explosions over Abortion." *Time Magazine,* January 14. http://www.time.com/time/magazine/article/0,9171,962698,00.html.

McKeegan, M. (1992). *Abortion Politics: Mutiny in the Ranks of the Right.* New York, The Free Press.

Michael and Jayne Bray v. Planned Parenthood Columbia Willamette, Inc. Squires, Sanders and Dempsey L.L.P. *Judge John W. Rudduck,* Court of Common Pleas Clinton County, OH (2009).

Mohr, J. (1978). *Abortion in America: The Origins and Evolution of National Policy.* Oxford, Oxford University Press.

Murphy, J. (2003). "FBI: Abortion Bomb Plot Thwarted: Suspect Leapt into Biscayne Bay to Avoid Arrest." *CBS News,* November 13. http://www.cbsnews.com/stories/2003/11/13/national/main583390.shtml.

The Nashville Declaration of Conscience: The Struggle against Abortion: Why the Use of Lethal Force Is Not Morally Justifiable. (1994). Nashville, TN: Southern Baptist Convention. Nashville, TN.

Nelson, J. M. (1979). *Access to Power: Politics and the Urban Poor in Developing Nations.* Princeton, NJ, Princeton University Press.

Noonan, J. T., ed. (1970). *The Morality of Abortion: Legal and Historical Perspectives.* Cambridge, MA, Harvard University Press.

Norris, P. and R. Inglehart (2004). *Sacred and Secular: Religion and Politics Worldwide.* Cambridge, Cambridge University Press.

Olasky, M. (1992). *Abortion Rites: A Social History of Abortion in America.* Washington, DC, Regnery Publishing.

Pauker, B. (2007). "The Fog of Words." *World Policy Journal* 24 (1): 103–107.

Planned Parenthood of the Columbia Wilamette Inc. American Coalition of Life Activists. (1995). *Circuit Judge Kozinski.* http://cyber.law.harvard.edu/ilaw/Cybercrime/planned-parenthood.html.

Prabha, K. (2000). "Defining Terrorism." *Strategic Analysis* 24 (1): 125–135.

Reagan, L. (1997). *When Abortion Was a Crime: Women, Medicine and the Law in the United States, 1867–1963.* Berkeley, University of California Press.

Risen, J. and J. Thomas (1998). "Pro-Life Turns Deadly: The Impact of Violence on America's Anti-Abortion Movement." *Newsweek,* January 26, 68–69.

Risen, J. and J. Thomas (1998). *Wrath of Angels: The American Abortion War.* New York, Basic Books.

Robb, A. (2010), "Not a Lone Wolf: Scott Roeder Is Now Serving a Life Term for Murdering Abortion Doctor George Tiller. But Did He Really Act Alone?" *Ms.* Spring. http://www.msmagazine.com/spring2010/lonewolf.asp.

Robb, J. (2004). "Mapping Terrorist Networks." *Global Guerrillas.* http://globalguerrillas.typepad.com/globalguerrillas/2004/04/mapping_terrori.htm.

Robb, J. 2009. "Networked Tribes, Systems Disruption, and the Emerging Bazaar of Violence. Resilient Communities, Decentralized Platforms, and Self-Organizing Futures." *Global Guerrillas.* http://globalguerrillas.typepad.com/.

Rood, J. (2005). "Animal Rights Groups and Ecology Militants Make DHS Terrorist List, Right-Wing Vigilantes Omitted." *Congressional Quarterly,* March 25. http://www.cq.com/corp/show.do?page=crawford/20050325_homeland.

Said, E. (1980). "Islam Through Western Eyes." *The Nation,* April 26. www.thenation.com/article/islam-through-western-eyes.

Schaeffer, F. and E. Koop (1978). *Whatever Happened to the Human Race?* Old Tappan, NJ: Fleming H. Revell Company.

Scheidler v. National Organization for Women (04–1244) and *Operation Rescue v. National Organization for Women,* U.S. Supreme Court (2005).

Scheidler, J. (1982). *Closed: 99 Ways to Stop Abortion.* Charlotte, NC: Tan Books and Publisher.

Schwartz, R. M. (1997). *The Curse of Cain: The Violent Legacy of Monotheism.* Chicago: University of Chicago Press.

Scott, J. (1999). "From Hate Rhetoric to Hate Crime: A Link Acknowledged Too Late—Anti-Abortionists Alleged Crimes Not Investigated." *The Humanist,* January/February. http://www.thehumanist.org/humanist/articles/scott.html.

Shannon, S. (2007.) "Join the Army (Or How to Destroy a Killing Center if You're Just an Old Grandma Who Can't Even Get the Fire Started in her Fireplace)." *Army of God.* http://www.armyofgod.com/ShelleyJoinAOG.html.

Shannon, S. "Toward the Use of Force." *Army of God.* http://www.armyofgod.com/ShelleyForce.html.

Shannon, S. "Who Is Shelley Shannon?" *Army of God.* www.armyofgod.com/ShelleyWhois.html.

Stinchcombe, A. (2000). "Social Structure and Organizations." *Economic Meets Sociology in Strategic Management,* ed. J. Baum. Bingley, UK:. Emerald Publishing.

Suro, R. (1998). "A Most Dangerous Profile: The Loner." *Washington Post,* July 22, A01.

Tamney, J. and S. Johnson (1988). "Explaining Support for the Moral Majority." *Sociological Forum* 3 (2): 234–255.

Thomas, J. (2009)."FBI's Investigation of Tiller Killing Looks at Roeder's Jail Visitors." *Kansas City Star,* August 14. http://www.kansascity.com/637/story/1373179.html.

Thomas, J. (2010). "Federal Charges Possible for Scott Roeder." *Wichita Eagle* (Kansas), February 8. http://www.kansas.com/2010/02/07/1170334/federal-charges-possible-for-roeder.html.

Toscano, R. (2007). "More on Defining Terror." *World Policy Journal* 24 (3): 111–112.

Toscano, R. (2007). "A War against What?" *World Policy Journal* 24 (1): 40–43.

United States of America, Plaintiff-appellant, v. Stephen John Jordi, Defendant-appellee, U.S. Court of Appeals, Eleventh Circuit 418 F3d. 1212 (2005).

Zanini, M. (1999). "Middle Eastern Terrorism and Netwar." *Studies in Conflict and Terrorism* 22: 247–256.

Zimbardo, P. (2007). *The Lucifer Effect: Understanding How Good People Turn Evil.* New York: Random House.

Index

About the Author

JENNIFER JEFFERIS is assistant professor of government at Regent University. Her research focuses on religion and political violence and social movements in the Middle East. She has interviewed members of the Army of God, the Muslim Brotherhood, al Jama'at al Islamiyya, and Gush Emunim in an effort to understand the process by which religious ideology inspires violent action. She is the author of *Religion and Political Violence: Sacred Protest in the Modern World.*